D1247180

Aversion therapy
and behaviour disorders:
An analysis

—

Aversion therapy
and behaviour disorders:
An analysis

S. Rachman and J. Teasdale

Foreword by H. J. Eysenck

University of Miami Press

Coral Gables, Florida

Contents

	Foreword by Professor H. J. Eysenck	vii
	Introduction	xi
1	Current status	1
2	Varieties of aversive stimulation	8
3	Chemical aversion treatment of alcoholism	14
4	Other applications of chemical aversion therapy	24
5	The nature of chemical aversion therapy	29
6	Chemical or electrical aversion?	32
7	Electrical aversion: sexual disorders 1	39
8	Electrical aversion: sexual disorders 2	56
9	Treatment of alcoholism and of compulsive eating	72
10	Changes associated with electrical aversion therapy	78
11	The nature of electrical aversion therapy	86
12	Disadvantages of electrical aversion therapy	90
13	Beyond the aversion principle	94
14	Covert sensitisation and cognitive control	106
	Theoretical problems	
15	Theoretical analysis: punishment training	119
16	Theoretical analysis: avoidance conditioning models	134
17	Theoretical analysis: classical conditioning models	143
18	An analysis of aversion therapy for sexual disorders	153
19	An analysis of aversion therapy for alcoholism	165
20	Conclusion	172
	References and Author Index	175
	Index	185

Foreword

Behaviour therapy differs from all other types of psychotherapy by having close links with laboratory experimentation and theoretical models built upon the results of such experiments; it thus represents a first attempt to use the 'natural science approach' in psychiatric treatment. Attempts to link two such apparently remote and even antagonistic disciplines as experimental psychology and psychotherapy are of course difficult and complex, and give rise to problems which are both real and at first sight insoluble. Yet there are urgent reasons why we should shoulder the burden of reconciling these two more or less independent disciplines. In the first place there is suggestive evidence that many neurotic patients, suffering from very real disabilities and handicaps, can be treated by means of behaviour therapy when other methods have failed; for their sake the development of these new types of treatment is urgent and imperative. But in the second place there is also the likelihood that experimental science, which originally suggested the methods of treatment, may be repaid in turn by the opening up of new avenues for testing rigorously theories and hypotheses under more 'real' conditions than is possible in the laboratory, and with rat and other animal subjects. Both sides thus have something to gain from the integration suggested by behaviour therapy.

Very few people, unfortunately, possess both the clinical experience and *savoir-faire* which can only be acquired by long-continued practice of therapy with neurotic patients, and the theoretical and experimental knowledge of conditioning and learning theory which can only be acquired by long-continued work in the experimental laboratory. Most writers on the subject have either concentrated simply on the clinical success and failures of different methods of behaviour therapy, without attempting to view them in the light of the theories which inspired them, or have discussed the theoretical derivation of the methods, without sufficient clinical knowledge to evaluate properly the novel considerations introduced by the change from rat to man, and from laboratory to clinic. The authors are almost unique in combining these two sets of relevant but disparate skills, and they have put us into their debt by seriously discussing both the problems which one is forced to ask of these new methods: Do they work? and: How well are they justified theoretically? The answers to both questions cannot of course be a simple Yes or No; they require extensive discussion and consideration of many and varied types of evidence. In spite of their commendable conservatism the authors are by no means pessimistic about the practical applicability and the theoretical justification for the methods of aversion therapy which they discuss, but neither do they show the facile optimism which characterises so many clinical psychologists who have jumped on what threatens to develop into a bandwaggon. It would be a great pity if this should happen; serious scientific work, and fundamental advances based on close study of experimental evidence and theoretical models, do not flourish in an atmosphere where different 'schools' compete with each other on the basis of 'anything you can do, I can do better!'

Rachman and Teasdale indicate very clearly those regions where the clinical facts fit the learning theory model, and also those where the shoe pinches; in addition, they suggest ways and means of testing possible changes in the theory which might overcome existing difficulties. They do not disguise the fact that in such a new field, perfection is not to be expected, and that while the general outlines of a proper theory may be dimly visible, details are still to be worked out – both in the laboratory and in the clinic. Their book is thus indispensable to all those who are working in the psychiatric field and are using, or thinking of using, aversion therapy; it is equally indispensable to psychologists concerned with general theoretical problems of negative reinforcement, drive, habit formation and the general formulation of a behaviour system.

H. J. Eysenck, Ph.D., D.Sc.
Professor of Psychology
Institute of Psychiatry
London University

Acknowledgements

The views and ideas expressed in this book have been discussed with many of our colleagues over a period of years and we wish to thank them for their interest and co-operation. We are particularly grateful to Professor H. J. Eysenck, Dr. J. Bancroft, Dr. M. P. Feldman, Dr. I. Marks, Dr. M. Gelder, Mr. C. Blakemore and Mr. A. Mathews. In addition, Doctors Feldman, Bancroft, Marks and Gelder kindly supplied us with some unpublished information in order to clarify particular points.

Introduction

We have mixed feelings about aversion therapy. On the one hand, we are interested in it as a psychological process and welcome the introduction of effective treatment methods. On the other hand, we recognise that it is an unpleasant form of therapy and one which is open to abuse.

In this book we have attempted a constructive analysis and evaluation of the theory and practice of aversion therapy. However, we also argue that more acceptable substitutes should be sought and we look forward to an early replacement of current procedures.

Our evaluation of the available evidence is that aversion therapy is probably effective – but we have been unable to satisfy ourselves beyond all doubt. Nevertheless, at present, there is sufficient evidence to justify the judicious and enquiring use of aversion therapy. We do not feel that there are adequate grounds for employing aversion therapy as a routine procedure and therapists should consider alternative methods before opting for it. Where possible, the method should be employed as a 'research treatment' and every attempt should be made to obtain hard evidence regarding its efficacy.

In addition to evaluating its clinical effectiveness, we have attempted to analyse the theoretical nature of aversion therapy and, in particular, to relate it to aspects of the psychology of learning. Here we have placed greatest emphasis on punishment training, avoidance learning and classical conditioning. Aversion therapy is one of the methods of behaviour therapy which has clear links with experimental psychology. The historical and methodological connections are more direct than the theoretical ones, but we have been able to trace some interesting interrelationships between theory and aversion therapy practice. At various points, however, the gap between the experimental data and clinical practice is far too wide for comfort. The shortage of appropriate analogues is largely responsible for the untidy collage of procedures which constitute 'aversion therapy'. In extrapolating from experimental findings, especially studies conducted on animals, insufficient attention has been given to the cognitive variables involved in aversion therapy.

A major puzzle which we are unable to resolve is why patients refrain from carrying out their deviant behaviour after they leave the hospital. For example, a transvestite who has been treated by electrical aversion therapy *knows* that if he cross-dresses in the safety of his home he will not receive a shock. Even so, for long periods after the termination of treatment, many patients do not carry out their deviant acts.

As stated above, it is our view that the available evidence permits one to conclude that aversion therapy is often effective. The evidence is scanty and rarely meets the strict standards which must be applied in assessing therapeutic effects with most types of disorder. It is our contention, however, that the disorders which have been the prime target of aversion therapy respond so poorly to existing treatments (Feldman, 1966), and probably have such a low rate of spontaneous remission, that our standards of judgment must be tailored accordingly. Naturally, we are not advocating a general reduction in standards, and the accumulation of more substantial evidence will allow a mature assessment to be made at a later date. In the present circumstances, however, we are willing, in this interim judgment, to err on the side of optimism.

Aversion therapy is used predominantly for the treatment of those behaviour disorders (alcoholism and sexual deviations) in which the patient's conduct is undesirable but nevertheless, self-reinforcing. The appetitive characteristics of these disorders frequently involve the therapist in problems concerning the introduction of other suitable forms of satisfying behaviour. Sometimes it is not sufficient only to eliminate the unsuitable behaviour. One of the main themes of the present work is the desirability of developing a form of aversion therapy which seeks to suppress deviant behaviour *and* then to develop alternate forms of satisfying behaviour which will be incompatible with the unacceptable target behaviour. This necessity for generating alternate forms of behaviour is not often met in the treatment of neurotic disorders (Eysenck and Rachman, 1965).

In essence, aversion therapy is an attempt to associate an undesirable behaviour pattern with unpleasant stimulation *or* to make the unpleasant stimulation a consequence of the undesirable behaviour. In either case, it is hoped that an acquired connection between the behaviour and the unpleasantness will develop. There is a further hope that the development of such a connection will be followed by a cessation of the target behaviour. Ideally, the therapeutic programme should include attempts to foster alternative, acceptable behaviour patterns.

It is important to remember that aversion therapy is not the only treatment available for conditions such as alcoholism, sexual disorders and the others mentioned in this book. Although there are no doubt many cases in which aversion therapy is the treatment of choice, clinicians should not assume that all alcoholics or sexual deviates require this form of treatment. The alternative methods are discussed elsewhere (Eysenck and Rachman, 1965) and include systematic desensitisation, assertive training and operant conditioning.

In both the theoretical and clinical sections of this book, our aim has been to *clarify*, or simply *identify*, the prevailing problems and difficulties in order to prepare the way for further research and analysis. The process of identification gradually acquired a disproportionate amount of space.

1

Current status

The three most commonly used methods of Behaviour Therapy are desensitisation, operant conditioning, aversion therapy. Although it is the oldest of the three methods, aversion therapy is not the best established or most refined procedure (Eysenck and Rachman, 1965; Rachman, 1965; Rachman, 1967). Aversion therapy has been used intermittently over the past thirty years, but has never quite taken, and the limping progress of the technique probably can be attributed to the mixed results reported over the years (see Franks [1963, 1966] for a full account). The renewed interest in aversion therapy is a reflection of the Zeitgeist which has involved, among other events, a reappraisal of the accepted ideas of psychopathology and treatment. These changes are associated with the emergence of Behaviour Therapy.

In a lecture on the development of secondary reflexes, Pavlov (1927) mentioned an uncompleted study by Podkopaev in which a dog appeared to develop a weak conditioned nausea response to the sound of a tone. The dog was given an injection of apormorphine and one or two minutes later a tone was sounded for a prolonged period. While the tone was still sounding, the drug began to take effect – 'the animal grew restless, began to moisten its lips with its tongue, secreted saliva and showed some disposition to vomit' (p. 35). After several repetitions of this sequence, the tone produced these symptoms in a mild form (see Fig. 1).

Podkopaev's observation

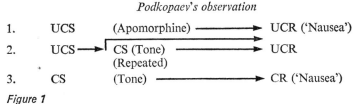

Figure 1

This observation was confirmed by Krylov (Pavlov, 1927), who noted that, after they were given repeated morphine injections, his experimental animals showed the symptoms of nausea, saliva secretion and sleep during the preparations for an injection.[1] A connection had been

1 In his recent description of a morphine-addict treated by apomorphine aversion therapy, Liberman (1968) observed that 'by the sixth session, he reported feeling waves of nausea as soon as he began injecting the morphine'. A striking similarity.

set up between the morphine and the preparatory activities – in some cases, the symptoms were evoked by the mere appearance of the experimenter. Although he presented no details, Pavlov claimed that there was a relation between the range of effective conditioned stimuli and the number of injections given. Actually, the implication was that the *latency* of the conditioned reactions (nausea, sleep, etc.) decreased with the frequency of injections given. This type of conditioned response is classified by Grant (1964) as 'Pavlovian Type B' and he suggests that a 'great deal of interoceptive conditioning and autonomic conditioning apparently follows' this paradigm.

Western writers generally credit Kantorovich (1930) with the first attempt to use aversion therapy (see Voegtlin and Lemere, 1942; Franks, 1963). This work is reported as a brief abstract and contains a clear indication that Kantorovich may *not* have been the first aversion therapist – he concludes his summary as follows: 'A comparison of this type of therapy with the other methods employed in the Leningrad Psychiatric Hospital indicates its superiority' – the implication is that aversive treatments were being used elsewhere. Kantorovich treated twenty alcoholic patients with electrical aversion therapy and claimed that after treatment most of them did not use alcohol for months. The alcohol was 'presented with a strong electrodermal stimulus' and this formed a 'stable defensive reflex to the alcoholic excitant. This reflex took the shape of a withdrawal of the hands and body and mimio-somatic responses of repugnance'.

One of the earliest Western accounts of aversion therapy was provided by Max in 1935. This brief report describes the diminution of a patient's homosexual fixation by the administration of electric shocks. The fetishistic stimulus (presumably, imaginal) was presented 'in conjunction' with an electric shock and Max noted that low shock intensities were ineffective. On the other hand, high intensity shocks 'diminished the emotional value of the stimulus for days after each experimental period'. Although some 'backsliding' occurred, the effect of the treatment 'over a 3-month period was cumulative'. A remarkable feature of this note is that it mentions no less than four phenomena of importance; shock level, devaluation of the CS, punishment recovery effects and cumulative build-up. This highly suggestive paper was apparently ignored however, and the great majority of therapists used nausea-producing drugs as the aversive UCS (Voegtlin and Lemere, 1942). In view of the extensive use made of electrical stimulation in experimental psychology, it is curious that this early study was overlooked.

During the late thirties and forties, chemical aversion therapy was widely employed – predominantly in treating alcoholics. With a few notable exceptions (such as the determined work of Voegtlin and his colleagues at Shadel Sanatorium) most of these reports are of poor scientific quality (Franks, 1963, 1966). Voegtlin and Lemere (1942) described a number of these early attempts and it appears that applications of chemical aversion conditioning were attempted in Belgium, U.S.S.R., France, Britain and the U.S.A.[1] An amusing aspect of these reports is that the alcoholic conditioned stimuli are nationally representative. The Russian workers tended to use vodka, the British sherry or whisky, the Americans bourbon, and the French therapists used wine.

After this period of considerable activity during the forties, research workers appeared to lose interest in the therapeutic possibilities of aversion conditioning. The resurgence of interest in aversion therapy (in Britain at least) can be traced, to some extent, to the publication of Raymond's (1956) fascinating account of the treatment of a fetishist by apomorphine conditioning. The response to this paper was, of course, enhanced by the growth of Behaviour Therapy and, in the past few years, many successes with aversion treatment have been reported (see reviews by Rachman, 1961; Franks, 1963, 1966; Eysenck and Rachman, 1965; Rachman, 1965). The next significant development was the switch from chemical to electrical methods and the important publications were those of McGuire and Vallance (1964), Feldman and MacCulloch (1965), Blakemore *et al.* (1961), Blake (1965) and Marks and Gelder (1967). Anyone who contemplates using aversion treatment must first make a decision about the type of noxious stimulus which he is going to employ. To date most of the cases reported in the literature have been treated by chemical aversion methods but there are sound reasons for believing that electrical methods may be preferable (Eysenck, 1960; Rachman, 1961, 1965).

After selecting an aversive stimulus, the therapist has to decide on the timing of the stimulus and its mode of introduction. There are numerous variations of procedure and the therapist's choice can be made on the basis of practical precedent or by deduction from psychological theory. If he is guided by clinical precedent, presumably he will choose a method which has been used with success in the treatment of his patient's disorder. If he is guided by theoretical considerations, then he needs to

---

1 Miller *et al.* (1964) traced 169 references to conditioning procedures in the literature on alcoholism.

B

consider the merits and shortcomings of three models of learning: classical conditioning, avoidance conditioning, punishment training.

Until quite recently, the shortage of relevant data and clear paradigms made the design of treatment extremely trying. This task has been simplified in certain respects by our increased comprehension of the three models mentioned above. These advances in theoretical understanding must not be exaggerated, however, and therapeutic applications are still seriously limited by our ignorance. In particular, we have only the remotest notions about the operation of cognitive controlling factors.

Our evaluation of the clinical, experimental and theoretical literature leads us to propose that, for the present, treatment procedures should follow a 'punishment training' paradigm. The aversive stimulus should be administered contingent on the occurrence of the deviant response. For various reasons, however, we feel that a punishment model does not provide a sufficiently comprehensive *explanation* of the aversion therapy process. For example, it is of little assistance in accounting for the attitudinal changes which are observed during treatment.

Despite its limited explanatory value, the punishment model does provide a useful and practical schema for the design and conduct of treatment. Until our understanding of the processes involved in aversion therapy is extended, we recommend the use of the 'punishment training' paradigm.

Learning theory

In recent years the connections between 'learning theory' and behaviour therapy have come under critical examination (see Breger and McGaugh, 1966a, 1966b; Rachman and Eysenck, 1966; Weist, 1967). It is commonly argued that behaviour therapy bears little or no relation to 'learning theory' or, indeed, to experimental psychology. While it is true that 'learning theory' and behaviour therapy are by no means fully integrated, we feel that there are several important and necessary connections.[1]

The three most prominent techniques of behaviour therapy (aversion therapy, desensitisation, operant training) all have such connections. These relations can be grouped into five categories: historical, the

1 There are, of course, several theories of learning. The term 'learning theory' is used to include theories 'which overlap in many ways, and give rise to similar predictions, although experimentalists may show a preference for one or other of two ways of talking about phenomena. But both are agreed about most of these phenomena, and it is these which "are closest to reality", and which form the factual, scientific basis of behaviour therapy' (see Rachman and Eysenck, 1966).

provision of treatment paradigms, deductions and predictions based on learning theory, the provision of a therapeutic 'technology', the provision of an experimental basis for developing and assessing treatment procedures.

The historical connections between the main behavioural treatment methods and experimental psychology (especially 'learning theory') are clear and direct. It is fair to state that all three methods were developed from the findings of the experimental psychology of learning – in fact, they can be traced to Pavlov's work on conditioning. The historical emergence of chemical aversion has been mentioned above and the first (?) application of this method was derived explicitly from Pavlov's findings. The earliest use of electrical aversion was also based on Pavlovian findings but the recent developments of this method have been influenced by Skinner's work on operant conditioning and Solomon's studies of avoidance conditioning. Even though 'aversive' forms of treatment have been used for centuries (Hunter and McAlpine, 1963), it seems clear that *aversion therapy* as currently conceived and practised, would not have developed in the absence of Pavlov's findings and their consequences. Operant training methods are a direct application of the psychology of operant conditioning, and particularly the extension of this area as exemplified by Skinner's work. Again, it is highly improbable that the clinical operant procedures would have developed in the absence of Pavlov's, Bechterev's and Skinner's work. Wolpe's (1958) major contributions to behaviour therapy, including the design of desensitisation treatment, were based on several sources within 'learning theory' and most particularly, the work of Pavlov, Watson and Hull.

'Learning theory' has provided *methods* of operation which are of therapeutic value. The best example of this is seen in operant training 'technology'. The administration of aversion therapy also involves the use of experimental techniques, but to a lesser degree. Desensitisation treatment, however, only retains some elements of the operations involved in learning psychology studies (e.g. Mary Cover Jones' feeding inhibition method). In order successfully to apply the theory to clinical problems, Wolpe (1958) found it necessary to extend and elaborate his early methods of practical retraining by introducing imaginal stimulation.

'Learning theory' has provided *paradigms* on which to base treatment techniques. For example, Wolpe's account of the genesis and role of anxiety in neurotic disorders was based on the work of Pavlov and Hull, extended into the sphere of experimental neuroses. In aversion therapy, most clinicians work within the context of Pavlovian classical conditioning. The present work examines the value of this and other models. Clinical workers who employ operant procedures tend to use Skinner's view of behaviour as their model.

'Learning theory' enables clinical psychologists to make *deductions and predictions* about abnormal behaviour and the effects of therapeutic interventions. In the present work, for example, we will attempt to show how a punishment model generates numerous predictions about the effects of treatment (see Chapter 15). For instance, electrical aversion therapy will produce more prolonged suppression of deviant sexual behaviour if the aversive stimulus is of moderate intensity. Mild shocks will lead to a temporary suppression of such behaviour. Response-contingent aversive stimulation will produce suppression of deviant behaviour, but non-contingent stimulation will fail to do so. In the use of desensitisation, Wolpe was able to predict that the inhibition of anxiety provoked by treated stimuli will generalise to similar but untreated stimuli. In operant training procedures, we can predict the effects of positive and negative reinforcement on abnormal behaviour (e.g. Ayllon, 1963; Ayllon and Houghton, 1962; Ayllon, Houghton and Hughes, 1965).

'Learning theory' has helped to provide an experimental basis for *designing and assessing* treatment procedures. In operant training procedures, clinicians assess change in the same way as laboratory experimentalists. They also assess the effect of particular procedures by conventional means (e.g. test probes, see Wolf and Risley, 1964). In desensitisation treatment, a great deal of our knowledge has been acquired by the use of experimental designs ordinarily employed in studying the psychology of learning (Rachman, 1967), but it must of course be acknowledged that these methods are common to all branches of experimental psychology. The experimental design of studies in aversion therapy are generally of the same character and hence not exclusive to 'learning theory'. Moreover, the recent advances in experimental methods employed in aversion therapy studies (e.g. penile plethysmography, semantic differential tests) derive largely from physiology and personality studies.

Having argued for the existence of five clear links between 'learning theory' and behaviour therapy, it is also necessary to draw attention to the limitations of these associations. Firstly, the attempts which have been made to construct treatment methods from 'learning theory' have not always been successful. It can be argued, for example, that Feldman and MacCulloch's (1965) deduced 'anticipatory avoidance conditioning' treatment for homosexuals is unsatisfactory on many counts (see Chapter 7). Secondly, the 'learning theory' models which are used can only account for some of the clinical evidence which is currently available. Thirdly, our methods of assessing therapeutic improvements are still miserably inadequate. Naturally, more limitations could be mentioned. This should, however, be unnecessary as there are few psychologists who would contest the view that behaviour therapy (and 'learning theory' for that matter) has not yet reached the stage where full explanations are possible.

It is our contention nevertheless that the links between 'learning theory' and behaviour therapy are genuine and useful. Certainly, in the present work we have found that 'learning theory', or more accurately, the experimental psychology of learning is both relevant and helpful in attempting to understand aversion therapy.

2

Varieties of aversive stimulation

The search for noxious stimuli antedates the growth of modern psychology. Numerous examples of the nastier products of human imagination are described in the historical text prepared by Hunter and MacAlpine (1963), and some startling and disreputable antecedents of aversion therapy were also related by Castell (1967).

Aversion therapy (modern style) has involved the almost exclusive use of electrical or emetic noxious stimulation. In compiling a list of all the types which have been used within the last ten years, however, we were surprised at the size and variety of the inventory. It must be noted, however, that most of these variations have only been used on rare occasions and that not all of them actually fall into the category of *aversive* stimulation – 'negative reinforcers' is probably a more accurate label. The list is given here as a matter of theoretical interest and brief accounts of each type of stimulation are provided.

Noise

High intensity auditory signals have been used quite commonly in experimental psychology (Azrin, 1958) and can produce aversive effects. Azrin and Holz (1966) state that the main disadvantage of aversive noise is that its range of effective variation is restricted. To this limitation we must add the observation that subjects generally adapt to auditory signals fairly rapidly – unlike shock.

A few clinical applications of aversive noise have been reported and, broadly speaking, it was found that although behavioural suppression did occur, these effects were transient. Flanagan *et al*. (1958) explored aversive noise effects on three stutterers and Barrett (1964) studied a tiqueur. With the exception of one stutterer, the suppressive effects of noise were not observed to persist after the termination of the aversive conditioning sessions.

The clinical value of aversive noise appears to be minimal. If a signal of moderate intensity is used, then the patient is likely to adapt to it. Moreover, Azrin (1958) concluded that auditory signals of less than 105 decibels produce little suppression. Even extremely high intensity signals (up to 135 decibels) cannot be relied upon to produce total suppression. As the practicable upper limit of auditory stimulation is approached at 135 decibels, there seems to be little value in pursuing the possibility of employing aversive noise.

Time-out from positive reinforcement

Ferster (1958) has argued that the aversive controls encountered in social situations generally involve the removal or discontinuation of positive reinforcement. Five common social punishments – disapproval, imprisonment, isolation, fines, criticism – fit into this scheme and can also be viewed as 'time-out'. After a careful consideration of the problem, Leitenberg (1965) reached the tentative conclusion that 'time-out satisfied sufficient criteria to conclude that it belongs to the class of stimuli called "aversive" '.

Time-out procedures have been applied in a number of clinical studies with disturbed children and there can be little doubt about their potency (e.g. Lovaas, 1966; Wolf, Risley and Mees, 1964; Burchard and Tyler, 1965). A full description of the technique, with clinical examples, is provided by Tyler and Brown (1966). It appears that swift, brief isolation can successfully eliminate long-standing and severe behaviour problems but, in the experience of the present writers, the method needs to be applied with great consistency and promptitude.

Traumatic respiratory paralysis

The infusion of a 20-mg. drip of scoline (a curare-like drug) produces a temporary traumatic respiratory paralysis in human subjects. Sanderson et al. (1963) showed that extraordinarily powerful conditioned responses could be established on the basis of the paralysis induced by this drug, and then explored the possible use of scoline injections as an aversive stimulus for treating alcoholism. They compared scoline-based aversion therapy with two control treatments in three groups of fifteen alcoholics each (Madill et al., 1966). The scoline-group of patients were given alcohol to smell, taste and see immediately before and during the period of respiratory paralysis. The second group received scoline injections without the presentation of alcohol, and the third group received placebos. The only significant alteration in drinking noted in the scoline-conditioning group was a change in venue and this change was also observed in the patients who received scoline only. The clinical value of this radical method is therefore doubtful. Moreover, the effects cannot be attributed solely to conditioning in so far as the scoline-only group responded in the same manner as the conditioned group.

Holzinger, Mortimer and van Dusen (1967) tried out the Sanderson–Madill method on twenty-three male alcoholics and obtained clinical improvements in only two of them. Clancy, Vanderhoff and Campbell (1966) failed to find significant differences in abstinence rates when comparing patients treated with scoline or saline injections. The most recent report (Farrar, Powell and Martin, 1968) shows two successes out of twelve patients treated by the respiratory paralysis method. The two successfully treated patients were still abstinent one year after the administration of the treatment.

On the present evidence it appears that patients treated with scoline as the UCS make an initial response to the treatment; there is also vidence that a similar response can be obtained simply by administering coline or when saline injections act as the UCS. The necessity for using scoline conditioning (or scoline alone) is thus undermined.

One of the most disturbing features evident in some of these reports is the failure of the therapists to give their patients a frank explanation of the proposed treatment. In our view this omission is ethically questionable (see page 94 ff.). As there is no longer any reason for supposing that the scoline-conditioning method is particularly effective in treating alcoholism, we feel that this is the right moment to terminate investigations of this type.

Aversion relief treatment

In 1964, Thorpe *et al.* described a method of treatment which combines aversion therapy and relief-from-shock (used as positive reinforcement). The technique is an extension of aversive conditioning in which the 'relief response which inevitably follows the cessation of aversion conditioning is utilised'.

A series of words and phrases is presented to the S and then followed by shock – a classical conditioning procedure. The innovation consists of presenting a *relief* word as a signal that the aversion trials are finished; the hope is that the S will develop a positive reaction to the relief stimulus. For example, a homosexual patient was shocked in the presence of slides such as 'sodomy', 'flapping wrists' and the relief stimuli consisted of heterosexual phrases such as 'female breasts', 'girl friends', etc.

Although Thorpe *et al.* achieved some useful therapeutic results, it is not yet possible to determine either the overall effectiveness of their method or, more pertinently, the value of their innovation. In their sexually disordered patients, masturbatory practice was included as part

of therapy. There is evidence that aversive conditioning alone is successful, and there are also data on the combined effects of aversion plus
masturbatory changes. Consequently, the separate contribution (if any)
of aversion-relief will need to be demonstrated before its clinical use is
contemplated.

A move in this direction has been made by Schmidt, Castell and
Brown (1965), but as their data were not collected systematically, all
that one can conclude is that the case for aversion-relief has not been
disproved. In fact, their retrospective analysis of fourteen patients (with
mixed diagnoses) showed that aversion-relief produced an 87% improvement rate. This figure does not, however, include the eight patients
who refused treatment or defected.

Some incidental observations reported by Thorpe et al. (1964) are
worth mentioning. Apparently as a consequence of the aversion-relief
therapy, one of their homosexual patients (Case No. 1) reported that his
reaction to homosexuals had changed from pleasure to 'aggression and
disgust'. His indifferent attitude to women also changed and he now
regarded them as 'desirable sexual partners' (as assessed on the Osgood
Semantic Differential Test). The second case, a latent homosexual,
reported that as treatment progressed he spent increasing amounts of
time thinking about girls, whereas he found thoughts of homosexuality
'frightening and sickening'. Their fifth case was treated for latent homosexuality and motor-cycle fetishism. As treatment progressed, he
reported the loss of his interest in motor-cycles and was no longer
sexually aroused by them. His homosexual fantasies disappeared and
he developed heterosexual interests.

Unfortunately we cannot be sure what aspects of the treatment
produced these interesting changes. The patients received shocks in the
presence of deviant stimuli, relief after heterosexual stimuli and were
also asked to masturbate to heterosexual fantasies. At best, one can
account for the loss of interest in the deviant stimuli by the administration of shocks and the development of heterosexual interest by aversion-
relief and masturbation. It is difficult to explain, however, why the two
patients developed feelings of *disgust* or *revulsion* in regard to homosexuals. These reactions are, of course, fairly often encountered after
chemical aversion.

Combination methods

It has to be pointed out that aversion therapy has often been used in
combination with other forms of treatment. Sometimes this is done

explicitly (e.g. Blake's [1965] use of relaxation-plus-aversion), but more often additional therapy is given as a matter of course and usually consists of counselling, reassurance or brief psychotherapy. Some writers have firmly recommended that aversion therapy always be accompanied by adjuvant therapy. In some cases the use of additional methods seems to be essential, but the best combinations and the circumstances which demand extra treatment are by no means clear.

The three types of adjuvant treatment which offer most promise are: desensitisation, alterations in masturbatory practice, drugs. It is to be hoped, however, that research into the effects of supplementary techniques will not obscure the specific and separate consequences of aversion therapy itself.

Miscellaneous methods

An intriguing new method of treatment, covert sensitisation, which uses imaginal aversive stimulation, is discussed in Chapter 13. The health hazards associated with smoking have provoked some new aversive methods (e.g. Wilde, 1965, 1966; Franks *et al.* 1967), but none of them has yet received a full evaluation. Weiner's (1962, 1966) excellent research on response-cost may, in time, produce some clinical 'by-products' – probably in the field of therapeutic token-economies (e.g. Burchard, 1967; Liberman, 1968) and the technique of 'satiation' has been ingeniously applied by Ayllon (1964) in a limited number of cases.

Repugnance

The preliminary findings on the effects of covert sensitisation give rise to a re-consideration of the possible value of *overt* sensitisation. Electrical and chemical aversion therapy, both of which can be regarded as instances of overt sensitisation, use painful or nausea-inducing stimulation. Covert sensitisation methods employ approximations of these painful or nausea-inducing stimuli. They seem also to suggest that feelings of *revulsion* or *disgust* may prove to be effective aversive consequences. It should be possible, for example, to associate drinking or deviant sexual behaviour with real or imaginal stimuli which provoke revulsion or disgust – without pain or nausea. In practice, of course, it is likely that disgusting or offensive stimuli will frequently induce nausea. The important point, however, is that everyone has some stimuli (verbal, visual, olfactory, gustatory) which can produce feelings of revulsion. In exploratory interviews with a few patients we find that they can all be 'put off' their food by the intrusion of a disgusting stimulus.

Whether the deliberate and repeated introduction of these stimuli, contingent on abnormal responses, can suppress deviant behaviour is as yet unknown. The potential aversive value of offensive stimuli seems worth considering and we suspect that disgusting olfactory stimulation may prove to be particularly powerful.

Summary

Aversion therapy almost always involves the use of aversive electrical or chemical stimulation. Other types of aversive stimulation which have been used or suggested, include: intense auditory stimulation, time out from reinforcement, traumatic respiratory paralysis, aversion-relief, covert sensitisation, combination methods, satiation, response-cost procedures. Of this list, only one is in fairly regular clinical use. Time-out procedures are apparently of considerable value in reducing disruptive behaviour, particularly in children. Aversion-relief is a promising method, but has not yet been adequately studied, and covert sensitisation has fascinating possibilities. It is recommended that the treatment of alcoholism by traumatic respiratory paralysis be terminated.

3
Chemical aversion treatment of alcoholism

In 1942, Voegtlin and Lemere published an extensive review of the effects of available treatments for addiction to alcohol. They concluded that the conditioning procedures were among the most promising. According to these writers, the purpose of conditioning treatment is as follows:

Treatment of alcohol addiction by establishing a conditioned reflex depends fundamentally on the creation of an aversion or distaste for alcoholic beverages by virtue of their association during treatment with some sort of noxious stimulus. The latter stimulus is usually concerned with the elicitation of nausea or vomiting and is called the unconditioned stimulus. The conditioned stimulus is represented by various alcoholic beverages. The repeated association of these two stimuli, under appropriate circumstances, will result finally in the ability of the conditioned stimulus (liquor) to elicit the (noxious) response formerly elicited by the unconditioned stimulus (*p. 770*).

It can be seen from this quotation that Voegtlin and Lemere viewed the treatment procedure in terms of a classical conditioning paradigm.

Voegtlin and Lemere attributed the earliest attempt to treat alcoholism by conditioning to Kantorovich (1935), who used electric shock as the unconditioned stimulus. In 1933, Sluchevsky and Friken apparently treated seven cases of alcoholism by a chemical method employing apomorphine as the unconditioned stimulus. The effects of this treatment were not reported. Two years later Galant employed a modified version of this procedure and reported the results which he had obtained in twenty-two cases. Three of his patients relapsed immediately after completion of treatment, but the other nineteen were abstinent for varying periods, while two (less than 10%) were still dry one year after the termination of treatment. Slightly more encouraging results were apparently obtained in France and in England. As Voegtlin and Lemere pointed out, these early results were far from being impressive. None the less they argued that, with proper application of the technique, improvements could be expected in as many as 70% of patients treated. Their optimism was derived largely from their own experiences with the conditioning technique.

In 1950, Lemere and Voegtlin described their own results with more than 4,000 alcoholic patients treated during a period of fourteen years at the Shadel Sanatorium in Seattle. The Sanatorium was devoted exclusively to the treatment of alcoholics, and their patients, who were all voluntary, were 'advantageously circumstanced types of alcoholic patient'. They stated that their treatment technique 'does not offer much hope' to inadequate alcoholics and those whose motivation for treatment is low. Their method consisted of producing nausea and vomiting to the sight, taste, smell and thought of alcoholic beverages by administering emetine as the unconditioned stimulus. Treatment sessions lasted from thirty minutes to one hour and approximately six sessions were given to each patient, usually on alternate days. The average length of hospitalisation was ten days. Between two and four booster treatments were given as necessary, or, routinely, at the end of six and twelve months. They noticed that relapses were often treated 'with better success the second time'. Surveying their results with patients treated between 1935 and 1948, they were able to obtain follow-up data on 4,096 of the original group of 4,468 – an admirable model of efficiency and perseverance. Forty-four per cent of the patients who were followed up were found to have remained totally abstinent since their first treatment. Of the patients who relapsed, 878 were re-treated, and of these, 39% remained sober after their last treatment. 'This gives an overall abstinence rate of 51% for the 13-year period covered by this survey.' An analysis of the abstinence rates for varying periods revealed a slow rate of attrition. After their first treatment, 60% were known to have remained abstinent for at least a year, 51% for at least two years, 38% for at least five years and 23% for at least ten years. As the authors point out, these results compare very well with other methods of treatment – none of which, in their review, yielded abstinence rates of more than 24%.

Their experience with apomorphine led them to conclude that it was too short-acting and that its sedative action interfered with the process of conditioning. In their procedure, emetine produced superior results, but the relevant data were not given. They also point out that in the three years preceding their 1950 report, they introduced an adjuvant treatment for those patients who showed evidence of neurotic disturbances. They calculate that approximately 30% of their patients received adjuvant pentothal treatment and argue that this addition is 'definitely helpful'.

This work by Lemere and Voegtlin has many admirable qualities and provides substantial support for the notion that aversion conditioning therapy can be effective – or more accurately, chemical aversion treatment – in the management of alcoholism. Their findings cannot, in the strictest sense, be regarded as definitive proof, however, because their sample is atypical of the alcoholic population and it is not possible to attribute the improvements which they obtained simply to the effects of the conditioning treatment. One would need to know what the spontaneous remission rate in a population of this type would have been and, also, one needs to know what therapeutic benefits were derived from the experience of hospitalisation and its associated influences. Neither is it possible to accept unquestioningly their conclusion that apomorphine is less effective than emetine. In regard to their use of booster treatments, however, some information is provided in an earlier paper. Voegtlin, Lemere, Broz and O'Hallaren (1942) followed up 285 patients for one year after the completion of treatment. Of these, 197 had from one to four booster treatments spaced at approximately one to two months after the original treatment and thereafter at ninety-day intervals. These booster treatments consisted of one further session which was completed over twenty-four hours. It was found that those patients who received two or more booster treatments had abstinence rates above 90%, whereas those who did not receive booster treatments had an abstinence rate of only 74% (over a one-year follow-up). It is interesting to observe that many of their patients showed a marked reluctance to return for booster treatments (this parallels a recent finding with electrical aversion treatment [Bancroft, 1968]). The authors also reiterate that patients who show positive motivation for improvement generally do well on the treatment. Unfortunately, however, no separate analysis of the data is made in terms of the patients' strength of motivation prior to and during treatment.

An important question raised by the apparently successful results obtained with this treatment is whether or not such effects can properly be ascribed to a conditioning process. As is the case with other types of psychological disorder, a proportion of alcoholic patients improve without formal therapeutic assistance. It is of course very difficult to determine a spontaneous remission rate for all types of alcoholic patient and considerable variations are known to occur among patients from differing social groups and with varying types of personality. For this, and other reasons, it is highly desirable that any attempts to assess the effectiveness of any type of treatment for alcoholism should include a matched control group. In the absence of this type of data it is impossible accurately to determine the extent to which the results obtained by Lemere and Voegtlin were solely determined by the conditioning treatment and to what extent peripheral factors played a part, e.g. hospitalisation, contact with experienced medical staff and so forth. It should also be remembered that in the three years prior to their report on the overall effectiveness of this treatment, these workers introduced an adjuvant treatment for a third of their patients (pentothal treatment). There is one strong indication that conditioning *is* the effective process. On the basis of the evidence discussed in their general review of the literature, Lemere and Voegtlin (1942) convincingly argued that neither emetine nor apomorphine, given in the absence of the conditioned alcoholic stimuli, were effective.

The problem of determining the extent to which improvements can be assigned to aversion conditioning alone is unfortunately an almost universal feature of the clinical reports on the subject. Thimann (1949) described the results obtained with emetine aversion conditioning in 245 patients who were followed up for periods of one or more years. One hundred and twenty-five (51 %) were found to have remained abstinent and seventy-three of these were found to be abstinent after a four-year post-treatment period. These figures, which are reasonably similar to those reported from the Shadel Sanatorium, are likewise moderately encouraging. The problem of interpretation is similar to that mentioned in regard to the Shadel studies in that the aversion treatment was supplemented by psychotherapy and/or group therapy. No control data were obtained. Thimann listed a number of contra-indications for conditioning treatment which can be divided into two main categories: unstable premorbid personality and/or various types of physical disorder.

A fairly typical example of the type of report which features in the literature on chemical aversion treatment of alcohol is that of Williams (1947). He reported on the effects of the treatment in thirty-five patients. Only eighteen of the original group completed the treatment and of these, sixteen made a reasonable degree of improvement. Eleven of the sixteen had 'returned to moderate drinking but have never become intoxicated while five showed a definite aversion to alcohol'. Of the seventeen patients who did not complete treatment, three were found to have ceased drinking altogether, two drank in moderation and twelve had returned to their former drinking pattern. An interesting aspect of this otherwise unsatisfactory account is the fact that the sample consisted of 'hard cases'. All of the patients showed evidence of 'marked debilitation so that treatment was necessary to put these patients in the best physical condition'. Despite the fact that an aversion to alcohol was observed in a proportion of these cases, it is not possible to attribute the therapeutic results solely to the conditioning technique. In addition to aversion therapy, the patients also received medical treatment, psychotherapy and social rehabilitation procedures. Furthermore, the timing of the treatment leaves a great deal to be desired (see below).

In 1957, Wallerstein and his colleagues described the results obtained in a trial which compared chemical aversion treatment, hypnotherapy, antabuse treatment, milieu therapy. In their introductory discussion Wallerstein and Chotlos quote, with seeming approval, a criticism made by Carlson to the effect that it is not possible to conclude from the work of the Shadel group or of Thimann that the treatment effects described by these people can be attributed to the conditioning procedure – 'He concludes that it seems inaccurate to ascribe any special merit to aversion therapy' (p. 3). However, the Wallerstein group themselves were not entirely successful in avoiding this type of contaminating effect. Hammersley (1957, p. 62) describing the method used in the study states that the fifty patients who received conditioning treatment also 'continued to attend weekly group therapy sessions and to participate in a full activities programme'. On the other hand, they did attempt to obtain control data by the inclusion of two comparison treatment groups and a fourth group which received only milieu therapy. Unfortunately, the study, in addition to being open to the contamination effect mentioned above, contains three major weaknesses. The patients in the four groups were not appropriately matched. For example, the patients in the conditioning group were categorised as containing 62% with character disorders and 14% with psychotic or psychotic-like disorders, the milieu group had 26% psychotic disorders and 52% character disorders, the antabuse group had 32% psychotic or psychotic-like disorders and 47% of character disorders, the hypnotherapy group contained 28% psychotic type disorders and 51% character disorders. Apart from the fact that these broad groupings cover as many as thirteen disparate diagnostic labels, it can be seen that the aversion therapy group had the smallest proportion of psychotic or psychotic-like patients (14% vs. 32% in the antabuse group) and the largest proportion of patients with character disorders. These disproportions might have played some part in determining the overall outcome in that one of the sub-analyses carried out by the authors reveals that the patients with character disorders did worst on all types of treatment and those with what they describe as psychotic-like problems responded rather well to the aversion therapy procedure. Another difficulty in assessing these results arises from the fact that a large minority of the patients were lost at follow-up. For example, in the aversion therapy group, twenty-one of the fifty patients treated were not assessed at follow-up. Consequently the results which the authors describe are subject to the possible effects of unknown biases. The loss of this follow-up information is extremely unfortunate. It also tends to have misleading consequences in that one may erroneously quote the overall improvement figures in terms of the number of patients seen at follow-up. In point of fact, the authors themselves appear at times to be confused by their own data analysis. Hammersley quotes an improvement rate of 41 % who are 'significantly improved' after conditioning therapy (p. 65) and later, in the same book, Wallerstein (1957) gives a percentage of 'total patients improved' for the conditioning group of 24 % (p. 156).

The third limitation of the Wallerstein study centres on the problems of timing and the identity of the aversive event – is it nausea or vomiting? Both of these problems are discussed in relation to other studies on page 29 below. The four groups in this study consisted of the following numbers of patients: Antabuse – 47, Aversion therapy – 50, Hypnotherapy – 39, Milieu therapy – 42. Of the patients who were followed up, twenty-five treated with antabuse were improved and fifteen were unimproved. In the aversion therapy group, twelve were improved and seventeen were unimproved. In the hypnotherapy group, fourteen were improved and fourteen were not improved. In the milieu therapy group, eleven were improved and fifteen were not improved. Taken at face value these results seem to indicate that the antabuse treatment was superior to the other three types which did not differ among themselves. The results give no indication that the conditioning aversion therapy made any additional contribution above that obtained from milieu therapy. However, in view of the weaknesses of the study mentioned above, it cannot be concluded that the aversion therapy was wholly ineffective.

Franks (1960, 1966) has argued that the large variations in success claimed by therapists using aversion therapy can probably be accounted for by the poor quality of much of this work. In particular he draws attention to the frequent disregard shown for the importance of temporal factors in conditioning. For example, he quotes Spencer Patterson as recommending that the alcohol 'should be given after the patient feels nauseated'. He comments that 'of the many possible procedures there is no doubt that this form of conditioning (backward conditioning) is the

c

least easy to develop and the most readily extinguished' (p. 284). To this one can add an example of therapists who allowed as long as twenty minutes to elapse between the drinking of the alcohol and the onset of vomiting – Williams (1947) mixed the emetine in the patient's drink and then waited until the nausea and vomiting occurred. It is interesting to notice, however, that despite this time-lag, all of his patients who completed the treatment developed an aversion to alcohol – 'usually after the fourth treatment, he would begin to show marked aversion to alcohol' (p. 192). Under these badly timed conditions it is surprising that the aversion developed at all, but one can reasonably assume that the strength of the conditioned response is unlikely to be very great when produced under these conditions. Another example of aversion developing under sub-optimal treatment conditions is given in a recent study; Beaubrun (1967) found that 'some patients developed a genuine conditioned aversion, but many who did not appeared to benefit from the treatment nevertheless'. As he failed to state what his criteria were, this potentially interesting distinction is lost. This is a pity as the treatment method diverges markedly from the usual classical conditioning model and some hard data on a so-called 'conversion' method would be welcome. The results from this study add little to our evaluation of chemical aversion therapy because the treatment method does not follow the conditioning paradigm and the data were assessed retrospectively. No controls were available and the statement that 'A.A. alone seems better than emetine alone' is misleading because (among other reasons) the emetine treatment 'was only given to patients who requested it, and usually only if they had failed with more conservative methods, e.g. disulfiram and A.A.'. However, the suggestion that post-treatment attendance of A.A. is therapeutically beneficial may be worth following up.

Reviewing the literature on this subject one cannot help being struck by the mixture of methods which have been used and by the prevailing confusion about what the unconditional response should be. Most writers appear to assume that it is the act of vomiting which is the crucial event. There are good grounds for believing, however, that it is the onset of nausea which forms the basis for the development of the conditioned aversion reaction (see p. 29 below). If this is indeed the case, then many therapists have undoubtedly been using a backward conditioning procedure. In one of the largest of the trials of chemical aversion treatment (that reported by Wallerstein and his colleagues) Hammersley (p. 60) described their procedure as follows: 'As a strong wave of nausea

developed, and before actual vomiting began, the patient was given
1½ ounces of whisky and told to swallow it directly or briefly smell of
it first and then swallow it. If the administration of whisky was properly
timed, emesis occurred in less than 30 seconds after ingestion of whisky.'
It can be seen that here the clear assumption is that the unconditional
response (or more properly, event) is the act of vomiting and *not* nausea.
It is instructive to notice, however, that 'there was almost without
exception a strong aversion to alcohol' developed in their group of fifty
patients. In fact, 25% of their cases vomited immediately they were
given whisky after they had undergone five days of conditioning treatment. It is clear, therefore, that even if nausea is the crucial event (and
hence Wallerstein and his colleagues were using a backward conditioning procedure), some measure of conditioned aversion was being
developed. It is likely, however, that the relatively poor therapeutic
outcome in these patients can be explained partly by their faulty technique. It would, incidentally, have been rather interesting to know
whether these workers observed a relationship between the establishment of a conditioned vomiting reaction and eventual therapeutic
outcome. In other words, did those patients who developed a conditioned vomiting reaction show better long-term results than those
patients who developed an aversion which did not involve actual emesis?
Hammersley found that in 25% of their cases the conditioning of nausea
and vomiting to the CS was effective. When the patients were given some
whisky to drink, vomiting followed very quickly. In the remaining 75%
a number of disturbed reactions were observed – nausea, flushing,
perspiration, palpitation and so on. He states that, 'Even though emesis
did not occur in these cases, there was almost without exception a strong
aversion to alcohol.' Over the follow-up period, the improved patients
reported that when they tried to drink they rarely experienced emesis, but
that they frequently felt ill and nauseous and that these reactions became
more severe if they continued to drink. One patient reported a spread
of the conditioning effect to pills and even to water! Another patient
however, deliberately 'broke' his aversion to alcohol by subjecting himself
to four hours of 'dogged drinking' – despite recurring emesis. One of the
clearest observations to emerge from this work is the fact that patients
with unstable home backgrounds or of disturbed personality, responded
rather badly to all forms of treatment. This factor almost certainly contributed to the poor results obtained by Wallerstein and his colleagues in
comparison with the Shadel group which, it will be recalled, treated
private patients who were generally from the higher social groupings.

Wallerstein (1957, p. 163) mentioned two patients who were not improved by conditioning treatment and 'paradoxially claimed an increased desire and capacity for alochol after conditioning'. This may possibly be an example of 'punishment contrast' (see p. 53). Another incidental finding which is worth noting is the occurrence of two apparent cases of symptom substitution. Hammersley mentions one patient whose alcohol consumption was markedly reduced but who displayed disordered and anti-social behaviour after the completion of treatment. Another patient was successfully conditioned but later developed a 'disabling, hysterical paralysis of the right arm, attributed by him to one of the many hypodermic injections administered during the course of the hospitalisation'. As in all instances of presumed symptom substitution, it is extremely difficult to be certain that the phenomenon observed is truly a substitution rather than the development of a new problem consequent upon some further stress. This possibility is unfortunately not considered or discussed by Hammersley.

In his 1960 review, Franks criticised those writers who claim that the conditioned response established by this treatment 'is absolutely specific so that the subject may be in the happy state of having an aversion to spirits, but be able to enjoy the pleasures of drinking wine' (p. 285). Actually, this state of bliss has in fact been reported. Voegtlin and Lemere (1942) quote examples of this type, as do MacCulloch et al. (1966). Most recently Quinn and Henbest (1967) found that their ten alcoholic patients who had been treated by chemical aversion methods to a conditional stimulus of whisky developed an aversion to this drink, but not to other types of alcohol. The significance of this type of selective effect is discussed in some detail on page 49.

In our opinion, the most fair-minded interpretation which can be given to the evidence on chemical aversion therapy is as follows. There is a strong possibility that chemical aversion therapy is effective in the treatment of certain types of alcoholic patients. However, we have been unable to locate adequately convincing evidence to *prove* this possibility beyond any doubt. It must also be added that the treatment is, at best, somewhat inefficient. Furthermore, it appears that the best prospects for a satisfactory response to this treatment include adequate motivation and a stable personality and background.

Summary

Chemical aversion therapy has been used quite extensively in the treatment of alcoholism. In well-conducted studies, the abstinence rate observed one year after treatment is in the region of 60%. The relapse rate is a continuing problem but can be reduced with booster treatments. The majority of relapses occur within one year.

Patients with a stable pre-morbid personality and/or a cohesive home background probably respond better than other types of patient. Alcoholics who voluntarily seek treatment and are well motivated to recover, probably respond better than other types of patients.

Although this observation requires special attention, it appears that many (most?) patients develop an aversion to the alcoholic CS after treatment. This reaction takes the form of distaste or even revulsion. The aversive event involved in treatment is primarily the occurrence of nausea and it is not known what contribution, if any, is made by the onset of vomiting.

Does the conditioned aversive reaction generalise to all types of alcohol and/or all external situations? The evidence on 'spread of effect' is equivocal. Some observers claim that the treatment effects are widespread but there are a few clear examples of highly specific treatment effects.

Although there is strong evidence that aversion therapy is frequently effective in terminating alcoholism, it is not definitive. In particular, we require conclusive demonstrations that aversion therapy contributes more to the therapeutic process than the non-specific factors involved in general treatment and rehabilitation procedures.

4
Other applications of chemical aversion therapy

Until about ten years ago, chemical aversion treatment had been used almost exclusively in the management of alcoholic patients. Against a background of the emergence of behaviour therapy, Raymond's (1956) publication of a successful attempt to treat a fetishistic patient by apomorphine aversion conditioning aroused considerable interest. Since 1956, a sprinkling of similar case-reports have appeared in the literature but for present purposes we will concentrate only on those publications which seem to us to be of particular concern – either as landmarks or if they made some special contribution.

Raymond's patient was a thirty-three-year-old married man who was given treatment on probation after having been convicted of causing damage to a perambulator. Since the age of ten he had been attracted by prams and handbags. These objects aroused him sexually and he obtained a release of tension by attacking them. These attacks on prams had resulted in several convictions and he spent several periods in mental hospitals. He had not benefited from previous therapy, including psychoanalysis. Raymond's aversion treatment programme was similar to that used in the treatment of alcoholism. The patient was shown a collection of handbags, prams and coloured illustrations, 'after he had received an injection of apomorphine and just before nausea was produced'. Treatment was given two-hourly day and night, the patient was allowed no food and he was kept awake with amphetamine. Treatment was suspended after one week and the patient went home temporarily. He returned eight days later and reported some progress. Treatment was then continued for a further nine days and by this time he was showing a strong aversion to the fetish objects.

After the patient had been followed as an out-patient for a period of six months, he was given a booster course of treatment in hospital. Nineteen months later he 'still appeared to be doing well'. He no longer had fantasies concerning handbags and prams, his sexual relations with his wife had greatly improved, his probation officer reported very noticeable progress and he had no further trouble with the law. He reported that he no longer required his old fetishistic fantasies to enable him to have sexual intercourse with his wife and he had also ceased to masturbate with these fantasies. His wife confirmed that their sexual relationships had greatly improved.

During the course of the treatment and immediately after its completion, the patient explained that he was no longer sensitive to prams or handbags. That is, he ceased to be particularly attentive to them. After five days of the treatment, he had said that the 'mere sight of the objects made him sick' and when the treatment was terminated, he handed over a number of photographs of prams, saying that he had carried them with him for many years but would no longer need them. It is not clear, however, whether his reported aversion to the fetish had weakened when he was seen at the follow-up $1\frac{1}{2}$ year's post-treatment. Incidentally, Raymond's method of withholding food and preventing sleep does not appear to be essential. The rationale behind this aspect of the treatment, as given by Raymond, is that the modification of attitudes and 'psychological conversions are more easily obtained in states of exhaustion and hunger'. As became quite evident when this type of work was further developed, depriving the patient of food is apparently an unnecessary elaboration and one which can very readily be dispensed with. Similarly, there has been no support for the idea that it is necessary to keep the patient in a state of exhaustion – or, for that matter, that the treatments need to be given in such a concentrated form. These elaborations, like that of food deprivation, can be excluded. From a recent publication, it would appear that Raymond himself has now omitted these aspects of the treatment (Raymond and O'Keeffe, 1965).

In his discussion of the fetishist, Raymond makes the point that, despite the prognostications of various psychologists and psychoanalysts, the removal of the fetish objects was not followed either by impotence or homosexuality or sadism. In other words, no symptom substitution was observed.

Prompted by Raymond's success, a number of other therapists used his technique in attempting to treat other types of sexual disorder. Glynn and Harper (1961) and Lavin et al. (1961) successfully treated two transvestite patients with apomorphine aversion conditioning. In both cases the patients reportedly developed an aversion to the female clothing. Morgenstern, Pearce and Linford Rees (1965) offered aversion treatment to nineteen patients with transvestism. Six of these patients failed to attend for treatment and of the remaining thirteen, seven appear to have been cured while a number of 'relapse incidents' were reported by the other six patients after completing the course of treatment. All of the thirteen treated cases showed much improvement. The seven cured patients entirely ceased cross-dressing.

The actual treatment consisted of thirty-nine sessions, repeated three times daily. At each session the patient was given an apomorphine injection and then required to carry out his cross-dressing ritual during the onset of nausea. A number of difficulties arose during the administration of the treatment, including outbursts of aggression, and these are the subject of a separate account (Morgenstern and Pearce, 1963). At follow-up (which ranged from eight months to four years) the patients were given prolonged and detailed interviews. Three interesting points emerged from this undertaking. Firstly, most of the patients stated that the formerly exciting clothing had lost its appeal. Secondly, no symptom substitution was observed – on the contrary, it was found 'with astonishing uniformity, they reported better social contacts, less anxiety, and most gratifying for them, improvement in occupational adjustment' (Morgenstern *et al.*, 1965). Thirdly, the relapses which occurred tended to be episodic and could always be related to specific events in the patient's life (e.g. enforced sexual deprivation during wife's pregnancy, etc.). It seems clear from these results that it is unnecessary to keep patients in a state of exhaustion or food deprivation during the treatment.

Raymond (1964) gives a detailed and useful account of his treatment technique, explains how he determines the onset of nausea period, and reiterates the importance of introducing the conditioned stimulus before the feelings of nausea subside. In this report he also describes the successful treatment of two patients with addictions. One of these addicted patients developed a very strong conditioned nausea reaction to the CS (cigarettes) and also to similar or associated stimuli such as cigarette smoke, etc. Exposure to cigarettes or cigarette smoke reportedly made him feel ill.

Freund (1960) has been engaged in a protracted investigation of the effects of aversion therapy on homosexual behaviour. His treatment technique was adapted and developed from the aversion procedures commonly used in the treatment of alcoholism. After injecting emetine, he waited for the patient to experience the onset of nausea and then presented slides of dressed and undressed males to the patient. In the second phase of the treatment, the patient was shown films of nude and semi-nude females approximately seven hours after the administration of testosterone. Freund reported the results of this type of therapy on forty-seven patients. Follow-up studies carried out three and five years after treatment, indicated that 51% of his patients showed no improvement, 14·9% showed a temporary improvement, 25·5% were permanently improved; the remaining 8·5% were not adequately investigated.

Freund concluded that this form of aversion therapy did not produce results which were different in quality or degree from those claimed by other methods. This rough comparision does not, of course, take into account variations in the selection of patients, the evaluation of outcome (and particularly the prolonged follow-up carried out by Freund) and other important but uncontrolled variables. The value of this study would have been greatly enhanced if a matched control group had been studied at the same time. Nevertheless, on the face of it these results offer very little promise for this method of treating homosexuality.

In a later publication Freund (1965) reported that although his sample had been increased, the poor results had not altered. A five- to eight-year follow-up study of sixty-seven patients who had undergone this type of treatment revealed that only twelve of them showed long-term improvements. A further ten patients had shown a temporary heterosexual adaptation but then relapsed. Freund draws particular attention to the fact that no patients who were referred from the courts made a successful response. On the other hand, sixteen of the thirty-one patients who volunteered for treatment without any external pressure, and whose motivation for change was high, showed either long-term or temporary improvements.

Despite the disappointing therapeutic effects of Freund's treatment programme, he nevertheless made two contributions. His patients were subjected not only to aversion treatment but an attempt was also made to foster or generate heterosexual interests and activities. In this part of the treatment, the patients were given injections of testosterone and then seven hours later presented with films depicting nude females. While this attempt can scarcely be said to have produced fruitful results, it nevertheless draws attention to the importance of trying to help patients to develop alternative, acceptable and satisfying forms of sexual behaviour. In the course of his investigations Freund also developed an extremely useful instrument which enabled him to record the patient's involuntary sexual reactions. This penile plethysmograph produced a number of intriguing findings which are beyond the scope of the present book. It has, however, featured quite prominently in some of the more recent applications of electrical aversion therapy (see Chapters 6 and 7) and also offers numerous possibilities as a method for investigating many aspects of male sexual behaviour (see, for example, Rachman, 1967; Rachman and Hodgson, 1968). A simple and inexpensive modification of Freund's plethysmograph was developed by Bancroft, Jones and Pullan (1966) who described its use in the treatment of a case of paedophilia.

Chemical aversion therapy has also been used in treating a variety of other disorders (e.g. addiction; Raymond, 1962; Liberman, 1968), but as this literature consists almost entirely of isolated case histories, they will not be described here.

Summary

To conclude, chemical aversion therapy appears to be at least moderately successful in treating sexual disorders – with the possible exception of homosexuality. It should be pointed out again, however, that there is a notable absence of control studies and we are not therefore in a position to reach a definitive conclusion on its effectiveness. For reasons which will be discussed below, we feel that for the most part, electrical aversion therapy is the preferable technique.

5
The nature of chemical aversion therapy

It seems clear that chemical aversion therapy generally falls into a classical conditioning paradigm in which a repeated association is made between the stimuli associated with the undesirable activity and an unconditioned nausea reaction provoked by an emetic. The explicit intention of most therapists has been to set up a conditioned connection between the conditional stimuli and the unconditional reaction of nausea, such that, after treatment, the patient will cease carrying out the undesirable activity. It is hoped in fact that the appearance of the conditioned stimuli will be followed by feelings of nausea. Although this aim has been achieved in many instances by the time that treatment is terminated, the learned connection is not always stable.

Chemical aversion treatment does not follow the punishment model in that the aversive consequences are not necessarily 'response-produced' or 'response-contingent'. Chemical therapy is also distinguished from avoidance conditioning for a number of reasons. During the treatment the aversive consequences can neither be eliminated nor *avoided*. In addition, a prime feature of avoidance conditioning is the development of a new response pattern – this does not occur in chemical aversion therapy. The patient does not acquire a new type of response but instead is making much the same sort of response to a new *stimulus*. It would seem, therefore, that the most appropriate model is that of classical conditioning. It is worth bearing in mind, however, that the actual treatment techniques often incorporate some measure of instrumental activity, including punishment. A rigid classification into classical or instrumental conditioning is neither possible nor desirable.

Unfortunately, however, we cannot yet be absolutely certain that chemical aversion therapy is a true conditioning process. We can rule out the possibility that the treatment effects are produced simply by the action of the emetic drugs – at least in the case of alcoholism (Voegtlin and Lemere, 1942). And, clearly, the repeated presentation of the conditional stimuli does not eliminate alcoholism or sexual deviations. It then follows that *the treatment effects are a consequence of the repeated pairing of the CS and the UCS.*

This conclusion supports the view that the therapy is a conditioning process. Further positive evidence comes from the fact that a new stimulus-response bond is established. After successful treatment, patients are frequently reported to experience nausea or other negative reactions when they come into contact with the previously attractive CS.

In addition, there are numerous pieces of evidence which suggest that the usual phenomena associated with conditioning processes can be detected in aversion therapy – e.g. the effects of repeated trials, extinction, spontaneous recovery, booster effects, generalisation, etc. It must be pointed out, however, that these phenomena have not been subjected to deliberate inspection during and after aversion therapy. It is possible that they may not stand up to systematic testing.

At this stage of the discussion, it may seem that we are being needlessly pedantic. There remains one observation, however, which is potentially rather embarrassing to the argument that chemical aversion therapy is a conditioning process. In recounting the clinical data, we drew attention to the fact that some therapists (e.g. Williams, Hammersley) used backward conditioning sequences or excessive interstimulus delays, but nevertheless obtained some therapeutic successes. Strictly speaking, these patients should not have developed conditioned reactions or, at best, their CR's should have been very weak. While it is true that the majority of the patients who received this type of treatment either relapsed or failed to respond in the first place, some of them *were* successfully treated. This fact needs to be explained.

We would like to consider three possibilities. Firstly, the successful patients may have improved as a result of non-specific therapeutic influences (e.g. the milieu therapy group in the Wallerstein [1947] study). If this explanation is correct, then the claim that aversion therapy is a form of conditioning would be weakened. It is not, however, a fatal objection because it cannot encompass the fact that many patients who experienced the therapy, later exhibited nausea or vomiting in the presence of the CS.

A second explanation for the occasional success of backward aversion conditioning rests on the observation that the nausea produced by emetics lasts for some time and therefore the patient will experience *some* forward conditioning even if the CS is presented after the *onset* of nausea. In chemical aversion therapy, the UCS is *not* a discrete and brief event.

The third explanation invokes the role of cognitive factors and is complementary to the second explanation. It seems likely that human subjects quickly learn to regard the entire treatment session as being aversive and therefore the precise timing of stimulus sequences which is necessary in other types of conditioning situation (e.g. eye-blinks) is not essential in aversion therapy. The treatment situation may easily acquire secondary reinforcing properties. The animal experiment reported by Pavlov and mentioned on page 1 is an example of this type of secondary spread. There is, however, an even more pertinent observation recently reported by Ashem and Donner (1968). In an experiment on covert sensitisation (see Chapter 12) they found it impossible to use a backward conditioning method because their patients soon learned to make 'an automatic association' between the CS and the unpleasant UCS, *irrespective* of the actual sequence of stimulus presentations.

Summary

It is highly probable, but not certain, that chemical aversion therapy is a form of conditioning. Although a rigid classification is neither possible nor desirable, the therapy appears to be primarily a type of classical conditioning.

6
Chemical or electrical aversion?

Aversion treatment, particularly chemical aversion, can be an unpleasant and arduous form of therapy and this fact, coupled with the often equivocal results obtained in the treatment of alcoholics, has probably contributed to its decline in popularity. Franks (1960, 1963) has drawn attention to the poor quality of much of the early work on aversion treatment of alcoholics.

> . . . unfortunately, not all modern practice is sound . . . for example, some clinicians advocate giving the alcohol after the patient reaches the height of nausea. This, of course, is backward conditioning (since the unconditioned stimulus of the apomorphine or the emetine is preceding the conditioned stimulus of the alcohol) and backward conditioning, if it occurs at all, is at best very tenuous . . . (*Franks, 1963*).

In any conditioning situation, the time intervals which elapse between the presentation of the various stimuli and the response are of importance, and some aversion therapists appear to have been ignorant of this fact or have tended to ignore it. Franks writes that '. . . under such circumstances, it is hardly surprising that reports of evaluation studies range from virtually zero success to 100 per cent success'. Even if the timing is *not* crucial, temporal proximity of the CS and UCS is desirable.

The choice of nausea-producing drug has also given rise to difficulty. Some of the drugs which have been used to produce nausea also act as central depressants. This type of drug would interfere with the acquisition of the conditioned response. There is, furthermore, some confusion about the nature of the particular response which one is attempting to attach to the sight, smell and taste of the alcohol. In some of the earlier studies therapists stressed the action of vomiting rather than the feeling of nausea. As Raymond (1964) has shown, however, the action of vomiting is not the important event – apparently it is the feeling of nausea which influences the acquisition of an aversion reaction to alcohol. In regard to Raymond's clinical observations, it has been noted that 'a considerable number of studies have dealt with the effector aspect (of conditioning) and, with several notable exceptions, all agree that the response is unnecessary for conditioning' (Young, 1965). For example, the salivation response to morphine can be conditioned 'even though salivation itself is inhibited by atropine' (Young, 1965).

The problems involved in chemical techniques of aversion conditioning are multiplied by the existence of individual differences in reactivity to the various nausea-producing drugs. People differ in the speed and extent of their reactions to the various drugs and, furthermore, the same person may react differently to the same quantity of drug on different days or even at different times on the same day. Individual differences in reactivity, therefore, make the planning of a carefully controlled form of conditioning treatment extremely awkward. The use of chemical noxious stimuli also precludes the possibility of making accurate measurements of the unconditioned and conditioned responses which are being elicited. While it is possible, of course, to obtain measurements of reaction latency, it has proved extremely difficult, if not impossible, to obtain measures of magnitude of the responses produced.

Because of the arduous nature of the chemical aversion conditioning sessions, it is impractical to provide frequent repetitions of the association between the conditioned stimulus and the unconditioned stimulus. The number of conditioning presentations and the number of sessions which can be provided are, therefore, inherently restricted. These restrictions not only increase the duration of the treatment period, but they also limit the number of conditioning trials which can be carried out.

The treatment is unpleasant, not only for the patient, but also for the therapist and the nursing staff. It is not uncommon for attendants to object to participating in this form of treatment and there can be no doubt that it arouses antagonism in some members of the hospital staff. Complaints about the method being unaesthetic and even harrowing are not without justification – it is certainly a method which does not lend itself to popularity. The nature of this treatment also makes it rather difficult to arrange for patients to be treated on an out-patient basis.

There is some clinical evidence to suggest that chemical aversion treatment brings about increased aggressiveness and hostility on the part of the patient (Morgenstern and Pearce, 1963). It should be pointed out, however, that some of these reactions to chemical aversion therapy are not entirely surprising; experimentally, it has been observed that the administration of aversive stimulation of *various kinds* can give rise to an increase in aggressive behaviour (Ulrich *et al.*, 1965). It may indeed prove necessary to develop special methods for managing the occurrence of aggression, if and when it occurs. A second difficulty which may be anticipated in most forms of aversion therapy concerns the anxiety which it arouses in some patients. On the one hand it has been suggested (Eysenck and Rachman, 1965) that there is a possibility that highly anxious patients may respond unfavourably to aversion treatment while Bancroft (1966) postulates that a high level of anxiety is necessary for successful treatment. Finally it should be mentioned that some of the drugs which have been used in chemical aversion treatment have unpleasant side effects and can be dangerous. Certainly, chemical aversion cannot be used for the treatment of patients with gastric ailments or cardiac complaints.

Despite the difficulties enumerated above and the indifferent quality of a great deal of the work on chemical aversion treatment, some useful successes have of course been achieved. Although the value of this method is at present decreased by the size of the relapse rate, it seems probable that many otherwise untreatable patients have obtained benefit from chemical aversion treatment. It should also be emphasised that the types of disorders that have yielded successes are precisely those kinds of abnormalities which are ordinarily resistant to change. Certainly until the advent of aversion therapy there was little that could be offered to patients with sexual perversions.

The bulk of the available laboratory evidence on the conditioning of negative reactions (and there is a considerable amount of such evidence) concerns experiments in which the aversive stimulus was an electric shock. This is the first, and potentially the most important of all the advantages offered by electrical methods of aversion treatment. Over the past few decades, psychologists have accumulated much detailed information about the effects of electrical stimulation on behaviour, and while it is true that there are many problems which have yet to be resolved, there is also little doubt that the information which is already available can assist in the design and conduct of aversion treatment. A start in this direction was made by Feldman and MacCulloch (1965) who attempted to construct a therapeutic programme from findings in the field of avoidance conditioning. Important contributions to the understanding of the effects of aversive stimulation on behaviour have been made by Solomon (1964), Church (1964), and by Azrin and Holz (1966).

Electrical stimulation can be precisely controlled. The therapist is in a position to administer a discrete stimulus of measured intensity for an exact duration of time at precisely the required moment. In this respect electrical aversion stimulation is clearly superior to chemical aversion. Each of these variables can be manipulated according to requirements and the entire treatment process becomes considerably more flexible. Variations in the patient's subjective reactions and general adaptation effects are, however, continuing problems. *Nevertheless, the increased control which is possible with electrical stimulation should permit more effective treatment, closer definition of the treatment process and increased theoretical clarity.*

Chemical techniques do not provide much scope for modifications which might be introduced on the basis of the patient's personality. Individual differences tend to be blotted out because the chemical aversion procedures cannot be manipulated with precision. For example, the observation that extraverts have a greater tolerance for pain than introverts (Lynn and Eysenck, 1961) could not be used to advantage. Lynn and Eysenck obtained a correlation of 0·69 between extraversion and pain tolerance in a group of thirty students and Poser (1960) reported a correlation of 0·53. Other relevant reports are quoted by Lynn and Eysenck, and these, coupled with the suggestion that extraverts can tolerate more intense electric shocks than introverts (Eysenck, 1967), may produce useful modifications of the electrical method. Certainly, individual differences in reactivity to, and tolerance for, electric shocks can be incorporated in electrical aversion treatment. When the relationships between personality and these variables have been worked out in greater detail, it should be possible to design treatment schedules which will meet the needs of the individual patient.

In addition the increased therapeutic control provided by electrical stimulation permits the therapist to make accurate measurements of the progress of treatment. Measurements of the patient's reactions at each stage of the treatment are valuable in their own right and also because of the information which they provide about the relationship between imagery and action. With the accumulation of research on this topic it should be possible to work out in some detail the relationship between, say, images of sexual perversions and the real act.

Unlike chemical aversion treatment, electrical stimulation permits frequent repetitions of the association between the unwanted behaviour and the noxious stimulus. It is perfectly feasible to present a large number of trials to the patient during one session and also to provide for numerous conditioning sessions within the same day. This should enable treatment to progress more quickly.

It is also feasible to construct portable apparatus for the delivery of

D

shocks and this allows treatment to be carried out on an out-patient basis. In some cases the patient can even administer the noxious stimulus to himself, if and when the necessity arises. A recent example of self-administered electrical stimulation was reported by Wolpe (1965). In this report, he described the partially successful treatment of a patient who was suffering from a drug-addiction. It was possible to bring about a temporary suppression of drug-craving by getting the patient to administer the electric shock to himself whenever the craving arose. The apparatus used in this case was that described by McGuire and Vallance (1964).

Experience with chemical aversion methods leads us to expect a rather high relapse rate in aversion treatment generally. A similar situation has, of course, been encountered in the conditioning treatment of enuresis (Gwynne Jones, 1960; Turner, Rachman and Young, 1967). In an attempt to obtain greater stability of nocturnal continence in the patients treated by the bell-and-pad method, Lovibond (1963) administered his conditioning programme on an intermittent reinforcement schedule. Although it is not yet possible to reach a firm conclusion about the long-term effectiveness of the intermittent reinforcement schedule used in this type of disorder, it is worth investigating the value of this schedule in helping to reduce the relapse rate in aversion treatment. Another possible technique for reducing the relapse rate is the use of booster treatments and these, too, are more feasible with the electrical method.

Another difficulty which can be overcome by the substitution of electrical for chemical aversion methods concerns the staff problems mentioned earlier. Electrical treatment does not require more than one therapist to be present and it is considerably less arduous and cumbersome (see McGuire and Vallance, 1964, for example). *With the exception of patients with cardiac complaints* there is virtually no danger involved in the application of electrical stimulation, providing that the equipment is well designed and constructed.

Unlike drug treatment, electrical stimulation does not give rise to unpleasant side-effects. Electrical stimulation also avoids the possibility (encountered in some drug treatments) of inducing an unwanted suppression of the developing conditioned response by depressing central nervous activity. The hypnotic effects produced by the administration of the commonly used nausea-producing drug, apomorphine, can be entirely avoided.

Electrical techniques are likely to have a wider range of application than chemical methods. For example, it would be impossible to use chemical aversion in the treatment of writer's cramp.

Having argued the case for electrical aversion therapy, we should, however, make one qualification. The chemical method can be retained as an alternative procedure and, in the conditions of alcoholism and compulsive eating, may even be the first choice. Intuitively it seems more appropriate to use the feeling of nausea to counteract over-eating or excessive drinking. Secondly, it is conceivable that *mild* anxiety induced by electrical stimulation may be reduced by imbibing alcohol. If, however, a patient treated by the chemical method later attempts to drink alcohol when he feels only *mildly* nauseated, the alcohol itself may produce strong feelings of nausea and vomiting.

Selecting an aversive stimulus: non-clinical considerations

In discussing the qualities of aversive stimuli, Azrin and Holz (1966) proposed a set of requirements for the 'ideal' punishing stimulus. Interestingly, many of their conclusions parallel those derived from a consideration of the clinical data which are presently available.

Among the properties which they regard as being desirable in an aversive stimulus are the following: in the first place, 'the punishing stimulus should have precise physical specification. Unless the relevant dimensions of the stimulus can be measured accurately and in physical units, we have imposed limits on studies from the outset in terms of replicability and reliability' (p. 384). To this we may add that an aversive stimulus also needs to be controlled for periods of time. In all of these respects, of course, electrical aversion is superior to chemical aversion. The second important feature mentioned by Azrin and Holz is 'the constancy of the stimulus in terms of the actual contact it makes with the subject'. Here again, electrical aversion (while not entirely satisfactory on this point) is superior to chemical aversion. The third characteristic of a satisfactory stimulus concerns 'the ability of a subject to escape or minimize the stimulation by means of some unauthorized behaviour'. In this respect neither chemical nor electrical appears to have an advantage. The fourth characteristic in the list given by Azrin and Holz is that there should be few skeletal reactions to the stimulus. The elicitation of strong and enduring skeletal reactions may physically interfere with the emission of the behaviour under study. Once again, electrical aversion is preferable to chemical aversion. The fifth characteristic is that the stimulus should be of a kind that can be 'varied over a wide range of values' because a limited range prevents a full investigation of the effectiveness of the stimulation being employed. In this respect electrical aversion is obviously superior.

It can be seen, therefore, that both from the clinical and experimental point of view, electrical aversion is preferable to chemical aversion.

Summary

Chemical aversion therapy has many disadvantages. It is difficult to control the timing of the CS and UCR and there is confusion about identifying the UCR. The method is arduous and unaesthetic. There are considerable individual variations in reaction to emetic drugs and no agreement about the best drug to use. The duration of drug-effects limits the number of trials which can be given and also makes out-patient treatment difficult. Staff problems are often encountered and patients with cardiac or gastric complaints cannot be treated.

Although electrical aversion treatment also has its limitations, it offers some advantages over the chemical method. As a great deal of experimental work on the effects of shock has been conducted, the link between laboratory and clinic is closer. Shock is a discrete stimulus with measurable attributes and increases the extent of therapeutic control. It permits greater precision, a closer definition of the treatment process and improved theoretical clarity.

The selection of a suitable aversive stimulus must be made on clinical and theoretical grounds. It is reassuring to find that both types of consideration favour electrical over chemical aversion.

7

Electrical aversion: sexual disorders 1

As mentioned in Chapter 1, two attempts to condition aversion reactions by means of electric shock were reported in the 1930s. The report by Max (1935) contained four particularly interesting features. These were: suppression of the deviant sexual reaction occurred only when an intense shock was used, the effect of the conditioning trials was to bring about a devaluation of the deviant sexual stimulus, some measure of recovery from the effects of shock-conditioning occurred between treatment sessions and the effects of repeated treatment sessions were cumulative. The punishment recovery effects and the cumulative build-up over successive treatment sessions were also noticed by Rachman in 1961. In a brief description of the treatment of a fetishistic patient, he reported a moderate degree of improvement.

The patient was a 32-year-old bachelor who was sexually aroused by women's buttocks and bloomers. He had never had intercourse but masturbated with fantasies concerning these fetishes. The patient was given five aversion conditioning sessions. Three stimulants were used: the patient's photographs of women wearing bloomers, visual images of women with attractive buttocks, visual images of bloomers. The electric shocks were administered with an induction coil and finger electrodes. The patient was given 10 to 15 trials with each stimulus at each session. The strength of the shock was gradually increased after every four trials. During the first session the patient complained that the visual image of buttocks was constantly with him. At the fifth session he could only obtain the images with great difficulty. The time elapsing between the instruction to obtain the image and its appearance was found to increase significantly from session to session. After the final session the patient reported feeling better and said he no longer felt attracted by buttocks, had ceased having his former fantasies and had disposed of his numerous pornographic photographs.

A proper evaluation of this pilot study was not possible because of a number of extraneous conditions. It is worth noticing, however, that two of the four features noted by Max are evident in Rachman's report as well. With increasing conditioning trials, the latency period prior to the patient obtaining the sexual image lengthened. Although some punishment recovery effects were in fact observed (but not reported in the earlier paper) the cumulative result of repeated treatment sessions was similar to that found by Max – namely, the patient's fantasies disappeared and he no longer felt attracted by women's buttocks. One aspect of the treatment procedure employed in this case which, in retrospect, appears to have been misguided, was the gradual elevation of the shock intensity. Increasing the intensity of shock in a punishment situation may inadvertently produce adaptation effects and even 'immunity' to the shock (Chapter 7).

Blakemore et al. (1963) described the treatment of a transvestite patient by electrical methods. As this case-study has been discussed in detail elsewhere (Blakemore, 1964; Eysenck and Rachman, 1965) we will restrict ourselves to a summary of the main findings and their implications. The patient was a married man of stable personality who had made a successful career in the civil service. He had been cross-dressing since the age of twelve and this activity was usually accompanied by masturbation. He also masturbated with transvestist fantasies. The treatment was administered by delivering electric shocks to the patient's feet by means of an electric floor-grid. The patient was required to dress in his favourite female clothing and at various points during this procedure he received either an electric shock or a buzzer signal. Each of these acted as an instruction to the patient to begin undressing and, either the shock or the buzzer, was repeatedly presented at various intervals until he was completely undressed. Five trials of this type, with short rest intervals between each one, were administered at half-hourly intervals from early in the morning until late in the afternoon, over a six-day period. At the end of treatment a total of 400 trials had been given and in half of these the electric shock had been the signal while in the remainder it was the auditory stimulus.

The treatment was immediately successful and brought about a termination of the deviant sexual behaviour. This was also associated with an increase in his normal sexual behaviour with his wife. Of particular interest is the observation that 'he experienced at times a dull testicular pain while in certain situations which would previously have acted as a stimulus for cross-dressing, and that this could only be relieved by intercourse with his wife or by masturbation' (Blakemore, 1964, p. 171). An unexpected observation made by these therapists was that the patient's behaviour in the presence of the auditory signal and the shock signal did not differ. Why the patient failed to make this discrimination is by no means clear and one might conclude that he had become conditioned to the entire treatment situation, including the electric floor-grid, the treatment room and so on. In discussing their results, Blakemore *et al.* (1963) argue that the treatment procedure involved both classical conditioning factors and instrumental-escape factors. The importance of the latter factors are emphasised by the authors who point out that a partial reinforcement scheme such as they employed would be expected to facilitate an instrumental conditioned response and to impede the development of a classical conditioned reaction. This point seems, however, to be inadequate as there is no way of determining what the strength of the conditioned reaction might have been if another schedule of reinforcement had been employed. The respective contributions made by instrumental and classical factors can only be determined by a comparison trial of two methods which are based on models derived from an instrumental scheme and a classical scheme. They point out that the patient received an unpleasant shock during the act of putting on female garments and that 'this provides us with the basic essentials for the development of a conditioned aversion response along classical Pavlovian lines'. They then go on to say that instrumental learning could have been mediated by the fact that the patient 'was repeatedly shocked during the act of undressing, and therefore was positively reinforced, by the cessation of these shocks, for behaviour which involved the escape from and avoidance of female clothing'. This interpretation seems to be not entirely accurate as the patient was *successful* in escaping from the shock only at the *end* of each treatment trial. During each trial the patient was receiving shocks *during* the act of undressing and consequently a number of the movements and activities involved in *undressing* would, within a short space of time, be *followed* by an electric shock again. The act of undressing would only have brought about a successful escape response at the end of the trial, i.e. when no more shocks were delivered during that particular trial. The avoidance response which was being conditioned was only successful on a comparatively small number of occasions. The authors argued that 'here we have the basic requirements for the development of an instrumental conditioned avoidance response'. Strictly speaking, however, they were conditioning escape and avoidance reactions on an intermittent reinforcement schedule – which incidentally may in the long-term prove to be a good method for establishing stable conditioned reactions. At present the evidence on this subject is equivocal (see Chapter 15 below). In the case of this particular patient the treatment was both successful and stable, although he did experience one brief and atypical relapse within a year after the termination of the treatment.

This case-study helped to demonstrate the therapeutic possibilities of electrical aversion treatment and also raised the problem of selecting the most suitable learning paradigm – instrumental or classical conditioning?

In 1964 McGuire and Vallance published a remarkable paper in which they described the very encouraging results which they had obtained by a 'simple technique' of aversion therapy. Their results at termination of treatment are shown in Table 1, and it can be seen that 56% of their patients showed either 'good improvement' or 'symptom removed'. Particularly good results were obtained with the fourteen patients complaining of sexual disorders. Of these, no fewer than ten responded well to the treatment. One of the noteworthy aspects of this report is the simplicity of the apparatus and of the procedure. The components used in constructing the apparatus cost £1 (2·4 dollars) and fit into a box approximately 6 inches square and 2 inches deep. They describe their procedure as follows:

The use of the apparatus follows a classical conditioning technique. The stimulus to which aversion is to be produced is presented, often by having the patient imagine the stimulus, and then a shock is administered. This procedure is repeated throughout the treatment session of 20 to 30 minutes, which can be held from six times a day to once a fortnight.

They point out that the shock level is determined by the patient himself and can be adjusted during the session. With a majority of their patients, the treatment was self-administered after the therapists had given them a demonstration session. From the authors' description it seems likely that their treatment method also embodied punishment training inasmuch as the aversive stimulus was often (?) administered after the patient had imagined the stimulus or carried out the deviant activity. In our view it is preferable to regard the image which the patient produces to instruction as a response rather than as a stimulus. The instruction given by the therapist seems better to fit the description of a stimulus than the imaginal production obtained by the patient. Even if this distinction is not acceptable,[1] however, it should be remembered that some of their patients administered the shocks to themselves (or received a shock via the therapist) when they had carried out the deviant activity. In this type of procedure there seems little doubt that the most relevant model is a punishment one rather than a classical conditioning one. From the information provided in this regrettably short account, McGuire and Vallance appear to have been punishing activities which

1 The image, even though it is a response to instructions, contains stimulus elements.

the patient engaged in, and only rarely to have built up a purely classical association between the CS and the UCS (shock). In all five of the short case histories given in this publication, a punishment technique appears to have been used – at least part of the time.

Table 1 Immediate follow-up results on 39 cases treated by aversion therapy

Symptomatic improvements	Smokers	Alcoholics	Sexual Perverts	Others	Total
Discontinued treatment	0	3	3	0	6 (15%)
None	3	2	0	1	6 (15%)
Mild improvement	0	1	1	3	5 (13%)
Good improvement	1	1	4	3	9 (23%)
Symptom removed	6	–	6	1	13 (33%)
Totals	10	7	14	8	39

Source: Reported by R. McGuire and M. Vallance, British Medical Journal p. 152, 1964.

In regard to the behavioural consequences of electrical aversion treatment, McGuire and Vallance report the following interesting observation:

Another alcoholic patient who had been given whisky to drink during aversion treatment accused the therapist of adding a chemical to the whisky to give it a bad taste. The same patient went into a bar against advice during treatment, but on trying to raise a glass of whisky to his mouth he had a panic attack and returned to hospital in an anxious state.

In their description of the effects of this treatment on a patient with fetishism, they noted that as treatment progressed the patient reported that he found it 'more and more difficult to conjure up the fantasy that was being treated. This was confirmed by an increased interval between shocks from three to fifteen seconds'. The behavioural and subjective consequences of the treatment were that the patient 'entirely lost interest in his fetish and in his masochistic practices'.

This contribution by McGuire and Vallance undoubtedly generated a great deal of interest in the therapeutic possibilities of electrical aversion treatment.

Bancroft, Jones and Pullan (1966) made a significant addition to the investigation of electrical aversion treatment of sexual disorders by monitoring the changes which occurred during the treatment session, on a penile plethysmograph. This instrument which is an improvement on the one originally described by Freund (1963) is simple and inexpensive and has already helped to expand our understanding both of sexual disorders and their treatment. The paper by Bancroft *et al.* also contains a fascinating case-study of a paedophiliac patient. A twenty-five-year-old clerk was treated because of his abnormal sexual interest in girls of approximately nine to twelve years of age. 'He masturbated to fantasies of young girls and would wander around housing estates watching them and talking to them. Spontaneous ejaculation would occur as a result of this. . . .' He was treated by electrical aversion therapy and photographs of children were used as the conditioned stimuli. On presentation of the photographs the patient was asked to concentrate on sexually stimulating fantasies. When an erectile response above an arbitrary, predetermined level occurred, he was given a painful electric shock to his arm. Although brief, this case-report contains some extremely interesting observations, but here we will simply draw attention to the remarkable change in the topography of his sexual interests. 'By the 20th day he was showing interest in slightly older girls (thirteen to fourteen years) and his observation of them at the weekend resulted in ejaculation more delayed than usual.' By the 25th day he was reporting a definite reduction in interest in children and 'increased interest in adult women'. As the authors point out, the case was not a complete therapeutic success. Nevertheless, his paedophiliac inclinations were virtually eliminated and at the eighteen-month follow-up he no longer showed evidence of this deviation. Incidentally, the treatment of this patient was stopped on the 38th day as he was making persistent penile responses, which the authors describe as 'a stereotyped form of response'. It is possible that this development was a function of the treatment procedure used (this point is discussed in some detail below).

A valuable contribution to our understanding of the processes involved in aversion therapy was recently made by Marks and Gelder (1967). They described the clinical and psychological changes which occurred in a group of five patients during faradic aversion treatment. The five patients were suffering from fetishism and/or transvestism and were all submitted to a concentrated course of therapy conducted on an in-patient basis. The importance of their contribution lies in the fact that they made careful quantitative and qualitative assessments of the behaviour, physiological reactions and attitudes of the patients both before, during and after treatment. In addition to undergoing a full psychiatric examination prior to treatment, all the patients were assessed on the semantic differential test, and their penile reactions to appropriate and deviant sexual stimuli were gauged. Frequent applications of these assessment procedures during the treatment enabled Marks and Gelder to determine the nature and timing of the changes which were associated with the treatment. Before discussing their findings, however, we need to present a detailed account of their therapeutic procedure.

All of the patients were treated on an in-patient basis over a two-week period during which they received two aversion therapy sessions per day, each lasting approximately one hour. After their discharge they were given booster sessions when possible – usually weekly to begin with, and then monthly thereafter for several months. The aversive stimulus was produced by a simple shock-box run off batteries; the electrodes were attached to the patient's forearm or leg. At the commencement of each treatment session, the patient was asked to select a shock level which was just above pain threshold. In the initial stages of treatment, the shock was delivered when the patient imagined himself in a sexually provocative and arousing situation which incorporated some features of his sexually deviant behaviour. For example, a transvestite would be asked to imagine that he was putting on some of his favoured clothing, and when he reported that he had a clear image of this activity, the shock was delivered. In the second stage of treatment, which usually commenced on about the third or fourth day of treatment, the patients were shocked when they carried out the deviant behaviour in reality. In other words, a transvestite patient would be shocked when he actually put on the female clothing.

The shock was delivered on an intermittent schedule and approximately one quarter of all trials were not shocked. Throughout the treatment the patient was required to wear the penile plethysmograph (a refined version of Freund's [1963] original instrument). The plethysmograph recordings were used to monitor the progress of treatment throughout; in addition, a modified version of the Osgood semantic differential test was applied at various points in the treatment in order to assess the patient's sexual and other concepts. The effects of the treatment were assessed by reported changes in the patient's behaviour, plethysmographic recordings, concept changes and by reports from members of the patient's family (especially their wives).

All five patients had relatively sound personalities, were highly motivated and co-operative and three of them were able to engage in heterosexual relations prior to the commence of treatment. They all practised masturbation while cross-dressing[1] or while in contact with

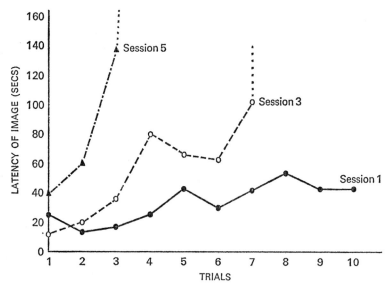

Figure 2 With treatment, patients take increasingly longer periods to obtain the deviant images. Reproduced from Marks and Gelder, *British Journal of Psychiatry*, 1967.

the fetishistic object and all of them had commenced their deviant sexual behaviour in childhood or early adolescence. The mean duration of the disorder in this group of patients was in excess of twenty years and all but one of them had been engaged in deviant sexual behaviour *for at least twenty years*.

One of the first observations to emerge from this study was that, with repeated exposure to the aversive stimulus, the patients experienced increasing difficulty in conjuring up the required images. The time taken to obtain the image increased and, in several instances, the patients eventually reached a point when they were unable to obtain the images

1 This type of masturbatory activity is assigned central importance in the theory of sexual disorders proposed by McGuire *et al.* (1965). See also, Evans (1968).

at all. The increase in latencies is clearly illustrated in Figures 2 and 3.

It will be seen from Figure 3 that Marks and Gelder checked the effect of simple repetition of the image and found that no change in latency occurred *except* when the image was followed by the delivery of electric

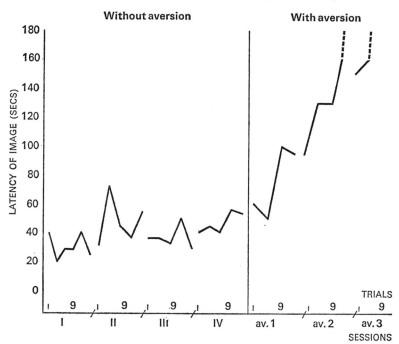

Figure 3 Increased latencies of image production are restricted to items which have been shocked. Reproduced from Marks and Gelder, *British Journal of Psychiatry*, 1967.

shock. In other words, the changes in ability to obtain the abnormal sexual image must probably be attributed to the effects of the aversive stimulation and not to simple habituation effects. This increase in latency observed in time needed to obtain the sexual images was paralleled by an increase in the time which elapsed before the abnormal stimulus produced an erection in the patients. In the early stages of treatment (and certainly before treatment commenced) patients generally produced fairly rapid and substantial erections when presented with the abnormal sexual stimuli. As the treatment progressed, however, the erectile response was increasingly delayed until, in many cases, the stimulus failed to produce any reaction. Figure 4, below, illustrates

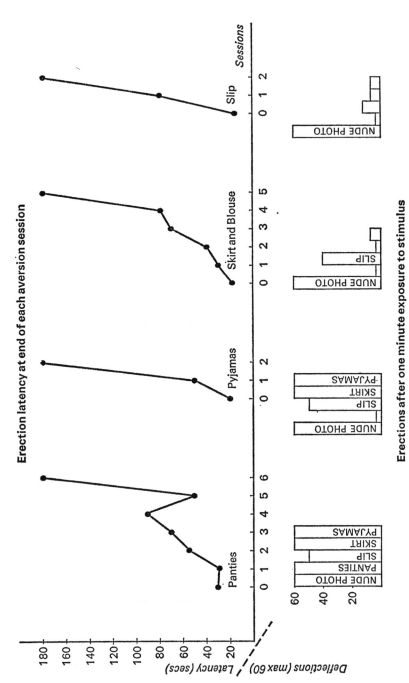

Figure 4 The selective effect of electrical aversion: Reductions in sexual reaction are restricted to treated items. Reproduced from Marks and Gelder, *British Journal of Psychiatry*, 1967.

the increasing erection latencies observed in one of the patients (a transvestite).

Another interesting aspect illustrated in this Figure is the remarkable specificity of the erectile changes which occurred during treatment. It will be seen from the Figure that the erection latency observed in response to a particular stimulus was fairly strictly related to the aversion treatment which had been administered. The first item treated in the case of this patient was 'panties', and it can be seen that erections in the presence of panties were totally eliminated after a few sessions of treatment. Notice, however, that the other sexual stimuli (skirt, slip, pyjamas) remained unaffected until they in turn were subjected to the treatment.

The patients continued to show erectile reponses to the stimuli until they had been associated with electrical stimulation. The second item which the therapist knocked out was 'pyjamas' and again, by referring to the Figure, one can see that the effect of treating this item was highly specific. The next items to be eliminated were 'skirt' and 'blouse', and finally, the therapist had to deal with the last item – a woman's slip.

This selective effect observed after aversion treatment has been noted on a few occasions. In their review of their treatment of alcoholism by chemical aversion, Voegtlin and Lemere (1942) quoted an early French report in which patients who had been conditioned with wine acting as the conditional stimulus, developed an aversion to this drink, but not for other types of alcohol. They also remark that they, too, had experience of specificity of this nature. More recent examples can be found in MacCulloch *et al.* (1966), and Quinn and Henbest (1967).

The selective effect of aversion treatment is also consistent with certain laboratory findings but not with others. At the same time, however, this selectivity introduces another paradox. How can we reconcile the specificity observed by Marks and Gelder during their treatment process with the general clinical outcome in their five cases of transvestism? The inhibition, or suppression, of abnormal sexual reactions *does* generalise to external circumstances and also to specific, but untreated, deviant sexual stimuli. It is evident that during the treatment only a very limited number of deviant stimuli can be dealt with. Nevertheless, the effects of aversion therapy appear to be widespread. These effects spread from the clinic to the external world and from a few selected sexual items to a wide range of stimulating conditions.

Azrin and Holz (1966) state that the generalised effects of punishment occur early in training but that 'this generalisation of suppression eventually disappears . . .' (p. 416). Although they are able to support this view with some experimental data, the work reported by Hoffman (1966) provides more detailed information. He was able to demonstrate clear gradients of stimulus generalisation in conditioning experiments with pigeons. After generating pecking responses by positive food reinforcement, the animals were shocked in the presence of a tone until the pecking ceased. The degree of suppression was then assessed by an examination of response rates in the presence of the original tone conditioned stimulus and variations thereof. Hoffman observed that while it is true that the stimulus generalisation gradient sharpens during successive testing periods, this process is fairly slow. The gradients obtained after the establishment of conditioned suppression were flat and high and only began to sharpen markedly after fifteen to twenty testing sessions. A particularly interesting feature of these studies is the extraordinary persistence of the conditioned suppression responses – they showed little change over a $2\frac{1}{2}$-year period (i.e. a fifth of the animal's life span). Furthermore, the generalised reactions were similarly persistent. In their experiment on traumatic conditioning in human subjects, Sanderson *et al.* (1963) also found broad, high and persistent gradients which bear some resemblance to those described by Hoffman.

Hoffman noted that a reduction of the generalisation gradient was obtained when the 'motivation for the ongoing, positively reinforced behaviour' (eating) was increased. The introduction of 'emotional stress', however, lifted and flattened the gradient. Hoffman correctly draws attention to the relevance of these findings for an understanding of anxiety reactions. In the present context, however, we are concerned with the relation between his experimental findings and the clinical observations of Marks and Gelder.

The specificity of their patients' reactions requires explanation. It seems possible that their observations are a function of the time of testing. It may be that if a patient's reactions to related sexual stimuli are tested after, say, the first and second sessions in which a single item (e.g. panties) is shocked, then generalised reactions would be seen. These generalisations would then be expected to decrease (i.e. the gradient would sharpen) with increasing shock sessions. This explanation, however, seems highly unlikely to be correct in view of the fact that the post-treatment gradients appear to be very wide indeed. A second possibility is that the specificity observed during treatment was a function of the patient's cognitive appraisal or of changes in their sexual motivation, or a combination of both these factors. It should be noted, however, that after these specific reactions had been detected, the patients were then given (in the final stage of treatment) shock stimuli while they were actually engaging in cross-dressing. In order to confirm that the specificity observed in the first half of the treatment programme is a general and enduring feature of the treatment process, it will be necessary to recheck the patients' stimulus generalisation gradient after the termination of the full treatment programme. If it is found that the stimulus generalisation gradients are flat at the termination of treatment then the apparent paradox will be resolved.

Hoffman's report that emotional stress lifts and broadens the gradient should also be checked in future clinical studies. From the therapeutic point of view, the finding that the effects of aversive training (both specific and generalised) are extremely persistent is, of course, encouraging. The complexity of the problem of stimulus generalisation is underlined by Hearst's (1965) comparisons of approach and avoidance gradients. Although his studies are less pertinent to the present discussion than Hoffman's (Hearst was studying Sidman avoidance behaviour) a few points are worth mentioning. He obtained support for the conclusion that avoidance gradients are usually flat and high but was not able to find confirmation of earlier reports that increases in shock intensity produce greater flattening of generalisation gradients. Hearst's work also raises the possibility that flat generalisation gradients are associated with increased resistance to extinction. If confirmed, this finding will be of considerable clinical interest. The shape of the generalisation gradients may provide a measure of progress within the treatment programme and also serve as the basis for general prognosis.

Marks and Gelder (1967) reported that their patients' sexual and other concepts changed in a way which paralleled their physiological changes and their imaginary productions. The patients' attitudes, erectile reactions and images all changed in the same direction but 'at rather different speeds'. The main attitudinal change observed in this group of patients was that the abnormal sexual stimuli became devalued as the treatment progressed. For example, the attitudes of transvestites to items like panties, corsets and so on changed from 'favourable' at the beginning of treatment to 'unfavourable' or 'neutral' at the end of treatment. The changes were often explained by the patients on the following lines. They said that the sexual objects, such as boots or dresses, no longer aroused them sexually, but neither did they produce a fear reaction. Their unfavourable evaluations of their deviations were not accompanied by the development of an anxious attitude. It was also noted in

E

this study that the changes in attitudes were, like the plethysmographic changes, highly specific to the nature of each phase in the treatment. That is, the patient's attitude towards panties would change only after

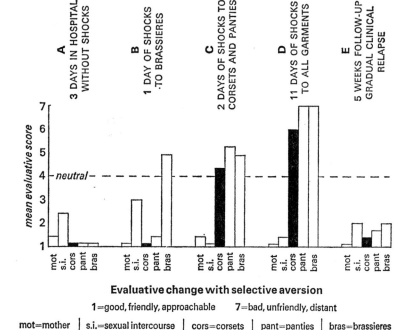

Figure 5 The selective effect of aversion treatment: changes in attitude are restricted to treated items. Reproduced from Marks and Gelder, *British Journal of Psychiatry*, 1967.

he had been subjected to electrical treatment in the presence of this object. The patient's attitudes to the other (and presumably related) sexual objects remained unaltered until they had been the subject of pairings with electrical stimulation. The interesting thing of course is that the specificity noted in the plethysmographic recordings and imagery is paralleled in the attitudinal change and it recalls the observations made by Azrin and Holz (1966) that punishment training is highly specific in its effects. The selective attitudinal changes are neatly illustrated in Figure 5.

It was noted above that the attitudinal and autonomic changes moved in the same direction at different speeds. Contrary to what one might have expected, on the basis of Festinger's (1957) work, in this study the patients' attitudes changed first and their autonomic reactions and sexual behaviour followed. Moreover, these attitudinal changes preceded the physiological changes in those cases where relapse occurred. The first signal that the patient was slipping back after he had completed a course of treatment and been discharged was a change in attitude.

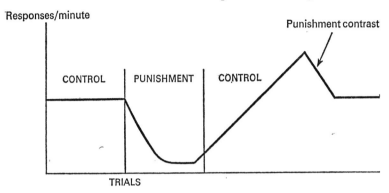

Figure 6 Theoretical graph illustrating recovery from punishment. The introduction of punishment produces a depression in response rate, but the withdrawal of shock is followed by a recovery of response rate and a brief period of excessive responding (contrast effect).

This was then followed by changes in physiological reaction and overt behaviour.

Another very interesting point which emerged was the comparative independence of the patients' normal and abnormal sexual activities. In no instance was the successful application of electrical aversion to the abnormal sexual behaviour associated with, or followed by, untoward changes in the patients' normal sexual outlets where these existed. In fact, in at least two cases their normal sexual behaviour was noted to improve shortly after the treatment had been completed.

There are a few indications in the Marks and Gelder report and in an earlier case-study (Marks, Rachman and Gelder, 1966) that some 'recovery from punishment' occurs during electrical aversion therapy. In his elaborate, interlocking series of experiments on the effects of shock punishment on rat behaviour, Estes (1944) detected a punishment recovery effect. This effect, which emerges most clearly under mild punishment, is an *increase* in responding when the shocks are withheld.

Under some conditions this recovery has been observed temporarily to *exceed* the original rate of responding (see Figure 6).

Despite the deficiencies in his studies (very small groups and some inconsistent control data), Estes also showed that the recovery from periodic punishment is probably slower than that seen when continuous punishment is used. The case for using intermittent punishment schedules is not clear but when comparisons are carried out, it will be worth while to attempt a confirmation of Estes' observation. It may also be the case that a high degree of 'punishment recovery' during treatment indicates unsatisfactory progress and/or a stimulus of inadequate intensity.

In the clinical reports of Marks and Gelder, the only published signs of punishment recovery are seen in latent periods which elapse before the patient obtains the deviant sexual image. With repeated shock trials the image latency increases. When the latencies are checked at the beginning of a new treatment session, however, decreases in latency are often observed. This phenomenon was clearly obtained by Rachman (1961) in a patient with fetishism, but the case was described briefly at the time and the parallel with Estes' work was missed. It was checked in a later case involving a homosexual fixation and, once again, clear punishment recovery effects appeared. The increase in latency obtained after a session of treatment was largely lost between (weekly) sessions. The patient was able to obtain approximately four to five clear images very speedily at the beginning of each session. This recovery effect soon dissipated when the intensity of the shock was increased. A punishment contrast effect in the form of increased masturbatory frequency was also noted prior to increasing the intensity of the aversive stimuli. These clinical observations are similar to the experimental conclusions discussed by Azrin and Holz (1966).

In general, the therapeutic outcome in Marks and Gelder's cases was encouraging. In all five cases the abnormal sexual behaviour was eliminated by the end of the concentrated course of treatment. Unfortunately, however, two of the patients showed some measure of relapse within a year of discharge.

Marks and Gelder (1968) have now increased their sample to twenty patients, and all but two of them 'showed marked to moderate improvement in their deviant behaviour by the end of treatment'. Ten patients were simple transvestites; nine of them were 'much improved' and the tenth 'improved' at the end of treatment. Six of the seven who were seen at the six-month follow-up period had retained their improvements. In the five transvestite patients with 'strong transsexual feelings', the long-term results were disappointing after clear improvements had been achieved by the end of treatment. The few patients with sado-masochistic urges responded surprisingly well to treatment, but the follow-up data on this group of five patients is not yet available.

The additional information reported by Marks and Gelder on their enlarged sample is, on the whole, consistent with their earlier findings. They have, however, found that in the majority of their patients the suppression of deviant *fantasies* is seldom complete. Secondly, they have now obtained some evidence that, in a minority of cases, the treatment produces 'conditioned anxiety or displeasure to their deviant behaviour'.

Of all the electrical techniques currently in use the one described by Marks and Gelder would seem to be the most satisfactory. It appears to be clinically effective and, except on some points, would seem to be entirely reasonable and justified in terms of the experimental information which we have regarding punishment training and classical conditioning. The only two queries which might be raised at this point concern (1) their use of an intermittent schedule of punishment (it may be more efficacious to use a 100% schedule – see Azrin and Holz 1966) and (2) their use of the development of the image as a signal for the administration of shock. This may very well prove to be the most efficacious procedure to use but, on the other hand, it can be argued that one should administer the shock when a *plethysmographic reaction* to the abnormal stimulus occurs. There is no certain way of deciding on this issue at present and we must await further experimental investigations. One of the features of this treatment which recommends itself most strongly is Marks and Gelder's careful assessment techniques and, in particular, their use of the semantic differential and the penile plethysmograph. The continued use of these monitoring instruments is strongly recommended. Ideally, the patients' autonomic reactions should be recorded both before, during and after treatment, e.g. cardiac rate, respiratory rate and so on. The purpose of including these measures would be to ascertain whether or not the patients acquire conditioned autonomic reactions.

8
Electrical aversion therapy: sexual disorders 2

Another important study of aversion therapy was recently completed by Bancroft (1966). He made a detailed examination of the effects of electrical aversion treatment on seven homosexual patients. All but one of the patients were treated on an out-patient basis and given two to four sessions per week; each session lasted for 1–1½ hours and the patients were given between thirty and forty such sessions. Five other patients who were offered the treatment declined to accept it and a further two defected before treatment commenced. The nature of the disorder meant that the treatment had to deal with fantasy material only and the subjects were shown photographs of sexually provocative males. In addition, at the beginning of every session, they were asked to look at photographs of sexually provocative women in order that their plethysmographic reactions to these stimuli might be assessed throughout the course of the treatment.

Bancroft's treatment differed from that of Marks and Gelder in one important respect – he administered the shock when the patient showed an erectile response of a certain predetermined amplitude. Marks and Gelder, it will be remembered, administered the electric shock when the patient reported that he had a clear and vivid sexually provoking image. In Bancroft's own description, 'when the threshold was reached a shock would be given. This would be repeated at 15-second intervals for the next minute provided that each time the amplitude was still above threshold and not actually falling. Thus a maximum of 5 shocks was given' (p. 102). The patients were also required to complete self-rating forms at the end of each treatment session in which they gave an account of their feelings of sexual arousal and anxiety. Apart from the therapeutic sessions, the patients were given no specific instructions other than being encouraged to masturbate to heterosexual fantasies between sessions. This instruction and the 'practice' which the subjects had with heterosexual pictures *during* the sessions, were designed to facilitate the growth of heterosexual behaviour as a replacement for the homosexual behaviour.

In every case behavioural changes have resulted which have been relevant to the therapeutic goal, but in at least 2 of the 7 patients these changes have been insufficient or too impermanent to produce significant long-term effects (*p. 231*). Patients C and E showed satisfactory results in that, in each case, the homosexuality was removed from the patients' behaviour and adjustments to heterosexuality are progressing slowly and steadily, (Bancroft, 1966).

Patient A showed a temporary improvement while patient B showed no significant therapeutic effect. Patient D was difficult to assess and while he benefited from a marked reduction in sexual anxiety he is still no nearer a heterosexual adjustment. In the remaining two patients, F and G, the follow-up period at the time of writing was too short to permit a reasonable assessment. However, patient F showed a 'dramatic' change in his heterosexual interest with some decrease in his homosexual interest and patient G showed a significant reduction in sexual anxiety with more manifest heterosexual interest, 'but no reduction in homosexual interest'. The treatment and monitoring techniques provided two measures of erectile response – the maximum amplitude of patient's response on the non-shocked trials to photographs of sexually provocative males and females and, secondly, the time taken to reach the threshold (response latency) when exposed to the photographs of males (both shocked and unshocked trials) and female photographs. Bancroft calculated that the two measures were closely related, that is, the amplitude and latency of the responses correlate significantly. He also noted that in those cases where homosexual interest was substantially decreased 'the treatment has been associated with considerable anxiety'. These and other observations led Bancroft to postulate that 'suppression of homosexual interest is dependent on a high level of anxiety' being generated or maintained.

The mixed clinical results obtained from this study, while disappointing, are not altogether surprising in view of the special difficulties associated with the treatment of homosexuality. In homosexuality the therapist is faced with a double problem. In the first place, he is attempting to suppress or eliminate the homosexual behaviour and, secondly, he needs to assist the patient in redirecting his sexual drive along heterosexual lines. This latter objective is, of course, immensely difficult to obtain and in a sense one of the most interesting points to emerge from Bancroft's study is the suggestion that certain types of practice may facilitate such an adjustment. A second difficulty which arises in the treatment of homosexual patients is the fact that one is obliged to restrict the aversion training to imaginal and photographic representations – a limitation which does not apply to the treatment of fetishism or transvestism.

One of the disturbing features of Bancroft's study, however, is that some of his subjects appear to have been simultaneously trained to make *homosexual* responses. An examination of the plethysmographic recordings made from session to session indicated that the patients, for the most part, continued to produce marked erectile responses to the homosexual photographic material despite the fact that they had been repeatedly shocked in the presence of these photographs. In fact, the main change that seems to have occurred (judging from the plethysmographic recordings) is that the patients began to respond sexually (i.e. produce erectile responses) to photographs of females as well as of males. There seem to be two possible explanations for this failure of the electrical aversion treatment to reduce the erectile responses to male photographs. In the first place it is possible that the shock intensity was not sufficiently great to produce suppression of the response (see Azrin and Holz, 1966). Secondly, Bancroft might inadvertently have been habituating the subjects to the administration of the shock by his method of re-applying the electric shock even when the erectile response remained unchanged. It will be remembered that he continued to apply the electric shock on up to five occasions during a one-minute period if the plethysmographic response showed no sign of declining. In this sense he may have been conditioning or training his subjects to endure the electric shock and causing them to maintain their erections *despite* the administration of shock. It is possible, therefore, that one should avoid using repeated shocks when the erectile response fails to decrease. Additionally, one can increase the intensity of the electric shock if the plethysmographic reactions do not decrease after the first few sessions.

On the positive side, the plethysmographic records indicate quite clearly that most of the patients developed erectile responses to the heterosexual photographs during the treatment. The two possible reasons for this improved reaction to heterosexual material (acting separately or in combination) are that they were instructed to masturbate to heterosexual fantasies between treatment sessions and, secondly, they were repeatedly exposed to female photographs and asked to attempt to obtain erections while in the treatment situation. In either event, both of these possibilities should be explored further because of the potential value which they hold in the development or redevelopment of normal heterosexual reactions in homosexual patients. Another suggestion arises from the observation that the two most successfully treated patients developed considerable anxiety in the treatment sessions. If this observation is repeated and extended it may follow that what one seeks to do in aversion treatment is to generate conditioned anxiety reactions to inappropriate sexual stimuli. If this proves to be the case, then one can take deliberate steps to increase the anxiety-evoking properties of the treatment session both directly (e.g. increasing shock) and indirectly (e.g. by using anxiety-provoking instructions) and so on. In view of the indifferent therapeutic outcome recorded by Bancroft, it might be worth while reconsidering the use of the erectile responses as the signal for administering the shock. The Marks and Gelder technique of shocking the appearance of a provocative image may be preferable. Obviously, however, the choice of the criterion signal for the administration of shock needs to be investigated far more thoroughly before one can reach a conclusion on this point.

Other possibilities which arise from Bancroft's study are that one should be careful to avoid the use of shock intensities which are too mild because one runs the risk of the patient becoming habituated to the shock or, worse, the shock stimulus may develop into a positive discriminative stimulus. In his discussion on the effects of punishment, Church (1963) presented a cogent analysis of the conditions under which the administration of an aversive stimulus may actually facilitate rather than eliminate the response. The administration of very mild electric shocks in aversion therapy should probably be avoided. As a result of Bancroft's experience, it may also be a sound procedure to avoid using a discontinuous sequence of shocking. That is to say, one should not continue to administer electric shock at regular intervals if the erectile response does not decline.

As has been stated above, one of the positive results to emerge from Bancroft's work is the fact that heterosexual responsiveness may be facilitated and improved by the use of one or both of the practice techniques which he employed; namely, the instruction to masturbate to heterosexual fantasies between sessions and the repeated presentation of provocative female photographs with the instruction that the patient must attempt to obtain an erection in their presence.[1] These potentially useful procedures for generating or improving heterosexual responsiveness should be borne in mind, particularly when one views aversion therapy as an attempt to suppress inappropriate sexual responses in order that more satisfactory sexual responses (of a competing nature)

1 The role of feedback to the patient is worth investigating in its own right (e.g. Valins and Ray, 1967).

be established during this period of non-responding. It is almost certainly the case that the best way of establishing a permanent elimination of unadaptive sexual behaviour will be to suppress the undesirable response and to generate a more satisfactory alternative response. With this aim in mind, the facilitation of heterosexual responses obtained by Bancroft is a useful pointer, although the value of simple exposures of nude-female pictures is brought into doubt by Solyom and Miller's (1965) findings. They found that increases in physiological responsiveness to female pictures did not always coincide with increases in heterosexual responsiveness. They were not, however, using a penile plethysmographic measure of responsiveness.

In 1965, Kushner described the successful treatment of a fetishistic patient who had been engaging in deviant behaviour for over twenty years. His fetishistic attachment centred on women's panties and he masturbated to fantasies concerning panties. On occasions, he dressed up in them. He derived considerable sexual pleasure from both types of activity. Kushner treated him by electrical aversion therapy and his method resembles that developed independently by Marks and Gelder (1967).

At each session the patient was presented with imaginal and photographic stimuli of panties and, on occasions, he was required to handle a pair of panties. At each session, from four to six stimuli were presented and these 'were immediately followed by shock . . . the patient was instructed to tolerate the shock until it became so uncomfortable that he wanted it stopped . . . he was then to signal for termination of the shock by saying 'stop' . . . twelve such stimuli were presented each session in random order' and approximately one minute elapsed between stimulus presentations. Each session lasted approximately thirty minutes and he was seen three times a week. After forty-one sessions the patient reported that he was no longer troubled by the fetish; however, changes in the intensity of his attraction to panties (and the associated behaviour) were reported as early as the second session. As treatment progressed, the patient reported that he was finding it increasingly difficult to obtain fetishistic fantasies while masturbating. After a partial relapse, shortly after the termination of treatment, he was given three booster sessions. He was also treated by desensitisation in order to overcome his inhibitions in normal sexual situations. When seen at followup, eighteen months after the termination of treatment, he appeared to be free of his fetishistic impulses. He reported that he experienced occasional and fleeting thoughts of the fetish object, but that he was no longer preoccupied with it and that he had successfully married.

In 1966, Kushner and Sandler described the effect of this treatment on a further three patients. In the second report, a slightly stronger shock intensity was used (from 1 to 7 milliamps) and the shock was delivered when the patient raised his finger to indicate that he had a clear and distinct image. This modification is the procedure used by Marks and Gelder.

Kushner and Sandler obtained a successful result with a thirty-two-year-old exhibitionist who had been troubled with this difficulty since the age of six. All the treatment was carried out by imaginal presentations and the patient was given 185 trials over a period of fifteen sessions. A partial reinforcement schedule was used and only 130 of the stimulus presentations were followed by punishment. A twelve-month follow-up revealed no resurgence of the exhibitionistic behaviour. Their third patient was a forty-eight-year-old man who suffered from depression and persistent, specific, daily suicidal ruminations. These ruminations focused on six distinct images which were amenable to reduction by means of punishment. The treatment procedure was similar to that used in the case of the exhibitionist mentioned above and the patient was seen for twenty sessions during which time he received 350 trials. A partial punishment schedule was introduced at the fourth session. After the twelfth session, the patient indicated that there had been a distinct improvement in that the ruminations had shown a substantial decrease in frequency. After some additional treatment the suicidal urges were eliminated almost entirely – apart from an occasional transitory thought experienced early in the morning. He was re-examined three months later and no recurrence had occurred.

The fourth patient described in this report was a forty-two-year-old man who complained of a 'hand contraction response'. The electrodes were attached to the patient's forearm and he was given some typing to carry out (this being a difficult task for him). Shock was administered whenever hand-contraction occurred and the treatment sessions lasted for about thirty minutes. Initially he made rapid progress and his speed and accuracy in typing improved as the number of contractions decreased. However, he later began to display erratic behaviour and in general showed a deterioration in efficiency. Eventually it was decided to terminate the treatment as he appeared to be making no further progress.

Solyom and Miller (1965) described the effects of electrical aversion therapy on six homosexual patients. Their method of treatment, which they describe as a 'double differential conditioning technique', involved the projection of photographs of semi-nude males. The presentation of these pictures was accompanied by an electric shock and the presentation of photographs of attractive females was 'positively reinforced by the termination of a continuous electric shock'. In addition, they recorded galvanic skin responses and finger plethysmographs. The intention here was to measure changes in autonomic functioning during and after treatment. They were only partly successful in bringing about a reduction or termination of homosexual activity, and apparently these changes were *not* accompanied by corresponding changes in autonomic responses to the male pictures. Instead they found that there was an increase in responses to photographs of sexually stimulating females – a result which is very similar to that obtained by Bancroft (1966) whom, it will be remembered, succeeded in increasing his homosexual patients' responsiveness to female stimuli even when it was not possible to reduce their homosexual inclinations.

Solyom and Miller gave their subjects an average of twenty-three treatment sessions and these lasted for approximately thirty minutes. During each session an average of fifteen stimulus presentations was given and the male and female pictures were interchanged at random. 'During the projection of nude male pictures, one to four electric shocks were administered at random usually when the (finger) plethysmograph curve began to descend, the final shock generally coinciding with the end of the male picture.' Prior to presenting the nude female pictures, an electric shock was given and this could be terminated by the subject. If he did so, his response in switching off the shock automatically triggered the projection of the nude female picture. The intention here was to associate the termination of shock with the appearance of an appealing female picture.

After treatment four of the six patients, while continuing to express homosexual interests, reported a significant increase in their control over these desires. Three of the patients had made social but not sexual approaches to females. Solyom and Miller point out that their plethysmographic results indicated that 'no change was found in the autonomic responses to male pictures but there appeared to be an increase in responses to sexually stimulating female pictures'. The group results certainly give this impression but two of the individual cases (D.R. and G.R.) showed parallel changes in overt behaviour and plethysmographic reactivity. Patient D.R., for example, dated two girls even though he retained some homosexual interest. His plethysmographic record shows an increased reaction to female pictures and a decreased reaction to male pictures. Patient S.B. on the other hand, produced clear increases in plethysmographic reactivity to female pictures but reported no sexual interest in his wife or other females.

Some aspects of the authors' physiological data are puzzling and serve to emphasise the need to improve our understanding of these phenomena. For example, the patients' pre-treatment GSR and plethysmographic responses to female pictures are not entirely consistent; the plethysmographic records of the six normal subjects show surprisingly little difference in response to female and male pictures, and so on.

Although the therapeutic outcome was not particularly encouraging, some of the observations made by Solyom and Miller are worth noting. As Freund (1960) had found earlier, the administration of a male sexual hormone appears to be of little value in stimulating sexual reactions to females. Secondly, they showed that there is a disjunction between the patient's physiological reactions and his overt behaviour. An increase in the patient's plethysmographic response pattern to female stimuli did not indicate that the subject was overtly heterosexual. In only three instances did the subjects show clinical improvements, whereas all six of the patients showed 'overall changes in plethysmograph response patterns'. As they point out, this discrepancy between overt behaviour and autonomic changes 'cannot be easily reconciled' and one cannot rule out the possibility that the failure of transfer might have resulted from an absence of the social skills and contacts which are a prerequisite for establishing heterosexual behaviour. Although Bancroft (1966) found a reasonable correspondence between overt behaviour and penile plethysmographic responses, there remains a great need for detailed physiological recordings to be taken during the conduct of aversion therapy – simply, it is essential to find out what is happening 'under the patient's skin' during aversion therapy.

Feldman and MacCulloch (1965) made one of the first attempts systematically to apply the evidence on the experimental application of aversive stimulation to clinical problems. The attempt, although admirable in many ways and apparently of considerable therapeutic effect, unfortunately contains a number of difficulties.

We feel that they have paid insufficient attention to the role of cognitive factors. This point can be illustrated by presenting a full description of their treatment and technique. After undergoing fairly extensive psychological investigations, the patient was asked to assess a large series of slides depicting males both clothed and unclothed and then to arrange them in a hierarchy of attractiveness. The hierarchy usually comprised about eight slides and treatment was commenced with the slide which was only mildly attractive. The patient was then worked up through the hierarchy in ascending order. The patient was also asked to compile a hierarchy of female slides and in this case the highest slide, i.e. the most attractive, was presented first and the patient then worked down the hierarchy in descending order. Feldman and MacCulloch then established a level of shock which was described by the patient as being very unpleasant. The treatment was carried out in a dark and quiet room at the hospital.

... The patient is told that he will see a male picture and that several seconds later he might receive a shock. He is also told that he can turn off the slide by pressing a switch, with which he is provided, whenever he wishes to do so, and that the moment the slide leaves the screen, the shock will also be turned off. Finally he is told that he will never be shocked when the screen is blank. It is made clear to him that he should leave the slide on the screen for as long as he finds it sexually attractive. The first slide is then presented. The patient has the choice of switching it off or leaving it on the screen. Should he switch it off within eight seconds he is not shocked and this is termed an avoidance response. Should he fail to turn it off within eight seconds, he receives a shock. If the shock strength is not sufficiently high to cause him to switch it off immediately, it is increased until he does so. In practice this has hardly ever been necessary. The moment a patient performs the switching off response the slide is removed and the shock is terminated. This is termed an escape trial. In addition to switching off, the patient is told to say 'No' as soon as he wishes the slide to be removed. It is hoped that a further increment of habit strength will accrue to the avoidance habit by means of this further avoidance response. The usual course of events is: several trials in all of which escape responses are made; a sequence of trials in some of which the patient escapes, and some of which he avoids; a sequence of trials in which the patient avoids every time.

After the patient has successfully avoided on three successive trials he is placed on a predetermined schedule of reinforcement. In addition to the attempt at suppressing sexual responses to nude males, Feldman and MacCulloch tried to make the patients more responsive to female photographs. This was attempted by introducing a female slide contiguous with the removal of the male slide. 'That is we attempt to associate the relief of anxiety with the introduction of the female.' They go on to say that the female slide was always removed by the therapist and never by the patient, 'so that his habit of avoiding females is not strengthened in the training situation'. It is evident from this description that we are here dealing with a situation which is a long way removed from Solomon's dogs jumping from one compartment to the next. As an extreme example we would draw particular attention to Feldman and MacCulloch's comment about the removal of the female slides. Their insistence that the patient should never remove the female slide seems to us to be stretching the analogy. We cannot see that there is anything but a very remote resemblance between pushing a button to remove a photograph of a female from a screen and what they describe as 'his habit of avoiding females'.

Had we been asked to predict, on purely theoretical grounds, the likelihood of such a treatment procedure effecting a major change in homosexual behaviour, we would undoubtedly have given it a low chance of success; we would of course have been entirely wrong had we made such a prediction – for the fact of the matter is that a substantial number of the patients treated by Feldman and MacCulloch did respond to this treatment. None the less, we feel that it might be worth while considering substituting some other stimulus representation in the treatment technique. As a possibility we would suggest that more effective results might be obtained by the use of imaginal stimulation in which the patient could be asked to produce fantasies concerning the *sexual behaviour in which he indulges* – in the manner of Marks and Gelder (1967). This view received some support by Evans' (1968) report on the treatment of ten exhibitionist patients by a method similar to Feldman and MacCulloch's. Evans substituted images for pictorial stimuli and obtained good results (see p. 69).

It could be said that the surprising thing about aversion therapy is *not* that its effects are uncertain, but rather that it works at all. One of the reasons for making this observation is the fact that patients know perfectly well that when they leave the clinic and approach the abnormal sexual object or indulge in the deviant sexual behaviour they will no longer receive electric shocks. In the Feldman–MacCulloch treatment, the patients were undoubtedly aware that when they left the hospital they would no longer receive electric shocks – for any reason, let alone for making homosexual responses or for that matter, when looking at photographs of attractive males. Nevertheless, a high proportion of their patients did 'make the generalisation' from the highly artificial clinical situation to the outside world. The operation of cognitive factors in aversion therapy is, we feel, therefore of crucial significance. Closely related to this problem is our need to understand what happens to the patient's autonomic reactions during a course of aversion therapy.

The clinical effectiveness of the procedure used by Feldman and

MacCulloch is satisfactory and offers considerable encouragement. In the first place it should be noticed that they offered treatment to *all* patients who were referred and this in itself is, as they comment, a very unusual procedure. In their report made in 1965 they had completed the treatment of nineteen patients. Of these, three defected from treatment, eleven were 'improved' at the end of treatment and the remaining five patients made very little response. At the time of publication, the follow-up on these patients was of short duration only and it was, therefore, impossible to assess the persistence of the observed changes, except to say that one patient in the series had relapsed. Feldman and MacCulloch have now extended their original sample and a more recent report (Feldman, 1967) indicates that their early successes are being maintained. They have not altered their selection procedure and have now completed treatment on forty-three homosexual patients. At the one-year follow-up period, twenty-five were improved, eleven were failures and seven defected from treatment. Patients of over thirty years of age, high Kinsey homosexual ratings and with personality problems, responded least well. Patients who had some heterosexual experiences and interests responded best.

Their results are exceptionally promising and there can be little doubt that Feldman and MacCulloch have made an important clinical contribution which needs to be extended and repeated. Incidentally, we feel that this report by Feldman and MacCulloch is an amusing example of the divergence between theory and practice, in that although the theoretical basis of their therapeutic method is, in our view, far from satisfactory, its clinical effectiveness is very encouraging.

MacCulloch, Feldman and Pinschoff (1965) have also provided some information about the changes which occurred during the course of treatment. They described the response latencies obtained for four of their patients and the pulse rate changes in two patients. The response latencies refer to the time which elapsed before the patient turned the switch to remove the male photograph. The writers claim that a regular pattern of responding occurred in patients who improved with treatment but did not do so in those who failed to improve or those who relapsed. The typical changes observed in the successful patients were of a similar nature to those described by Solomon and his co-workers in their studies (Solomon and Wynne, 1953; Turner and Solomon, 1962) namely, a shortish period of escape-responding followed by a sudden change to total avoidance which is then maintained at a consistent level. The pulse rate changes for only two of the patients were described and it appears that 'pulse rate changes to the conditioned stimulus were conditioned in one patient who improved with treatment but not in another', who failed to improve with treatment. They argue that their results 'suggest an association between pronounced pulse rate changes and successful avoidance learning, and conversely between an absence of pulse rate changes and avoidance learning'.

The information which they present is interesting and is a step in the direction of obtaining the vital but missing information on the underlying physiological changes which occur during aversion therapy. Unfortunately, however, their report suffers from two defects. In the first place, they provide information on a very small number of their total patient group (in the case of pulse rate changes, only two patients are described in any detail) and secondly, the information is almost all of a qualitative nature. No statistical analysis of the information was attempted and, particularly in the case of the pulse rate changes, this makes it extremely difficult if not impossible to draw any conclusions from the data.

In discussing the changes in response latency, they point out that as treatment proceeds, shorter response latencies are observed. They go on to say that

a naïve expectation might be that patients exposed to the anticipatory avoidance situation would eventually learn that there was an 8 second interval between the stimulus and the shock, and respond to this by 'sitting it out' for $7\frac{1}{2}$ seconds before switching off once they had learned that there was no simple relationship between their responses and what actually happened. In fact, only one patient out of over twenty treated to date has behaved in this manner.

It is 'a naïve expectation' and it is certainly one which the present authors would have made. The surprising thing is that their patients did not behave in a simple and adaptive manner by literally 'sitting it out' for the $7\frac{1}{2}$ seconds before switching off. The naïveté of our expectations appears to be exceeded only by the naïvete of the patients.

In many instances, a delay between the CS and UCS leads to the development of what Pavlov (1927) described as 'inhibition of delay' – a phenomenon akin to 'sitting it out'. After the presentation of the CS, the subject delays responding for a period of time which just anticipates the occurrence of the UCS.

First, the S quickly learns to relate the onset of the CS to an impending event of adaptive significance (food, trauma, etc.). This may take only one trial in some S's. It is manifested in a short-latency CR. Then, as the inevitability of the CS-UCS temporal relation begins to be experienced repetitively by the S,

F

a change in the CR pattern gradually occurs, in which the early portion of the CS-UCS interval is a time of inhibition of responding and the peak of the CR shifts out toward the time of occurrence of the UCS (*Kimmel, 1965, p. 170*).

A possible explanation of this unusual result noted by MacCulloch *et al.* (1965) is that their patients were experiencing considerable anxiety in treatment and more or less decided to 'take no chances'. As soon as the stimulus appeared they switched it off and thereby made certain that a shock would be avoided.

On the basis of the small number of patients presented, MacCulloch *et al.* postulate that there is a clear relationship between success in treatment and the rapid acquisition of the avoidance habit. They also point out that there is some suggestive evidence to indicate that a high degree of variation in response latency predicts a poor therapeutic outcome – as does the failure to acquire avoidance responses of consistently short latencies.

In regard to the information on pulse rate changes, the absence of quantification makes it very difficult to assess the role or importance of this information – particularly as only two patients are quoted in detail. Our difficulty in evaluating the information is further complicated by the fact that the authors appear to have been undecided about whether or not the pulse rate changes which they obtained constituted conditioned responses. Of the two patients described, one improved and the second did not. The authors argue that the patient who was successfully treated developed a mild cardiac response to the male pictures – even on non-shocked trials. Pointing out that this response was not present prior to treatment, they feel entitled to regard its emergence as evidence for the establishment of a conditioned cardiac response. They support their argument by showing that some of the increases in cardiac rate observed in this patient were of the order of twenty beats per minute or more. Certainly, on visual inspection, they appear to be justified in concluding that this patient did show cardiac changes during treatment and that his cardiac rate fluctuated a great deal. However, even though the patient quite obviously showed considerable cardiac rate fluctuation it is not possible, *on the data presented*, to decide whether or not a conditioned response had been developed. The authors point out that the cardiac response to the male picture which was observed on non-shocked trials was not present 'either prior to treatment or early in treatment'. Unfortunately, as the full data of all the trials in all the sessions is not presented either directly or in quantified form (summarised) one has to rely on visual inspection which is of necessity based on a small selection of the trials which the patient underwent (and that on one patient out of a group of more than twenty). The reliance on visual inspection methods is unsatisfactory in itself and also because of some comments made by the authors. In their discussion of the data from the patient who was unsuccessfully treated, they state that there was 'no change throughout'. In our view, however, even on the limited graphic information provided, this patient *did* show some cardiac fluctuations. We might point out that some of these fluctuations appear to be in excess of twenty beats per minute or more, a figure quoted by the writers in support of their argument that the successfully treated patient had developed a conditioned cardiac response. It is also noticeable that the two patients described in this paper had considerably different basal cardiac rates. The successfully treated patient appears to have had an exceptionally high basal cardiac rate (in the region of 100 to 110 beats per minute). This variation between the individuals simply emphasises the necessity for subjecting the data to proper quantitative analysis and until this has been completed it is necessary to suspend any conclusions.

Finally, it would appear that in the circumstances the best course which can be devised is that of regarding the tentative conclusions proposed by MacCulloch *et al.* more in the light of hypotheses. The hypotheses which one could construct might follow these lines: the successful conduct of aversion therapy is accompanied by what they call 'successful avoidance learning', i.e. the establishment of a conditioned cardiac response and rapid, consistent avoidance responses. The further investigation of these two possibilities will, we are sure, considerably advance our understanding of aversion therapy.

In their theory of sexual deviations, McGuire, Carlisle and Young (1965) placed great emphasis on the patient's masturbatory activities. They argued that sexual deviations are repeatedly reinforced by masturbation and drew attention to the prominence of deviant fantasies in the sexual life of a group of their patients. Some support for this potentially valuable theory was recently provided by Evans (1968) who noted a significant relation between masturbatory fantasies and response to treatment in ten exhibitionists. All ten patients were given electrical aversion therapy by a method which combined features of classical conditioning and punishment procedures. Shock was delivered three to six seconds after the presentation of phrases selected to evoke deviant associations. The patients were also asked to imagine the scenes suggested by the phrases. Six months after treatment, all ten patients were improved, but two of them still exhibited themselves occasionally.

These two patients generally used abnormal fantasies during masturbation. They also required more treatment sessions than the five patients who masturbated to normal, heterosexual fantasies. A comparison between patients, based on their typical masturbatory practices, showed that the five who used normal fantasies responded within five weeks. The remaining five used abnormal masturbatory fantasies and required far more treatment (range four to twenty-four weeks).

The role of masturbatory activity in maintaining or weakening abnormal sexual behaviour raises many interesting problems. If McGuire et al. (1965) are even partly correct, then the practice of aversion therapy can be improved. The evidence obtained by Evans (1968) supports their theory and also provokes two practical suggestions. In the first place, masturbatory practices can be investigated for their prognostic value. Secondly, it may prove possible to reduce abnormal sexual behaviour by altering the patient's masturbatory practices and fantasies. It would also follow that normal sexual practices can be shaped by altering the masturbatory activities of sexual deviates. In fact, Bancroft (1966) has already made an attempt of this nature and his results were sufficiently interesting to encourage further study. Research into the therapeutic effects of a combination of altered masturbatory practices and covert sensitisation (see Chapter 12) would seem to be particularly worth while.

Summary

Electrical aversion has been employed with apparent success in the treatment of transvestites, fetishists, homosexuals, masochists, exhibitionists – but the total number of cases reported so far is still small and there is a need for careful control studies.

At this stage of development it is impossible to recommend any particular treatment technique with confidence, but the Marks and Gelder method offers some apparent advantages. Like most other techniques, it involves punishment training of sexual fantasies. This phase is then followed by punishment of the actual deviant behaviour where this is feasible. Their use of plethysmographic monitoring and attitude-measurements is strongly recommended.

It appears that shock intensities need to be fairly high and the hope expressed earlier by Eysenck and Rachman (1965) that mild shocks may be adequate, now seems less probable. It is best to avoid building up from mild to strong shock as this procedure may produce habituation effects – or other complications. The use of discontinuous shocks seems undesirable, and it is likely that if the shocks are administered at the wrong time, untoward therapeutic effects may occur.

At least three treatment effects have been obtained often enough for us to have confidence in their reality. The repeated shocking of sexual fantasies produces an increase in image latency and penis erectile latency. Some punishment recovery may occur but the treatment effects on imagery and penile reactions are cumulative over a course of treatment. The diminution of fantasy strength is associated with clinical improvement. The diminution of erectile reactions to deviant stimulation is also associated with clinical improvement.

We need more information about the subjective loss of interest in deviant sexual stimuli and activities, consequent upon treatment. The possible development of aversive or anxiety reactions to deviant stimuli needs to be explored. On some occasions remarkable specificity of treatment effects have been observed and the problems thereby involved are considered.

No clear and unequivocal instances of symptom substitution have been reported. General improvements in adjustment have often followed successful treatment. Spontaneous (and prompted) improvements in normal sexual behaviour have followed successful treatment. Some attempts to re-direct and improve normal sexual behaviour are described and the encouragement of normal sexual fantasies during masturbation seems promising. The use of hormones has not been successful.

It is still not clear whether the presence of anxiety facilitates or impedes treatment. Nevertheless, some highly anxious patients have responded successfully. The effect of depression on electrical treatment is not known.

Further research into prognostic indices is required, but it seems probable that patients with stable backgrounds and personality will respond best. A positive heterosexual history and/or normal heterosexual outlets are probably favourable prognostic signs.

Apart from the problems already mentioned, it is emphasised that a great deal of research needs to be undertaken. The improvement of treatment methods is discussed and the use of monitoring during and after treatment is encouraged.

9

Treatment of alcoholism and of compulsive eating

After the encouraging results reported by McGuire and Vallance (1964), Blake (1965) described his experiences with a comparison trial between electrical aversion treatment of alcoholism and electrical aversion combined with relaxation training (as a preparatory step). The two methods concerned were employed on the grounds that Eysenck (1960), in discussing the possible applications of aversion therapy, had pointed out that in certain conditions it might be necessary to eliminate the unadaptive behaviour and the drive, usually fear, that motivates the actual response repertoire. Similarly, Metzner (1963) is quoted in support of the idea that aversion conditioning is only likely to succeed in the treatment of alcoholism either 'when the alcohol no longer reduces any drive except what is self-generated, or when the anxiety is simultaneously being extinguished by other methods'.

The patients who received aversion therapy combined with relaxation underwent a three-part therapeutic programme. The three phases of the programme were: relaxation training, motivation arousal, aversion conditioning proper. Once the patient had acquired the ability to relax successfully, he was given a few sessions of what appears to be counselling, and during these periods he was forcibly reminded of the undesirable consequences of his alcoholism. Attempts were also made to increase his desire to participate in the treatment and to rid himself of the disorder. The final phase of treatment consisted of the aversion conditioning procedure. The treatment was carried out with the subject and therapist in separate rooms. The shocks were, therefore, delivered when the patient was isolated. Each subject was supplied with a glass, water and alcohol of his choice and was instructed to mix his drink according to taste. The description of the method given by Blake is as follows:

He is told to sip his drink but not to swallow. A shock of increasing intensity, starting randomly above the threshold reported by him in a pre-aversion test to be unpleasant, is delivered contiguously with his sip on reinforced trials. He is instructed to spit out the alcohol (into a bowl provided) as a means of having the shock terminated. This is defined as an escape trial. Partial reinforcement on a schedule randomized around a 50% ratio is used. On non-reinforced trials the alcohol is ejected in response to a green light signal from the therapist. In this escape formula it has been observed that the alcohol is ejected with the same eagerness on non-reinforced trials, even when the green light has ceased to be presented, as when a trial is reinforced by shock.

Conditioning sessions extended over four to eight days and the whole programme took an average of 4·93 hours per subject.

This aversion treatment procedure was also used in treating the patients in the 'aversion therapy only' group. Attempts were made to reassess each subject at intervals of 1, 3, 6, 9 and 12 months. The success of the treatment was assessed in terms of the five criteria proposed by Knight (1941) where these were applicable. In addition, follow-up information was obtained wherever possible, from at least one independent person – usually the spouse or other close relative. The abstinent category included those individuals who were known to be abstinent during the one-year follow-up period. The improved category included 'those persons whose drinking was now of a social order . . . and appeared to be in no danger of pathological escalation'. The majority of the patients in this study belonged to social classes 1 and 2.

The full results available at the completion of the one-year follow-up were presented by Blake in a later paper (1967). Of the thirty-seven patients treated by relaxation and aversion therapy 46% were abstinent, 13% were improved, 30% had relapsed and 11% were unaccounted for. The twenty-two patients who were treated by electrical aversion therapy alone yielded the following outcome: 23% were abstinent, 27% were improved, 27% had relapsed and 23% were unaccounted for. Although the difference between the two groups in terms of the abstinent and improved categories was not statistically significant, it would appear that the relaxation-combined-with-aversion therapy produced substantially more patients who succeeded in abstaining for at least one year. Blake very fairly points out that the results give no grounds for complacency but that they are far from being discouraging.

It is, of course, very difficult to sort out the factors involved in the relaxation-plus-aversion therapy group as the patients were also receiving something akin to counselling. Nevertheless, this treatment programme would appear to deserve replication. In regard to the actual treatment procedure itself, it is possible that Blake's method of increasing the intensity of the shock is undesirable. Also, as we commented in regard to the Marks and Gelder paper (1967), the value of partial reinforcement schedules in this type of conditioning procedure has yet to be firmly resolved. Finally, Blake's observation that the patients responded very rapidly to the green light signal is reminiscent of the observation reported by Blakemore *et al.* (1964) in their treatment of a transvestite patient. This patient was observed to respond as rapidly to the sound of buzzer as he did to the electric shock trials themselves. The significance of these observations is not yet clear, but it does suggest the possibility that one might be able to dispense with the electric shock fairly early in the treatment procedure. Altogether, the finding that subjects respond so well to a secondary stimulus, such as a green light or a buzzer, raises numerous interesting possibilities. It may be that we are here observing an analogue to the experimental investigations of the effects of threat on autonomic conditioning (see Bridger and Mandel, 1964) for example. It should be remembered, however, that although it has proved possible to produce autonomic conditioned reactions to threat alone, these learned responses appear to be particularly fragile and easy to extinguish.

Blake (1966) also recorded GSR changes during the conduct of aversive therapy, and while he has yet to give a detailed report of these findings, it is interesting to notice that the great majority of his patients apparently did develop conditioned reactions during the course of treatment.

In 1966, MacCulloch, Feldman, Orford and MacCulloch reported on their unsuccessful attempt to treat four alcoholic patients by their technique of 'anticipatory avoidance learning' – which they had earlier used with some success in the treatment of homosexuals. They state that one of the main purposes in presenting their results was to introduce 'into the discussion a salutary note of caution'. They succeeded – but they also showed that their treatment technique does not appear to hold much promise for the treatment of alcoholics. In view of Blake's comparatively encouraging findings, it would appear that his procedure (particularly the relaxation-plus-aversion conditioning method) is the one which would best repay further investigation. It should be remembered, however, that a direct comparison between the Feldman and Blake studies is not possible because of the important differences between their patients. Feldman's patients were, from all points of view, distinctly unpromising material.

Although MacCulloch *et al.* (1966) state that the treatment procedure used with their four alcoholic patients was essentially similar to that employed in the management of their homosexual patients, it is not stated what instructions their patients were actually given. As we have suggested, the subjects' cognitive appraisal of the situation may be of considerable importance and the absence of this information is unfortunate. Their patients appeared to have difficulty in developing the anticipatory avoidance response of switching off the slide before the eight-second danger period had elapsed – and it is difficult to understand why they failed to do so. They were not permitted to drink during the treatment sessions and were merely exposed to photographs of alcohol, the sight of an open bottle and alcohol in a glass. None of these stimuli appear to be particularly reinforcing, and the patients would have gained nothing by permitting the slide to stay on beyond the eight-second danger period. It is in this light that their failure to develop the anticipatory avoidance reaction of switching off the slide appears to be so puzzling. Pulse rate recordings were obtained for two of the four patients but, as in their earlier reports, the authors did not provide a quantitative analysis of these observations. In consequence, it is impossible to ascertain whether or not a conditioned cardiac response did in fact develop in either of the patients. Certainly the graphic samples which they present indicate that there was, at least in one of the patients if not both, considerable fluctuation in pulse rate. In view of the difficulty in assessing this information (both in the report on alcoholics and the earlier ones on homosexuals) we are unable to accept at face value their conclusion that the pulse rate findings obtained from the alcoholic patients are 'in direct contrast to our successful homosexual patients'. It is, of course, perfectly possible that such a distinction can be made, but in the absence of further information their conclusion cannot be supported.

In 1965, Hsu described a new variant of electrical aversion therapy in which his alcoholic patients received a powerful (2 to 5 ma) shock within 0·5 to 5 seconds after swallowing alcohol. The shocks were administered to the *head* and lasted for 30 seconds. The initial treatment consisted of five daily sessions and was 'boosted' by two-day sessions given one month and six months later. Great anxiety was provoked by this unpleasant method and less than half of the original forty volunteers completed the first and second treatments. Quite reasonably, Hsu has refrained from giving detailed results until a prolonged follow-up is completed, but the method is exceedingly unpleasant and we can see no justification for its continuation. It comes as no surprise that the defection rate was so high.

Summary

Very little research into the effects of electrical aversion therapy on alcoholism has been carried out. In so far as it is possible to detect early trends, it seems likely that a punishment training method such as that employed by Blake (1965, 1966) may produce useful results. The use of supplementary relaxation training may increase the therapeutic benefits of therapy but, if so, its mode of action is not altogether clear. The further investigation of Blake's method, particularly with other types of patients, seems desirable and should include physiological monitoring and attempts to isolate the effective elements involved in the entire therapeutic programme. The subjective effects of the therapy should be carefully studied – during and after the training sessions.

It is premature to attempt comparisons between the theory, practice and effects of chemical as opposed to electrical aversion therapy in the management of alcoholism.

The treatment of compulsive eating

The experimental evidence, although limited, suggests that the passive association of food stimuli and shock may well produce a fear of the stimuli, but does not necessarily interfere with the act of eating (Lichtenstein, 1950). If the aversive stimulation is delivered during the sequence of activities which lead up to, and/or include eating, then the organism may cease eating – even for protracted periods (Masserman, 1943). There is also evidence that, under certain conditions, eating and anxiety are reciprocally inhibiting (e.g. Wolpe, 1958; Gale et al., 1966). At least three patients treated for compulsive eating by aversion methods have been reported in the literature and it is interesting to attempt a comparison between the clinical and experimental data.

Thorpe et al. (1964) used aversion-relief therapy (see Chapter 2) with a young girl who suffered from depression and intermittent bouts of compulsive over-eating. She 'felt that she wanted to eat continuously', thought about food constantly and had periodic bouts of excessive over-eating. These lasted for two to three days and were carried out in seclusion. When the bouts ended she felt exhausted, guilty and depressed. Her weight increased by approximately 6 kg. on each occasion.

She responded badly during the treatment sessions and experienced depressive and anxiety reactions; therapy had to be discontinued after eight sessions. The actual treatment consisted of presenting the word 'over-eating' on a card and then delivering a shock three to six seconds later. It was not possible to ascertain the effects of treatment on her pattern of over-eating, but she did report a reduction in her preoccupation with thoughts of food and eating. A direct extrapolation from

Lichtenstein's (1950) experiment would have led one to predict that the patient would become fearful of food stimuli, but that her excessive eating would not be altered. This prediction may have been supported, but the relevant data are unfortunately not available.

Meyer and Crisp (1964) treated two obese patients by punishing them with shocks when they approached 'temptation food' but not when they approached or ate their prescribed food. Case No. 1 received five shocks during her first treatment session but thereafter made only five more approaches during the thirty subsequent sessions. The treatment lasted for six weeks and the patient responded well. Her weight fell from 91 to 82 kgs. She was followed-up for six months and persisted in avoiding 'temptation foods'. Her weight steadily fell and then settled between 55 and 59 kg. A year later she still weighed 59 kg. This patient responded as might have been predicted – the punishment of eating or approach behaviour should lead to a cessation of the activity. In this case, moreover, the patient achieved a discriminated response. She avoided fattening 'temptation food' but continued to eat her prescribed diet.

Meyer and Crisp's second case was unfortunately a 'non-starter', and after receiving one preparatory practice shock she consistently refrained from approaching the temptation foods. In this way she prevented the treatment from being carried out. Meyer and Crisp satisfactorily explained her refusal, but they comment that, 'the difference between the cases indicates the necessity of precise and absolute pairing of unconditioned and conditioned stimuli'. This statement is plausible and it probably is important to ensure careful pairing of the CS and UCS. Their observations do not, however, provide support for such a conclusion.

It can be seen that there are practically no clinical findings relevant to the problem of eating and punishment. Until such data are forthcoming we have to rely on the experimental results obtained with animals. These suggest that if compulsive over-eating is to be treated by aversion therapy, the aversive stimuli should be delivered during the approach to food or very soon after eating is commenced.

10

Changes associated with electrical aversion therapy

Anxiety

It is not certain that all patients who undergo aversion therapy develop anxiety reactions during treatment. Nevertheless, there are sufficient clinical reports to suggest that this is, at least, a common occurrence. Bancroft (1966) made a particular study of the arousal of anxiety in his homosexual patients and found that it was typically, but not necessarily, encountered. He observed that two of his patients who responded well to the treatment experienced significantly large anxiety reactions. Whether this is a necessary concomitant of successful aversion therapy seems to be doubtful at this point and the role, if any, of anxiety development prior to or during the course of the treatment is a matter which needs clarification. In their analysis of eight patients, Marks and Sartorius (1968) found little sign of anxious attitudes emerging during or after electrical treatment. The measure which they used (Semantic Differential Scales) is not particularly suited for assessing anxiety, however, and more direct forms of measurement will be required. In an enlarged study of aversion therapy, Marks and Gelder (1968) later found some evidence that anxiety does occur in a minority of cases.

Physiological changes

As was pointed out earlier, there is a great need to find out more about the physiological changes which occur during therapy. The information available so far, while suggestive, is inadequate to permit one to draw conclusions. Solyom and Miller (1965) reported their findings on finger volume plethysmography and on GSR; however, as they did not present the full quantitative results it is difficult to assess the significance of their findings. MacCulloch and Feldman (1965) found that one of their two homosexual patients developed a conditioned cardiac rate reaction (he was successfully treated) and the other failed to show evidence of consistent cardiac changes (this patient did not respond to treatment). As mentioned earlier, however, failure to quantify these results makes it difficult to evaluate their importance. Once again we can only emphasise the importance of this type of information and the need to obtain quantitative measures of the data.

The most interesting information to emerge so far concerns the changes in penile volume which occur during the treatment of patients with sexual disorders. Bancroft *et al.* (1965) and Marks and Gelder (1967) found it to be an extremely useful measure of changes in sexual behaviour. Bancroft found it similarly useful in his 1966 study on homosexuals, but his results were somewhat puzzling in that some patients tended to show increased penile plethysmographic reactions to female stimuli but did not show consistent reductions in their plethysmographic reactions to male sexual stimuli. These findings, although they were consistent with the clinical outcome of his seven cases, need clarification. They may have been a function of Bancroft's treatment procedure (see p. 56), but this interpretation requires confirmation.

Marks and Gelder (1967) found that as the aversion therapy began to take effect (e.g. when the patient's other reactions diminished) the presentation of deviant stimuli failed to evoke penile plethysmographic changes. In particular, the plethysmographic changes were closely related to attitudinal changes and therapeutic outcome.

The patient's plethysmographic reactions can also be used as a monitoring device within treatment sessions – or even as the response upon which punishment is made contingent. In fact, Bancroft's (1966) treatment method is punishment training in which the aversive stimulus is delivered contingent on penile volume increases. The advisability of using this method cannot be decided until further investigations have been completed, but the value of plethysmographic *monitoring* has been demonstrated beyond doubt. For example, the persistence of plethysmographic reactions to deviant stimuli can be taken as a sign that therapy is not complete. Incidentally, penile plethysmography is an extremely useful diagnostic procedure (see Freund, 1963; 1967). Feldman (1966) has also made the useful suggestion that pupillary responses to sexual stimuli, as measured by Hess *et al.* (1965), could be employed as a method of assessing therapeutic change – and diagnostically.

Imagery

It has been shown in various studies that the time taken to achieve deviant fantasies increases with aversive training. These increases in the latency period tend to grow with repeated aversion trials.

Although some decrease in the latency period is frequently

encountered in the first few trials of a new treatment session, the overall trend within and across sessions is for latencies to increase. There is a *cumulative* increase in latency and the patient is sometimes taken to a point where he is no longer able to obtain the image at all. As this stage of total suppression is approached, patients tend to complain that the image keeps 'evading' them or 'sliding out of my mind'. They appear to have lost the ability to control the image. The increase in the latency period tends to be associated with alterations in sexual fantasies outside of treatment. Patients report that they are less concerned with the deviant images and 'don't think about them' as often as they had prior to treatment.

In his review of the effects of punishment, Church (1963) suggested that, as the intensity of the UCS is increased, the organism's behaviour goes through the following sequential changes: detection of the stimulus, temporary response-suppression, partial suppression and, finally, total suppression. If we make the reasonable assumption that the shock stimuli typically employed in aversion therapy are of moderate intensity, then the four stages described by Church should appear during treatment. The data on image-latency increases certainly seems to follow this pattern – temporary suppression, partial suppression and usually but not always, total suppression.

Sexual behaviour

In some instances, and especially in the treatment of homosexuals, therapists have made a deliberate effort to foster alternative sexual behaviour. These attempts have met with slight success and are discussed in Chapters 6 and 7. Here we are concerned with the changes in related and unrelated sexual behaviour which appear to be produced by the aversion therapy. There is sufficient evidence to make it safe to conclude that deviant sexual behaviour can be suppressed by aversion therapy. This suppression can be long-lasting but relapses have also been noted.

What happens to the patient's sexual drive if the aversion treatment is successful? Some patients appear entirely to refrain from sexual activity (e.g. some of the homosexuals treated by Feldman and Mac-Culloch, 1967). Others begin to develop heterosexual activities, albeit inadequately (e.g. Bancroft *et al.* 1965; Feldman and MacCulloch, 1967). There are other patients, however (and they might well prove to be the majority), who develop or resume satisfactory heterosexual activities (e.g. Marks and Gelder, 1967; Evans, 1968; Kushner, 1965; Blakemore,

1964, etc.). The likelihood of a patient resuming or developing hetero-sexual relationships appears to be related to his pre-treatment hetero-sexual experiences (and other factors, such as general stability, etc.). It will not be surprising if patients who have never been able to establish satisfactory heterosexual relationships are found to require considerable assistance after treatment. Such assistance may involve social training, counselling and desensitisation. In addition, specific sexual guidance may be required (perhaps along the lines proposed by Bancroft, 1966, regarding masturbation).

On theoretical and clinical grounds it seems unwise to terminate the patient's sexual deviation and then leave him in a vacuum – this despite the fact that *some* patients appear to manage abstemious lives after overcoming their sexual problems. Therapists should find ways of capitalising on the suppression of the deviant behaviour produced by the aversion therapy. If, during this period, acceptable alternate sexual behaviour is established, then the probability of the deviant behaviour returning will, almost certainly, be reduced.

Subjective consequences

The subjective consequences of aversion therapy are fascinating. Elec-trical treatment does not necessarily produce an *aversion* to either the deviant stimuli or the deviant activity itself. Electrical aversion therapy employs an aversive stimulus, but it does not follow that an 'aversion', in the ordinary sense, develops.

The changes in conceptual meaning attached to the objects involved in the patients' sexual deviations have been studied by Marks and Gelder (1967) and by Marks and Sartorius (1967). Marks and Gelder observed that the patients' attitudes towards the sexual objects and activities involved in their abnormal behaviour were selectively devalued as the treatment proceeded. No significant changes occurred in other concepts – even in sexual concepts which were unrelated to the patients' particular disorder. Although their attitudes always changed in the direction of devaluation, not all of the patients developed *un*favourable attitudes to their deviations. Some patients did develop strongly unfavourable atti-tudes towards the previously attractive sexual stimuli, but others tended to adopt a neutral attitude towards them. In this sense, then, aversion treatment does not always produce an aversion. Another interesting finding to emerge in this study was the observation that changes in attitude tended to precede the changes in physiological and behavioural measures both during the course of treatment and also when relapses occurred; the attitudes changed first and the sexual behaviour later. In the second study by Marks and Sartorius, a principal components analysis of a semantic differential scale was carried out and two dimensions emerged. These were the factor of general evaluation and a new factor named 'sexual evaluation'. The changes observed after treatment were confined to the sex evaluative scales. Other dimensions, including anxiety, showed no significant change (this finding is of course relevant to the point discussed above, namely, the occurrence or non-occurrence of anxiety during aversion treatment). Marks and Sartorius also demonstrated that the semantic differential scales showed good stability over a 24-hour test–retest period. Finally, they proposed a simple two-dimensional measure of sexual attitude which can be used in assessing the progress of treatment. Marks and Sartorius note that one of the main drawbacks to the use of the semantic differential technique is that patients can, without too much difficulty, simulate their responses on these scales. They point out quite reasonably, however, that it would be equally easy for patients to falsify information in an ordinary clinical interview. Our own view is that in some respects it might be easier to falsify (if one chooses to do so) when filling out a paper-and-pencil test than when face to face with one's therapist. However, it should be remembered that these patients are all accepting a distressing form of treatment voluntarily and it would be quite contrary to their interests to falsify the information with the risk of thereby misleading the therapist and perhaps invalidating the entire treatment procedure. Presumably if they are willing to undergo the discomfort and stress of aversion therapy they will be most unlikely to 'sabotage' the therapist's attempts to assess progress. Nevertheless, such occurrences cannot entirely be ruled out. Other workers who have observed a devaluation of deviant sexual stimuli include Max (1935), Blakemore (1964, 1968), McGuire and Vallance (1964), Kushner (1965). In addition to the two transvestite patients described in his 1964 paper, Blakemore (1968) obtained clear indications of a loss of interest in female clothing in two more transvestite patients. After aversion therapy they found that previously attractive clothing failed to arouse them. One of these patients actually cross-dressed some months after treatment in order to reassure himself that the desire or pleasure had gone. He said that he had totally lost interest in cross-dressing, was no longer aroused by it and regarded his *former* deviant behaviour with repugnance. McGuire and Vallance (1964) provided another example of the type of reaction reported by patients. After a fetishistic patient had completed ten treatment sessions, he said that he had 'entirely lost interest' in his fetish and the associated practices. The fetishist–masochist described by Marks, Rachman and Gelder (1966) had much the same experience – although the fetishism later returned.

We have found three clear examples of a patient developing an aversion to the CS. McGuire and Vallance (1964) described an alcoholic patient who complained that the therapist had made his whisky distasteful. The same patient later experienced a panic when he attempted to drink whisky at a pub (see p. 43). The second example comes from Blakemore (1964). The transvestite treated by him and his colleagues sometimes experienced a 'dull testicular pain' in previously provoking situations and this could only be relieved by intercourse. It is, however, impossible to know whether this 'pain' was a component of an aversive reaction or whether it was simply a residue of sexual arousal provoked by transvestite stimuli. One of Bancroft's (1966) homosexual patients (C) showed anxiety reactions to homosexual stimuli during and after treatment.

At present the evidence indicates that although a marked aversion sometimes develops after electrical treatment, many patients seem to experience a loss of interest in the deviant stimuli and associated activities (neutralisation). It must be noted that the available evidence is scanty. Secondly, the development of an aversion may prove to be a function of the amount and intensity of the treatment administered. Further trials and/or stronger shocks may move the subjective consequences from 'favourable' through 'neutral' to 'unfavourable'. Thirdly, it is quite possible that the subjective consequences of chemical aversion therapy differ from those encountered in electrical therapy – genuine aversion seems to be a fairly common consequence of the chemical method. Some of the numerous examples of patients developing an aversion to the conditioned stimuli after chemical treatment are given in Chapter 3. Unfortunately, we are not in a position to assess the frequency of this phenomenon as the subjective consequences of chemical treatment have also been reported inadequately.

Hammersley's (1957) robust and determined alcoholic patient whom we mentioned earlier, 'broke his conditioning' by forcing himself to drink through successive waves of nausea and vomiting. The point here is that the alcohol was acting as an effective CS. Raymond's (1956) fetishistic patient developed an aversion to the CS's handbags and prams, which he said made him feel sick. Glynn and Harper's (1961) transvestite patient developed a revulsion for female clothing and all of

G

Williams' (1947) successfully treated alcoholics reportedly showed a 'marked aversion to alcohol'. A morphine-addict treated by Liberman (1968) developed anticipatory anxiety before sessions, was made nauseous by thoughts of the drug and, for a period, lost the craving. This patient later relapsed, however. The fullest report on chemical therapy comes from Hammersley (1957) who found that 'there was almost without exception a strong aversion to alcohol' (including palpitation, perspiration, etc.) produced in a group of fifty patients. Twenty-five per cent of them actually vomited when given whisky to drink after five days of treatment. As the long-term results in this study were rather disappointing, we can only conclude that even when an aversion is successfully produced, the persistence of this effect is uncertain.

Before concluding this discussion it is necessary briefly to examine the nature of aversion. In the dictionary sense it means a dislike. It is an attitude. It can be argued, however, that within the present context such a definition is too narrow. Even if a patient does not express an unfavourable *attitude* to alcohol when it repeatedly produces feelings of nausea in him, it should still be permissible to say that he has developed an aversion to alcohol. When one considers the effects of electrical aversion therapy, however, the position is more difficult. As we have shown, patients do not always develop a dislike of the CS. The development of conditioned physiological reactions to the CS has yet to be demonstrated. But would the arousal of sweating or palpitations, for example, constitute an aversion? Another way to approach the subject is to define the patient's subsequent avoidance of the CS as an aversion. For example, a fetishist who ceases masturbating in the presence of boots might be described as avoiding a previously attractive stimulus. Our view is that a distinction between devaluation and avoidance should be retained and the term 'aversion' reserved for instances where a dislike is evident and/or clear negative reactions (e.g. nausea) are provoked by the CS. Unless this distinction is retained, we may incorrectly label a cessation of activity as an avoidance reaction – just as it was previously assumed that a cessation of deviant sexual activity implied an attitude of aversion. It seems clear that some patients simply lose interest in the deviant stimuli and cease their practices without actually avoiding previously arousing situations.

From a clinical point of view, it does not appear to be necessary for the patient to develop an aversion in the strict sense. It would, however, be extremely valuable to examine more fully the relationship between attitudinal, physiological, behavioural and therapeutic changes. Clinically, the prognostic significance of an aversion developing is of considerable interest.

Summary

Many, but not all patients, develop anxiety reactions during electrical aversion therapy. There are suggestions that physiological reactions, such as cardiac rate and GSR, are conditioned during treatment. Penile volume increases to the CS usually decline or disappear. The clinical significance of a failure to produce penile volume changes is not yet clear. The time taken to achieve deviant fantasies increases during treatment. These changes show some inter-session recovery but are cumulative in the long-term. Related sexual behaviour declines with treatment. Unrelated sexual behaviour may or may not change but some notable improvements in normal heterosexual behaviour have been reported. Some patients develop a dislike of the CS, but it is fairly common for them simply to lose interest in the CS. Following the administration of chemical aversion therapy, negative reactions (especially nausea) have been noted, in some studies, frequently to occur. The relationship between attitudinal, physiological and behavioural aversion is briefly examined and it is concluded that electrical aversion therapy does not necessarily produce an 'aversion' – even when it is therapeutically successful.

11

The nature of electrical aversion therapy

The existing therapeutic procedures can be analysed into three types of learning paradigm: classical conditioning, punishment training, avoidance conditioning. In the case of chemical aversion therapy, it was argued that a classical conditioning model provides the 'best fit', but that elements of the other two types of learning also play a role. The electrical method is primarily a form of punishment training which almost always includes elements of classical conditioning. The Feldman–MacCulloch method was developed on an avoidance learning model, but there are reasons for concluding that it is essentially a classical model in which the avoidance training elements are of lesser significance (see Chapters 8 and 16).

The punishment training model appears to fit many of the available facts. In virtually all of the clinical procedures, the delivery of a shock stimulus is contingent on the occurrence of a deviant response. For example, in sexual disorders the shock is generally administered when a penile reaction or a deviant fantasy occurs. This part of the therapy is *sometimes* preceded by classical training in which the shock is administered in association with a sexual stimulus irrespective of the occurrence of any particular response. However, with the exception of the Feldman–MacCulloch method, response-contingent shock is *always* used – at some stage in treatment. The definition of punishment implied in this analysis derives from Skinner (1953) and Dinsmoor (1954) and was recently elaborated by Azrin and Holz (1966) who state that 'an unequivocal aspect of punishment seems to be that punishment reduces a behaviour when the punishment is arranged as a consequence of that behaviour' (p. 381). This inelegant formulation is then developed succinctly in their 'minimal definition' of punishment as 'a consequence of behaviour that reduces the future probability of that behaviour' (p. 381).

Azrin and Holz point out that a simple decrease in responding is not a sufficient criterion as drugs, satiation, etc., can also produce response decrements. 'A specific event must be produced by a specific response in order to be considered a punishing stimulus' (p. 381). It is on this point that our classification of electrical aversion therapy as punishment training is vulnerable. In order to demonstrate the *specific* link between the response and its consequences, one normally institutes a test probe (e.g. a period of non-contingent shock). With the exception of the Marks and Gelder (1967) study, this has not yet been attempted. Although their observations are consistent with the present analysis they are not sufficiently extensive and will need substantiation. This requirement is easier to state than to provide. In the nature of clinical work it is usually impossible to conduct probes of this type. Hence the confirmation of this point may need the indirect approach of control treatment methods and therapeutic analogue studies of the type employed in investigating desensitisation treatment (e.g. Rachman, 1967).

In regard to the Feldman–MacCulloch method, we have already discussed the theoretical problems raised by their adherence to an avoidance model (Chapter 7). Here we need only mention that electrical aversion therapy rarely involves the learning of a new avoidance response. After successful treatment the patients do not avoid any particular stimulus – rather they cease responding to it. In other words, the behaviour is suppressed. If, as seems to be the case, the electrical method can be made to work effectively without avoidance training, then Feldman's advocacy of an avoidance model as the most appropriate guide for planning treatment is weakened (Feldman and MacCulloch, 1965; Feldman, 1966).

If the present emphasis on punishment training is justified, then it becomes necessary to specify the essential features which should be incorporated in any treatment method. They appear to be simple. Following the Azrin and Holz (1966) definition, a specific event (such as shock administration) must be produced by a specific response (such as a penile volume increase). Stated more concretely, the aversive stimulus must be delivered contingent on the occurrence of a deviant response. The relevant parameters such as timing, stimulus intensity and so forth, are discussed in Chapter 15. If the punishment model is appropriate, then the incorporation into the treatment procedure of existing knowledge concerning these parameters should facilitate reliable and satisfactory results.

The present account of electrical aversion therapy is not free of problems. Four important matters need clarification. Although we can specify the general form which treatment methods should take, it is not always certain *which* responses should be punished. In sexual disorders, for example, should the aversive stimulation be made contingent on penile volume increases or on deviant images or both? If both, then the phases of treatment need to be examined because the fantasies and penile reactions are not necessarily coincident in time. Secondly, this account has not incorporated the role of cognitive factors which must form an important part of any acceptable theory of aversion therapy (see Chapter 14). Thirdly, the viability of the punishment explanation needs to be tested in clinical trials which will compare the efficiency of treatment methods based on all the learning models – punishment, avoidance, classical conditioning. Lastly, the classical conditioning components of treatment have been acknowledged, but their function (or specific contribution) is not clear. Closely allied to this deficiency is the need for careful and extensive studies of the physiological changes which accompany punishment training.

It can of course be argued that punishment training *necessarily* involves classical conditioning. If one accepts this view then it becomes possible to re-cast our analysis and formulate a theoretical model in which classical conditioning provides the infrastructure. As we hope to show in our concluding chapters, this alternative framework offers some advantages. It certainly extends our analysis and allows an advance beyond the level of pragmatic description. It also provides a more satisfying connection between the processes involved in electrical and chemical aversion methods. This attempt to encompass punishment training within a classical conditioning model necessarily involves a fair amount of speculation and is likely to be of more interest to experimental and academic psychologists than to therapists. For the present, we suggest that the most *practical* choice is to continue to view electrical aversion therapy as punishment training and to design and conduct therapy within this framework.

An important attribute of the punishment model is that it generates clear predictions which are amenable to disconfirmation. For example, it should be possible to test the treatment effects of response-contingent shocks and non-contingent shocks – however, this check will have to be undertaken in an analogue study. For example, one possibility would be to test this proposition on volunteer, normal subjects, who wish to give up particular types of food. The importance of the shock-contingency prediction should not obscure the need to test the subsidiary predictions relating to stimulus intensity functions, temporal factors and so on.

On the practical side, electrical aversion therapy is not without difficulties. The most important problems are refusals and defections from treatment, the prevention of relapses and the avoidance of untoward emotional side-effects.

Summary

It is argued that for the present a punishment model provides the best practical guide for electrical aversion. In addition, it is noted that most procedures include some classical conditioning components. The implications of this model are discussed and some deductions are mentioned. Some ways of confirming or breaking the model are described.

12
Disadvantages of electrical aversion therapy

It will be some time before all the disadvantages of the electrical method become apparent. Even at this early stage it is worth drawing attention to some of the difficulties which have been encountered in chemical aversion therapy and which may be expected to arise when the electrical method is fully developed.

Firstly, the patient must be given a full medical examination; the treatment is not suitable for people with cardiac ailments.

The administration of aversive stimuli in laboratory experiments can give rise to aggressive behaviour. In clinical practice, aggressiveness, negativism and hostility have already been observed during the conduct of chemical aversion therapy. Secondly, there can be little doubt that most people have a fear of electrical shocks and that the method may prove to be exceedingly unpopular with some patients. The anxiety level of many patients certainly increases with the introduction of electrical stimulation and this may in turn interfere with the development of conditioned reactions. One example of this type of difficulty is reported by Beech (1960), who found that some patients reacted unfavourably to the administration of electric shocks involved in the treatment of writer's cramp. On the other hand, Bancroft (1966) concluded that anxiety probably facilitates the treatment and Thorpe et al. (1964) found that aversion-relief therapy was not influenced by the presence of anxiety.

If the presence of a high degree of emotionality does prove to be a stumbling-block in the application of electrical aversion treatment, the experimental work of Turner and Solomon (1962) on avoidance conditioning may be of some assistance. They concluded, on the basis of an interesting series of experiments on human subjects, that the conditioning of '. . . a highly emotional subject will proceed most rapidly if we start off with a short CS–UCS interval and then lengthen it, at the same time that we start with an intense UCS level then lower it to produce longer latency escape responses. When these procedures are combined, we should be able to produce rapid learning.' The possible application of these findings is discussed by Eysenck and Rachman (1965), but whether findings on avoidance conditioning can be applied to punishment training is doubtful. Moreover, it should be noted that one of the suggestions offered by Turner and Solomon, namely the progressive reduction in UCS intensity, is contrary to Azrin and Holz's (1966) recommendation that the UCS intensity should not be altered. Whether Turner and Solomon are correct in regard to the management of highly anxious S's will need general confirmation in a punishment situation, and this specific point can be given particular attention.

A major problem which looms in the background is that of relapses, and techniques will have to be developed to overcome them or to prevent their occurrence. Two possible methods which might be used, intermittent reinforcement and booster treatments, have already been mentioned. A third possibility is the use of stimulant drugs during the progress of electrical aversion treatment as there is experimental evidence that these drugs facilitate the acquisition of conditioned responses (Eysenck, 1960).

Another potential difficulty centres on the unpopularity of any method involving shocks. The refusal and defection rates can be expected to be comparatively large and, once again, ways of overcoming this potential problem will need to be developed.

Electrical aversion therapy fails with some patients. At this stage we do not have entirely reliable prognostic indices, but Feldman and MacCulloch's (1967) findings on homosexuals are worth bearing in mind. They imply, among other things, that patients with long-established homosexual behaviour respond less well. Although this is seldom stated explicitly, clinicians tend to assume that the chances of eliminating deviant or neurotic behaviour are determined to a considerable extent by the duration of the disorder. In the case of aversive training there is some evidence to support this assumption. Church (1963), for example, states that the degree of response suppression which can be attained by aversive stimulation is inversely related to the strength of the responses. Consequently, we might anticipate that patients with well-established deviant behaviour will respond less well to aversion therapy and also require more intensive treatment.

Ulrich, Hutchinson and Azrin (1965) recently published an account of pain-elicited aggression in which they convincingly demonstrated that pain may elicit aggression 'prior to any specific conditioning'. They also discussed the possibility of pain-elicited aggression occurring in man.

This phenomenon is not only observed during the administration of aversion therapy; it is regarded as one of the problems encountered by this form of treatment. Prior to the appearance of Ulrich's work, Eysenck and Rachman (1965), for example, stated that 'it has been observed experimentally that . . . aversive stimulation can give rise to an increase in aggressive behaviour (and) there is also some clinical evidence of increased aggressiveness and hostility on the part of the patient during the conduct of aversion treatment'. Elsewhere it has been suggested that 'it may, indeed, prove necessary to develop special methods for handling the aggression, if and when it occurs' (Rachman, 1965). Clear examples of pain-elicited aggression were reported by Lavin et al. (1961) and by Morgenstern, Pearce and Davies (1963) in their treatment of transvestites by apomorphine aversion therapy. Schmidt, Castell and Brown (1965) also observed occasional aggressive responses in their treatment of a variety of sexual and other disorders by electrical aversion-relief therapy.

Ulrich, Hutchinson and Azrin's delineation of the parameters involved in pain-elicited aggression should enable therapists to predict which factors in the treatment situation are most likely to instigate aggression. In regard to electric shock-induced pain, it would appear that the elicitation of aggression is a function of:

(a) shock frequency (the more often the shock is presented, the greater the frequency of aggressive responses);

(b) shock duration (the longer the shock, the greater the probability of aggression);

(c) shock consistency (the more consistent the shock, the greater the frequency of aggressive responses).

Shock intensity is related to aggression in a non-monotonic manner. Very weak or very strong shocks do not produce as much aggression as intermediate intensities (partly because powerful shocks are debilitating).

Other variables which may be of significance include chamber size, length of session and social isolation. Chamber size was of considerable importance in determining the amount of aggression – the more confined the area, the greater the frequency of aggression. It has also been observed that pain-elicited aggressive responses are extremely resistant to fatigue. Ulrich and Azrin (1962) found virtually no decrease in fighting responses after exposing a pair of rats to frequent shocks for 6 hours. Although the aggression decreased thereafter, the total number of fighting responses elicited during $7\frac{1}{2}$ hours of exposure reached the colossal total of 10,000.

It seems clear that most of the variables which produce pain-induced aggression are precisely those which are regarded as being important for the successful conduct of aversion therapy. There is, however, one possible improvement in the design of aversion therapy arising from the work of Ulrich et al. (1965).

Although pain can produce aggressive responses to inanimate objects (e.g. Azrin, Hutchinson and Sallery, 1964), there is evidence that rats performing in isolation do consistently better than paired rats. They learn more quickly, respond at higher rates and receive fewer shocks. The authors of this paper (Ulrich, Stachnik, Brierton and Mabry, 1964) point out that the 'poor avoidance behaviour which occurred in the social setting was related to the high incidence of shock-elicited aggression'.

It is possible, therefore, that the most effective way of preventing the occurrence of pain-elicited aggression during aversion therapy (which may, as Ulrich, Hutchinson and Azrin point out, interfere with the learning process) is to administer the noxious stimuli remotely. Presumably, patients treated in social isolation will display less aggression and acquire the appropriate conditioned responses more effectively and quickly. It is noteworthy also that in the apomorphine aversion method used by Morgenstern, Pearce and Davies (1963) at least one therapist and/or nurse was present during all the treatment sessions. Apparently, more aggressive reactions were encountered with this method than were elicited when the patients were screened off from the therapists (as was the case with the Schmidt, Castell and Brown [1965] technique). The possibility that pain-induced aggressive reactions during aversion therapy can be reduced by the method of isolation will require investigation. Other practical suggestions can also be derived from the theoretical and experimental analysis provided by Ulrich et al. (1965).

Summary

The observed and potential disadvantages of aversion therapy include aggressiveness and anxiety induction. Pain-elicited aggression is described and possible methods for dealing with the problem are mentioned. Three clinical problems which will be encountered are refusals, defections and relapses.

13
Beyond the aversion principle

Ethical considerations

The use of aversion therapy raises ethical problems which need to be examined – particularly as the method appears likely to be adopted extensively.

Our views on these matters are of course an expression of personal attitude. Psychologists, like other scientists, have a general responsibility to other people and this responsibility must be exercised. Detachment in scientific matters should not be confused with a detachment in ethical matters. In the first place, we feel that the *existence* of a problem must be recognised. Aversion therapy involves the deliberate application of painful or unpleasant stimulation – it involves 'punishment' in the technical sense, but this should not be allowed to become 'punitive' in the everyday sense. We have little sympathy with the argument that the use of aversion therapy does not raise ethical problems because other types of therapy also involve pain or discomfort (e.g. ECT in psychiatry, surgical procedures, etc.). Apart from the intrinsically fallacious quality of the argument ('one good abuse deserves another'), it is a counter which is irrelevant in the particular case. A patient who is about to undergo an unpleasant form of treatment derives no comfort from being reminded that there are other experiences which are even more unpleasant. Moreover, the unpleasantness of the other treatment procedures is incidental.

Aversion therapy *is* unpleasant, but psychologists must avoid becoming punitive agents. To do so would be both inherently objectionable and contrary to the nature and traditions of the discipline.

In our opinion, the treatment can only be given with the *knowledge and consent* of the patient. In addition, aversion therapy should only be advised if there are no alternative methods of treating the patient. However, ethical problems can also arise if a therapist refuses to offer treatment to a patient in distress simply because the therapist finds it difficult to administer. For example, we feel that aversion therapy could not justifiably be withheld in a case of intense self-inflicted injuries if the patient is 'inaccessible' and the therapist feels the therapy could terminate the danger.

Patients must be informed of the detailed nature of the treatment and the therapist is bound to give the patient a full and honest appraisal of the chances of success. Also, it is unthinkable that any form of coercion should be used in an attempt to induce a patient to accept treatment. While we agree that coercion comes in various packages, we nevertheless feel that in practice there is little difficulty in recognising 'undue influence'. We can illustrate this point by referring to two examples.

It is, we feel, quite wrong to make a prisoner's release or parole contingent on his consenting to undergo aversion therapy. A second instance is the use of aversion therapy without giving the patient a proper opportunity to refuse treatment. The experiment reported by Sanderson, Campbell and Laverty (1964) would seem to be an example of this type. In their study the patients were given an injection of a curare-like drug which brings about total paralysis for between 30 and 150 seconds. During this period breathing ceases and there is no doubt that it is a terrifying experience to undergo. Our specific objections are underlined by the fact that Sanderson *et al.* apparently did not give all their potential patients a full explanation of the nature of the treatment which they were to be given. As we have suggested, there are good reasons for recommending complete candour in describing the nature of any treatment which is being offered to a patient; in this instance the reasons are compelling because the experience is so harrowing. On the technical side, there is, in any event, almost certainly a relation between motivation and response to treatment. Unwilling patients are unlikely to respond well.

As a precaution against enforcing compliance in a patient, it is advisable to insist that he consider his decision for at least a week after the therapist has explained the procedure to him. In the long-term, however, the best ethical solution is to find an effective substitute for aversion therapy. With this aim in mind we will now consider some of the alternatives.

Beyond the aversion principle

Earlier we described some of the variations of aversive stimulation which have been attempted. These include isolation, verbal punishments, the withdrawal of reinforcement, intense auditory stimulation, time-out from reinforcement, covert sensitisation. Here we propose to discuss covert sensitisation in some detail and also to suggest a possible application of the extinction phenomenon which we feel may prove to be of some value in the treatment of specific types of sexual disorder.

Before we consider possible substitutes for aversion therapy, it must be mentioned that some cases of sexual disorder and other disturbances apparently respond well to established behavioural techniques. The method of systematic desensitisation (Wolpe, 1958; Rachman, 1967) is particularly useful in treating disorders in which anxiety plays a central role. There are some indications that desensitisation may be an adequate treatment for anxiety-mediated sexual disorders (Wolpe and Stevenson, 1961) and Bancroft (1968) is presently investigating the comparative effectiveness of aversion therapy and desensitisation in the management of homosexuality. Clearly, desensitisation is to be preferred over aversion, and if it proves to be widely applicable the problems attendant on the use of aversion will be of minor significance. None the less, there will almost certainly be a need for methods (aversive or non-aversive) which are capable of suppressing abnormal behaviour patterns in which anxiety plays an insignificant role.

The successful reduction and elimination of responses by the technique known as errorless extinction may provide an alternative to aversion therapy if it is applied along the following lines (or some variation of this). In the case of what we might call surplus and misdirected sexual behaviour, notably fetishism and transvestism, it seems worth considering the possibility that repeated unreinforced presentations of the stimulus may produce decrements in response strength. To particularise, the following method is one which appears to us to have some promise, but which we have not yet had an opportunity fully to explore. We are currently attempting this treatment with three patients (a sadist, a transvestite and fetishist). While they have all shown changes, the value of the method cannot be evaluated yet.

A thorough analysis of the patient's misdirected sexual responses would be carried out by means of the penile plethysmograph. Once a large range of imaginal, pictorial and real-life stimuli have been isolated, the patient would be exposed to each of the stimuli on a number of occasions in order to establish base rates of the magnitude of his sexual reactions. When these base rates have been established, the stimuli which produced the mildest sexual reaction would be presented for a very brief duration. Each stimulus would be withdrawn before a plethysmographic change became apparent. After a particular stimulus had been repeatedly presented at gradually increasing exposure durations *without eliciting a reaction*, the next stimulus in the hierarchy would be presented in the same manner. This second but mild stimulus, would likewise be presented for a very brief period to begin with. Providing that no sexual reactions are evoked at the rapid exposure time, the stimulus presentations would be gradually lengthened. When this stimulus is no longer capable of producing a sexual reaction, even at long exposure times, then the next most provocative stimulus would be presented in the same gradually extended manner. The therapist would work through the entire range of sexually arousing stimuli in this way until no plethysmographic reactions can be obtained in the presence of the deviant stimuli. It will, of course, be necessary to prevent the patient from elaborating a provocative image after the brief stimulus presentations. This can be ensured by making him do arithmetic problems as soon as the stimulus is withdrawn (and before the penile reaction occurs). Obviously this technique will be time-consuming but, if successful, would provide an acceptable alternative to painful aversive stimulation. Naturally, other types of extinction procedure are also worth considering.

Covert sensitisation

An alternative to aversion therapy which has already undergone some development is the technique which is sometimes described as 'covert sensitisation' or 'aversive imagery'. This procedure is actually an attenuated type of aversion therapy, but one which is undoubtedly less unpleasant. Instead of presenting the deviant stimulus and then administering an aversive stimulus, the sexual stimulus is followed by an *imaginary* event. In developing this procedure, Gold and Neufeld (1965) 'did a Wolpe' with aversion therapy; that is, they attempted to substitute an imaginal event instead of relying on overt occurrences, just as Wolpe (1958) did when he developed the therapeutic technique of systematic desensitisation. In this procedure the patient is exposed gradually to increasingly more disturbing, imaginal phobic stimuli. Gold and Neufeld successfully treated a sixteen-year-old boy who had been convicted in a juvenile court for soliciting men in the toilets of a railway station. Since the age of twelve years the patient had engaged in homosexual fantasies usually associated with masturbation. He then became involved in overt homosexual practices which he carried out with men whom he actively solicited in toilets, at swimming pools, cinemas or railway stations. Initially the patient was given six sessions of desensitisation treatment to overcome his feelings of anxiety. He was then given a few sessions of aversive imagery treatment (actually, their method is more accurately described as imaginal discrimination training). The writers describe the technique as follows:

Whilst relaxed, an emotive image was suggested of the patient in a situation of danger. He was encouraged to visualize himself in a toilet alongside a most unprepossessing old man. It was suggested that he would not under any circumstances solicit such a person. When the patient agreed to this suggestion (by signalling) he was rewarded with the words 'well done'. The image of the man whom he rejected in this way was slowly changed to a more attractive form, but at the same time surrounded by prohibitions such as the image of a policeman standing nearby. With this technique the patient quickly learned to reject an otherwise acceptable and attractive young man, even in the absence of prohibitions.

Later the patient was presented with alternatives in the form of an attractive young man and an attractive young woman. The image of the woman was associated with pleasant suggestions and the image of the attractive young man was associated with unpleasant imaginal stimulation. After 'frequent reinforcements of the correct (heterosexual) choice, the cues for punishing attributes could be reduced and finally, when given a completely equivalent choice without any extra cues, the patient was able to choose the heterosexual object consistently'. After the completion of ten treatment sessions the patient reported feeling considerably improved and said that he had been able to avoid homosexual contacts both in reality and in fantasy. He still retained some feeling of attraction for young men, however.

The patient was seen for seven more interviews over a period of twelve months and on the first three occasions was given booster treatments. At the end of the one year follow-up period, he had maintained his therapeutic improvement and successfully formed a relationship with a girl which involved petting but not intercourse.

It is impossible to be certain what the effect of the aversive imagery was in this case as a good deal of straight suggestion was given to the patient and he also received some counselling and desensitisation treatment. Furthermore, the patient was able to visualise situations very clearly and also experience associated emotions. His reactions generalised rapidly from the imaginal to the real situation. Gold and Neufeld point out that because of his age, the patient's homosexual habit was perhaps less firmly consolidated than is usually the case. Nevertheless, this case-report opened up a promising treatment possibility.

Another interesting case-history was recently presented by Davison (1968) in which a sadistic fantasy was eliminated by a combination of positive counter-conditioning and covert sensitisation. The first part of the treatment programme consisted of advising the patient to change his masturbatory activities. He was accustomed to masturbating with sadistic fantasies, and Davison was able to break this sexual pattern by giving the patient a series of assignments. He was told to masturbate while looking at pictures of provocative nude women and to refrain from masturbating with sadistic fantasies. If while masturbating in the presence of the appropriate stimulus, he began to lose his erection, he was to cease masturbating, use the sadistic fantasy to regain sexual interest and then begin masturbating in the presence of the provocative normal sexual material again. After a degree of improvement had been obtained in the patient's fantasy and masturbatory activity, it became necessary to direct attention to the sadistic fantasies themselves. He was instructed to imagine a sadistic scene and when he obtained this image clearly, was given a second and very disturbing image to conjure up instead. This disgusting counter-image evoked strong feelings of nausea in the patient and he required some time in order to recover. Thereafter his assignments for masturbation were increasingly shaped in the direction of normality. After eight treatment sessions, no sadistic fantasies had occurred for more than a month and the patient was therefore discharged. A one month follow-up showed there had been no reappearance of the sadistic fantasies (which had been present for ten years prior to the commencement of treatment). As in the case reported by Gold and Neufeld, it is not possible to determine the *particular* contribution made to the behavioural changes by the application of aversive imagery.

This interesting case contains a feature which is worth emphasising. Davison appears to have produced significant behavioural changes by getting the patient to alter his fantasies during masturbation – a technique which was also used by Bancroft (1966) and which is directly relevant to the theory of sexual disorder proposed by McGuire *et al.* in 1965. These workers assigned a place of central importance in the genesis and maintenance of sexual disorders to masturbatory practices and the accompanying fantasies.

Kolvin (1967) recently obtained two successes with aversive imagery in treating adolescents. The first patient was a fourteen-year-old fetishist and the second a fifteen-year-old boy who was addicted to sniffing petrol. After drawing up a list of dislikes which the patient reported, Kolvin relaxed the first patient and encouraged him to conjure up images according to an account given by the therapist. 'A colourful story of the crucial events was now presented and the patient was asked to visualise accordingly. By careful observation it became apparent when

H

the patient was just becoming affectively excited, i.e. motor tension, breathing, expression, etc. At this stage the aversive image was introduced in a suggestive and vividly descriptive manner. The response was immediate and in the main, reflected in the patient's expression of distaste. In this way the full erotically toned course of events was truncated and the sequence of events unpleasantly anticlimaxed.' The colourful story involved events of a sexually deviant nature which the boy had actually experienced and the aversive image was one of falling. (In passing, it is worth mentioning that the use of the penile plethysmograph in this procedure would provide a more accurate assessment of the arousal provoked by the sexually toned story and in this way the therapist could time the introduction of the aversive image more accurately.) After eight sessions of this form of treatment, coupled with some reassurance and brief psychotherapy, the patient was discharged much improved. A seventeen-month follow-up enquiry revealed that the patient was apparently quite well and had not experienced any recurrence of the fetishistic behaviour.

The second patient was treated over twenty sessions and the aversive image was also one of falling. Thirteen months after the completion of treatment the patient was apparently doing well and had 'not returned to his petrol-sniffing habits'.

Kolvin points out that aversive images are not ideal aversive stimuli and they have the disadvantage that 'the technique also depends on the capacity of the patient for visual imagery and for life-equivalent autonomic responses to pleasant and unpleasant imagery'. Kolvin's reservation about the method on the score of the precise timing of the application of the noxious stimulus has been dealt with above (i.e. this could be overcome by the use of the penile plethysmograph).

Cautela (1966) reported success in the treatment of two patients by the method of covert sensitisation. He trained his patients in relaxation and then gave them treatment sessions during which they were required to imagine that they were carrying out the compulsive, abnormal behaviour – at which point they were then asked to imagine that they were feeling extremely nauseous and actually vomiting.

The patient is then asked (while relaxed with his eyes closed) to visualize very clearly the pleasurable object (e.g. a highball). When he can visualize the object very clearly he is to raise his index finger. After he signals he is told to now visualize that he is about to take the object (to commit the compulsive act).

He is then asked to imagine the next step in the sequence of the compulsive behaviour – in the case of the first patient, that he was about to take a drink.

The glass is just about to touch his lips and then he begins to feel sick to his stomach. He is starting to vomit. The vomit goes up to his mouth and then he cannot stop it. He vomits all over the floor of the bar or restaurant or home, wherever he does his drinking. He is asked to visualize the whole scene again by himself and to raise his finger when he can visualize the scene and actually feel nauseous as the drink is about to go to his lips.

The next stage in the treatment is to get the patient to imagine that he feels nauseous as he is about to drink, but that he experiences immediate calm and relaxation when he puts the glass down. The final stage consists of training the patient to discriminate between the act of drinking and its associated image of vomiting on the one hand, and the feeling of relaxation and its associated image of rejecting the drink. Both of Cautela's patients, one with an alcoholic craving and the other with a disorder of compulsive eating, responded well to the treatment and follow-ups carried out more than six months after the termination of treatment showed that the improvements had been maintained. In a later paper, Cautela (1967) described the method in greater detail and reported some successes in managing obesity, alcoholism, homosexuality and conduct disorders. The importance of getting the patient to 'practice' at home is emphasised.

Cautela (1966) expressed an optimistic view about the possible applications of covert sensitisation and remarked that 'it seems quite likely' that the method 'can be effective in other compulsions such as smoking, gambling and even hand-washing. Obsessions could also be treated by this method.'

If the recent clinical report by Anant (1967) is anything to judge by, Cautela's optimism is well grounded. Anant used a procedure which he described as 'verbal aversion' in the treatment of a group of alcoholic patients. All twenty-six patients were successfully treated and follow-ups carried out between eight and fifteen months after termination of treatment revealed that there had been no relapse whatever. 'The technique involves asking a deeply relaxed patient to imagine scenes in which he sees himself drinking, feeling sick and vomiting, in that order.' After taking a full history of the patient's drinking, Anant trains him in relaxation. The covert sensitisation procedure is commenced in subsequent sessions. The patient is asked to imagine scenes in which he is drinking (these usually are confined to situations and beverages which he is accustomed to). While the patient is imagining himself in these situations, the therapist then gets him to imagine that he feels nauseous and that he begins to vomit. (As can be seen, the procedure is very similar to the one described by Cautela.) Anant's patients were also instructed to practise imagining the same type of scene at home. As the treatment progressed, the patient was asked to imagine that he felt sick at the mere smell of the liquor and then that he felt sick whenever he experienced a mere desire to drink, and finally he was taught to discriminate between liquor and soft drinks. 'He is asked to imagine that he feels sick whenever he wants to have liquor but feels all right as soon as he changes his mind and wants to have a soft drink.' One of the striking features of Anant's report is that the patients were apparently treated in comparatively few sessions. Although the exact figures are not provided it would appear that most of them received only half a dozen treatment sessions in all. Anant points out that several other factors might also have contributed to the treatment effect in addition to the covert sensitisation. These include suggestion and brief counselling which the therapist provided for the patient in the preliminary sessions. To this extent his procedure resembles that used by Kolvin (1967).

Anant's results are remarkable. Certainly they are the best which the present writers have seen reported for the treatment of alcoholism and they deserve close investigation and early replication. Such replication should control for the effects the suggestion and brief counselling. The deliberate insertion and exclusion of these factors should not be difficult to arrange.

Results from controlled investigations of covert sensitisation are in fact beginning to appear. One of the first reports comes from Ashem and Donner (1968) who attempted to compare the effects of covert sensitisation with two types of control treatment. Twenty-three alcoholic patients were allotted randomly to three experimental groups: covert sensitisation (forward conditioning), covert sensitisation (backward conditioning), no-treatment control. The treatment, which was given over nine forty-minute sessions, was preceded by relaxation training. The patients were told to then imagine that they were drinking (in a variety of situations); when they signalled that they were experiencing the taste of the alcohol, the therapist told them that they felt uncomfortable, then nauseous and, finally, that they were vomiting. This procedure (forward conditioning) was varied in the 'backward conditioning group' by requiring the patients to imagine the nausea and vomiting *before* they tasted the alcohol. In practice, it proved impossible to retain this temporal distinction and the two sensitisation groups were combined – it early became clear that the patients were making 'an automatic association' between the CS (alcohol) and the UCS (nausea) on subsequent presentations.

As treatment progressed, the patients were relaxed after imaginal presentations of alternate behaviour (e.g. 'imagine you are rejecting a drink – now relax').

A six-month follow-up comparison between the nine non-treated control patients and the fifteen who had been sensitised shows a clear difference between the groups. While six of the treated patients were abstinent (i.e. 40%), none of the controls were.

These results, while far from being as striking as those claimed by Anant, do support the idea that covert sensitisation may be a surprisingly useful therapeutic tool and that its effects are sometimes obtained in relatively few treatment sessions.

A notable feature of covert sensitisation is that it appears to produce results despite its apparent simplicity – like desensitisation. To date, covert sensitisation has been successfully used in the treatment of cases of sexual disorder, alcoholism, addiction and compulsive behaviour. Admittedly, very few patients in all have received this treatment. Nevertheless, it would seem that in certain instances (at least) it is effective. The substitution of this, or any other, attenuated form of aversion therapy would, of course, be extremely welcome. While guarding against excessive reserve (because of its simplicity), the method should, nevertheless, be approached with some caution. This must include experimental studies which investigate in considerable detail and with great care the range, nature and mode of action of the aversive images. In addition to experimental investigations of the procedures and mechanisms involved, the clinical effectiveness of the technique needs to be explored over a wide range of cases. Some encouragement can be drawn from the success which has now been achieved with Wolpe's method of systematic desensitisation (Rachman, 1967) – a procedure which also relies on *imaginal evocations* of anxiety-provoking stimuli and situations. It can be argued quite legitimately that if it is possible to evoke the 'negative' emotional reaction of anxiety by direct verbal instruction then there is no reason to suppose that similar verbal provocation should not be capable of eliciting 'negative' emotional and physical reactions such as nausea, embarrassment, disgust and so on.

The examples of covert sensitisation described so far, appear to be based on conditioned suppression. An explanation based on a classical conditioning model would need to label the therapist's instructions as the CS ('imagine a desirable act') and the UCS ('imagine feeling nauseous'). This approach is not obviously false but it is probably too superficial a view. The therapists' initial instructions give rise to a complicated chain of covert responses, and it is these responses which, when verbally conveyed to the therapist, produce the UCS. In this sense, the aversive consequences (unpleasant feelings associated with the second image chain) are response-produced.

Ashem and Donner's (1968) interesting attempt to confirm that covert sensitisation is a *conditioning* phenomenon unfortunately failed because of their subjects' cognitive appraisal of the situation. This factor, coupled with the covert nature of much of the treatment procedure, will make quantitative and reproducible investigations extremely difficult to design. The task is not insuperable, however, and the recent growth of knowledge concerning systematic desensitisation, which is also a partly covert process, encourages one's hopes. Even at this stage it is possible to control and measure certain aspects of covert sensitisation. The antecedent variables can be controlled and standardised and the overt consequences observed and measured. Some of the intervening changes can also be measured. The use of the penile plethysmograph, for example, is likely to prove very valuable in studying covert sensitisation of male sexual disorders.

The possibility that covert sensitisation does produce conditioned aversion reactions receives some small support from clinical observations. Ashem and Donner (1968), for example, quote an experience reported by one of their alcoholic patients . . . 'as I approached the liquor store I broke out in a sweat and could hardly open the door. When I finally got in I could hardly talk, for my throat was dry and choking and my stomach was flipping' (p. 11). A similar but less powerful reaction was reported by a patient under treatment by one of the authors. After four sessions of covert sensitisation, which involved associating feelings of nausea with masturbation to a fetish, the patient felt 'queasy in my stomach' during actual masturbation. These unpleasant feelings were not sufficiently strong fully to inhibit the abnormal masturbatory activities, but they did reduce the pleasure which the patient had obtained prior to being sensitised.

In addition to clarifying the therapeutic effects of this new method, it will be necessary to isolate the effective elements involved. This implies experimental analysis of the relative contributions made by supplementary counselling, suggestion, relaxation and the non-specific consequences of entering treatment. The effects of instructing patients with sexual disorders to alter their masturbatory-fantasy practices (Bancroft,

1966; Davison, 1967) are worth investigating both in their own right and as a contribution to covert sensitisation.

Kolvin (1967) has already drawn attention to certain disadvantages of the method. It depends on the patient's ability to obtain the required images and 'life-equivalent autonomic responses' (problems also encountered in systematic desensitisation, Wolpe and Lazarus, 1966). If Kolvin's views are confirmed then the method may need to be modified. We should, however, avoid the error of simply assuming that these factors *are* essential – despite the fact that their role appears to virtually be axiomatic. Finally, we need to confirm that the second image has to be *aversive*. It could be that any interfering image will produce suppressive effects and here we may note *en passant* that sexual images can be broken quite rapidly by making the subject do arithmetic calculations, for example. This phenomenon can easily be confirmed by observing the effect of such calculations on penile plethysmographic reactions.

In the long run it may be most profitable to view covert sensitisation in terms of the general relationship between cognitive functioning and learning (and particularly behaviour modification). We are undoubtedly in for a number of surprises. If, as seems to be the case, patients can acquire (conditioned?) aversive reactions (see the examples described by Ashem and Donner) through the manipulation of purely imaginal events then the implications of these clinical findings for general psychology are very considerable. A great deal of general psychology, and particularly the study of learning, is still peripheralist in conception. The findings on covert sensitisation underline the inadequacy of this type of approach and at the same time provide a striking example of the distance between learning in animals and in humans. Our traditional reliance on animal data in formulating theories of human learning is once again seen to be limiting.

Summary

Aversion therapy involves the deliberate application of unpleasant or painful stimulation, and therefore raises serious ethical problems. These are discussed and the necessity for avoiding coercion or deception is stressed. It is argued that the best solution to the problem is to find effective substitutes for aversion therapy. Two possible alternatives, extinction and covert sensitisation, are considered. Of these, covert sensitisation has already yielded some promising clinical results and it merits further investigation. The broader implications of this technique are mentioned.

14

Covert sensitisation and cognitive control

The nature of covert sensitisation will need to be studied with great care. If, as now seems possible, the therapeutic effects of aversion therapy carried out in *imagination* prove to be comparable to those obtained in ordinary aversion therapy, it will become essential to reconsider the *entire* subject. What is occurring in ordinary aversion therapy? What are the effective elements in covert and overt therapy? To what extent are these two methods similar? If they share common mechanisms, does the overt type of therapy contain anything of additional value? As virtually all of the covert sensitisation studies have so far involved nausea-producing reactions, this discussion will compare chemical aversion and covert sensitisation therapy. The common features of the two methods are: (i) they both involve the temporal association of two stimuli, (ii) they both involve cognitive changes in the patient, (iii) they both involve the arousal of unpleasant reactions in the patient, (iv) they both produce a learned connection between the real or symbolic deviant stimulus and autonomic reactions (?). The major differences between the two methods are (i) the use of real *v.* symbolic conditioned stimuli, (ii) the use of real *v.* symbolic unconditioned stimuli.

It is not surprising that a symbolic CS can be used to establish learning.[1] The therapeutic efficacy of symbolic UCS's in producing feelings of discomfort and even nausea, while fairly novel, is also not unduly remarkable. It is in fact based on an extremely common human experience (e.g. 'not while I'm eating . . .'). The striking finding is the apparent ease with which the learned connections can be established on a covert, symbolic level *and* how they can override complex, long-established, strong and rewarding behaviour patterns such as addictions, alcoholism, sexual deviations.

Recognising the power of symbolic functioning, we must now return

---

1 Pavlov's (1935) views on this are interesting – 'obviously for man, speech provides conditioned stimuli which are just as real as any other stimuli', and 'speech . . . can call forth all those reactions of the organism which are normally determined by the actual stimuli themselves' (p. 407).

to a consideration of ordinary aversion therapy. What advantages derive from the use of tangible conditioned and unconditioned stimuli? Theoretically, there are two advantages. Tangible stimuli remain within the therapist's control (and on a practical level, enable him to vary such factors as intensity, with some precision). Secondly, the learned connections established with tangible stimuli may well be stronger and more enduring. The comparative clinical value of the two methods can only be ascertained by experimental investigations.

It is also of some interest to consider the possibility that ordinary aversion therapy is (and always has been) nothing more than a cumbersome and roundabout technique for establishing symbolic connections between the CS (e.g. alcohol) and the CR (e.g. nausea). If this is so, then the (admittedly indifferent) results obtained with chemical aversion therapy under poor therapeutic conditions, such as backward conditioning, become more comprehensible. The interesting report by Ashem and Donner (1968) on the covert sensitisation of alcoholics is relevant here – it will be recalled that they were unable to carry out their intention to use a backward conditioning control because their subjects made 'an automatic association' between the 'images' of alcohol and nausea *irrespective* of the sequence of instructions given by the therapist. After brief experience with the two sets of 'images', their subjects automatically linked the two. In similar vein, it seems quite possible that after very few trials involving real alcohol and nausea, patients automatically link the CS and the UCR – irrespective of their temporal sequence.

It may seem that this discussion of some of the implications of covert sensitisation is flitting far in advance of the data and is altogether too fanciful. There is evidence from an entirely different source, however, which is not only consistent with the discussion so far, but is also important in its own right. The comparison between covert sensitisation and aversion therapy was, of necessity, restricted to chemical aversion therapy. So far, covert sensitisation procedures have not involved imaginal shock stimulation, but as will be shown below, there are good reasons for supposing that this type of imaginal UCS may also prove to be effective (practically, it may be a good idea to preface the imaginal presentations with a few real shocks).

It has become increasingly clear over the past few years that cognitive factors can influence autonomic functioning (including autonomic conditioning) in a remarkable fashion. In the first place, however, it is necessary to point out that conditioned autonomic reactions can occur without awareness and, furthermore, autonomic reactions are usually beyond cognitive control. In this sense, a wide range of neurotic conditions (particularly those in which anxiety is a central feature) can be viewed as *failures* of cognitive control – 'I know there is nothing to be frightened of – *but*. . . .' The occurrence of autonomic reactions in the absence of overt behavioural changes (or subjective changes) is pertinent to aversion therapy and work from Gantt's (1964) laboratory indicated some years ago how this process (which he calls 'schizokinesis') can occur.

I also want to emphasize this difference between the formation of the cardiac conditional reflexes, the visceral conditional reflexes and the more easily observable motor ones; but here we have a split between the functions of the organism so that the organism may be in adaptation with some of its organs and some of its reactions, but not with others. This phenomenon I term 'schizokinesis'.

Gantt has provided numerous examples of this phenomenon. He quotes the work of Newton who showed that dogs that had been given only one reinforcement of a faradic shock formed conditional cardiac reactions which were extraordinarily resistant to extinction. Even though the faradic shock was not readministered, the dogs continued to display the cardiac response for many months. There was no parallel motor response. In describing one of these dogs, Gantt says

if you were looking at this dog, as we used to do, without taking measurements of cardiac conditioning, if you were only observing his movements, you would say that he had not formed any conditional reflex, but that by the study of the heart rate you were able to see the conditional reflex appear after one conditioning event.

Is something like 'schizokinesis' occurring in aversion therapy? Are underlying, covert changes occurring during the course of therapy and are these related (perhaps even causally) to the patient's altered overt behaviour? When observations such as Gantt's are repeated on patients undergoing aversion therapy, we will be in a position to assess these questions. All we can do here is to raise the possibility that these patients are acquiring cardiac (and other) autonomic reactions to the deviant stimuli and that these are related to, or even mediate the overt behavioural and attitudinal changes. Certainly, most patients undergoing the treatment find it distressing and anxiety-provoking. At very least we wish to make the point that full autonomic recordings should be taken during the experimental investigation of aversion therapy if we are to get closer to an understanding of the processes which are involved. Any explanation of aversion therapy which relies exclusively on presumed cognitive changes seems to us likely to fail. Similarly an explanation which relies too heavily on the conditioning of behaviour which is under voluntary control is likely to be inadequate.

Nowadays it is commonplace that the setting and instructions which are given to a subject undergoing a course of conditioning may have a profound effect on the development of these responses (e.g. Grings, 1965; Spence, 1965). As far back as 1937, Cook and Harris[1] reported that the magnitude of a GSR was increased when the subject was told that he would receive a shock and decreased when he was instructed that he would not receive a shock. A more recent instance of the effects of threat of shock on an autonomic response is provided by Hodges and Spielberger (1966). The dramatic effect of the threat of shock on cardiac rate is clearly illustrated in Figure 7 below. Bridger and Mandel (1964) compared GSR fear responses produced by electric shock or by the *threat* of administering electric shock. They found that under *both* conditions their subjects acquired GSR's to a previously neutral stimulus – the verbally communicated threat of shock was as effective as a real electrical stimulus. It was observed, however, that the responses which had been produced by threat alone, extinguished after instructions had eliminated this threat. In Figure 8 below it can be seen that there is no obvious difference between the responses produced by shock or by threat of shock. However, once the subjects were told that no more shocks would or could be given (the shock electrodes were removed), a clear difference emerged. The responses which had been produced by threat were immediately eliminated when the subjects were informed that no more shocks were forthcoming. However, the shocked group continued to display responses during the extinction period even though they had been informed that they were in no danger of receiving further shocks. In fact, this last observation is unusual – in most similar studies it has been found that conditioned reactions (even those of an autonomic type) can be extinguished rapidly if the subjects are informed that they are no longer in danger of being shocked. The implications of these findings will be discussed further, below. Here we are simply making the point that cognitive factors may have a profound effect on the course of conditioning.

Another illustration of the effect of instructions on the course of

---

1 In 1938 Mowrer drew attention to the power of 'expectancy or preparatory set' in establishing and abolishing 'apparent conditioned responses'. As Grings (1965) pointed out, however, Mowrer's reluctance to call these changes 'proper learning' is not justified.

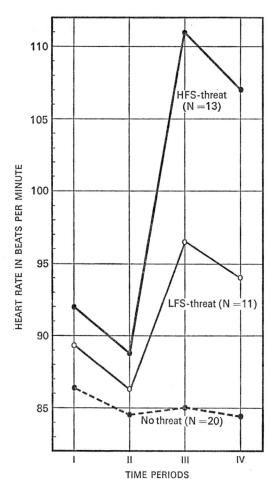

Figure 7 The effect of threat-of-shock on cardiac rate. Reproduced from
Hodges and Spielberger, *Psychophysiology*, 1966.

conditioning is seen in a study reported by Spence and Goldstein (1961).
They conditioned an eye-blink response in a group of subjects under
two levels of UCS intensity (puff of air). After the initial twenty conditioning trials had been completed, some subjects were informed that the
UCS would be increased to a very unpleasant intensity 'at some time
during the following 10 trials'. In their summary of the results, Spence
and Goldstein remarked that

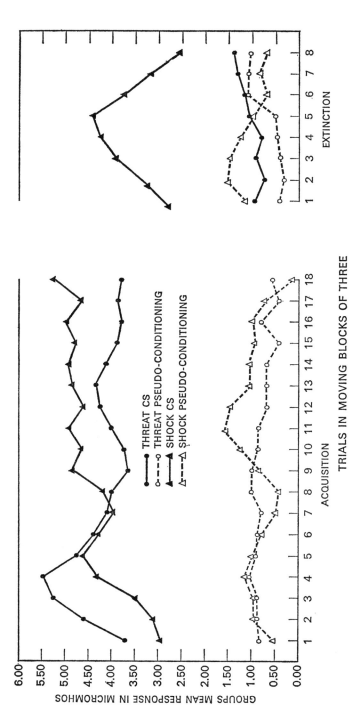

Figure 8 Conditioning and extinction when shock or fear-of-shock are used as the UCS. Reproduced from Bridger and Mandel, 1964, J. Psychiat. Research.

on the assumption that this threat would materially increase the level of emotional response and hence the level of drive of S it was predicted that the performance of this group over this block of trials would be significantly higher than that of a control group not given such a threat. This prediction was confirmed.

In 1957, Branca attempted to relate the subjects' expectations of shock, as well as their subjective evaluations of the intensity of shock, to the frequency and occurrence of conditioned GSR's. His results showed that

expectation of shock as a painful or fearful experience was necessary and sufficient to produce responses to the experimental and generalisation stimuli in this experiment and such expectancy was the result of awareness of the existing relationships between the experimental stimuli and experience with the unconditioned stimulus.

Confirmatory evidence was obtained by Chatterjee and Eriksen (1962), who noted a marked correspondence between their subjects' conditioned autonomic reactions (cardiac rate) and their verbalised expectancies.

In addition to demonstrating the profound influence of cognitive factors on the development of conditioned responses, including those of an autonomic nature, these findings parallel some of those on covert sensitisation.

In a way the most impressive and important aspect of the research which has been conducted on the relationship between cognitive factors and conditioning, relates to the data on the effect of the instructions and expectancy on the *extinction* of conditioned reactions. These findings are central to the apparent paradox involved in aversion therapy, namely the fact that patients who have undergone such treatment refrain from carrying out the deviant behaviour even after they have left the treatment situation and are fully aware that they are no longer in danger of receiving electric shocks. Cook and Harris (1937), in addition to demonstrating the facilitation of conditioning by means of instructions, showed that the GSR can be considerably reduced when the subject is told that he will not receive any further shocks. Bridger and Mandel (1965) demonstrated very rapid extinction of a conditioned GSR when the subjects were informed that they were to receive no further shocks. These results were compared with those obtained from subjects who were not informed that they were in an extinction period or that they were no longer in danger of being shocked. They described their procedure in the following way. The subjects in the two non-informed groups were told that the experimenter would not return until the experiment had been completed. The acquisition series was then presented and, for the non-informed subjects, the extinction series followed immediately without interruption. For the informed subjects the experimenter returned at the end of the acquisition series, removed the shock electrodes, wiped the subject's leg clean of electrode jelly, and reassured the subject that no further shocks could or would be given.

During the course of the experiment they also examined the differences which ensued under conditions of partial and continuous reinforcement. Their findings showed that subjects who were informed that they were in the extinction phase and that they would receive no more shocks showed a very rapid (almost immediate) extinction of the reactions. However, those subjects who were not informed of the change of conditions and the absence of shock required quite a few extinction trials. The results are shown clearly in Figure 9. The four groups involved are

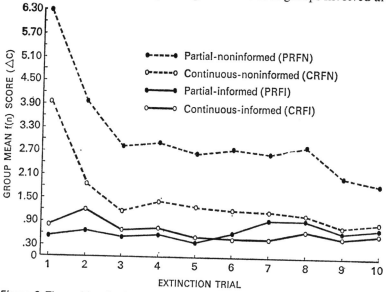

Figure 9 The rapid extinction of a conditioned GSR when subjects are informed that no further shocks are to be administered. From Bridger and Mandel, 1965, *J. of Experimental Psychology.*

indicated in the legend – PRFN indicates subjects who were not informed of the change in the experimental conditions and were conditioned under partial reinforcement, CRFN is the group which received continuous reinforcement but was not informed of the change in the state of the experiment, PRFI are those subjects who received partial reinforcement and were informed of the changed conditions, CRFI indicates the group of subjects who received continuous reinforcement and were also informed of the change from acquisition to extinction. Oddly enough, however, these results of Bridger and Mandel (1965) are somewhat contradictory of their earlier findings which were mentioned above. It will be recalled that in their earlier experiment, the elimination of the threat of shock did not produce immediate extinction.

Notterman, Schoenfeld and Bersch (1952) reported a quicker extinction of conditioned cardiac rate when subjects were told they would receive no further shocks; a comparison group of subjects who were not informed that the shocks were to be discontinued took longer to extinguish the conditioned reactions. In similar fashion Chatterjee and Eriksen (1962) found that extinction of a conditioned heart rate pattern could be brought about almost immediately if the subjects were informed that they would not be subjected to further shocks. They state that 'those subjects who were informed there would be no more shocks at the beginning of the extinction trials showed almost a complete loss of the conditioned reaction without experiencing non-reinforced presentations of the CES'. Simply informing the subjects that the shocks were to be discontinued was 'sufficient to produce almost complete extinction . . .'. The same observation was reported by Grings and Lockhart (1963) in an experiment on the conditioning of the GSR. They examined the effect of 'anxiety lessening' instructions on the course of the GSR and succeeded in bringing about rapid extinction of a conditioned reaction by the simple expedient of telling their subjects they would receive no more electric shocks and then presenting the CS in a normal extinction procedure. They found that the effect of these instructions was independent of either the number of reinforcements which had been given in establishing the conditioned response or of the intensity of the UCS which had been used. A very similar result was reported by Wickens, Allen and Hill (1963) in their experiment on conditioned GSR's. Like Grings and Lockhart, they obtained rapid extinction when the subjects were told they would receive no more shocks and they were also unable to find any relationship between UCS strength and speed of extinction after the instructions had been given. The generality of findings of this type is enhanced by Spence's (1963) report on the effect of cognitive factors in extinguishing a conditioned eyelid response. He demonstrated that the rate of extinction of the eyelid response is a function 'of the degree of discriminability of the procedural changes that occur with a shift from acquisition to extinction . . . extinction is greatly retarded when these changes are minimised or the subject is distracted by another task'. He used three groups of subjects and found that in the great majority of instances those people who noticed a procedural change occurring in the transition from acquisition training to extinction training showed a rapid extinction. The absence of such awareness on the part of the subjects was found to correspond with a markedly slower rate of extinction. These results are illustrated in Figure 10 where it can be seen that Groups 1 and 2 showed fairly rapid extinction while the subjects in Group 3 showed a markedly slower rate of extinction. Twenty-one subjects of Group 1 and nineteen of Group 2 observed the changeover from acquisition to extinction training, but only one subject in Group 3 reported noticing such a change (there were twenty-five subjects in each group). Although conditioned eyelid responses appear to be particularly fragile, the relevance of this experimental outcome to aversion therapy can be seen in the fact that an awareness of changes in stimulus conditions can markedly facilitate extinction of conditioned reactions and there can be no doubt that patients who undergo aversion treatment are able to discriminate between the clinical and non-clinical settings.

Although the major part of this chapter is concerned with the power of cognitive factors to influence autonomic reactions, it is necessary to reiterate that an explanation of aversion therapy which relies *solely* on cognitive factors is unlikely to be successful. There are four reasons why this is so. Firstly, there are experimental data which show that conditioned autonomic reactions can develop and persist even in the absence of observable behaviour change. Such reactions are frequently observed to be outside of cognitive controls (e.g. neurotic conditions). Secondly, autonomic reactions in general are exceedingly difficult to control voluntarily. It is true that under strict laboratory conditions such control can be obtained (e.g. Lang and Hnatiow, 1966) but specific training conditions are required and, even then, the *degree* of control obtained is not great. Thirdly, there are many examples of patients developing an actual aversion to the CS after therapy and this frequently includes highly unpleasant physical reactions. Hammersley's (1957) alcoholic patient for example had to undo his aversion by arduous repetition of the sequence alcohol→ vomiting. He was apparently unable voluntarily to prevent himself from getting sick when he drank alcohol. The fact that deviant sexual responses are frequently beyond cognitive control is of course attested to by patients requesting thera-

I

peutic assistance. Lastly, there is a major paradox which we find difficult to resolve. In view of the experimental evidence on the influence of cognitive factors in the extinction of conditioned autonomic reactions,

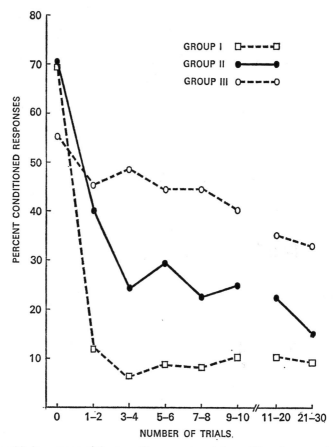

Figure 10 Awareness of the prevailing experimental conditions has a marked effect on the durability of eye-lid CR's. Subjects in Group 3 were 'unaware' (see text). From Spence, *Science*, 1963.

it is odd that patients continue to refrain from indulging in their deviant behaviour after leaving hospital. Like the subjects in Bridger and Mandel's (1965) experiment, patients *know* that they will not receive any more shocks when the electrodes are removed. Bridger and Mandel's subjects showed rapid extinction of a conditioned cardiac response when they knew that the shocks were to be discontinued. After leaving hospital, many patients nevertheless refrain from carrying out formerly appealing behaviour for protracted periods. It is possible that this paradox arises from the fact that patients who undergo aversion therapy receive not ten, twenty or thirty conditioning trials (as is customary in most of the experiments described) but something in the region of 300 to 750 conditioning trials. In any event, it seems clear that a purely cognitive theory will not provide an adequate account of aversion therapy. Similarly, any theory which fails to accommodate the influence of cognitive factors will be inadequate.

Summary

The theoretical implications of covert sensitisation are discussed and a comparison between this method and ordinary aversion therapy is carried out. The power of covert, symbolic processes as illustrated by covert sensitisation is then related to experimental findings on the ability of cognitive changes to establish or extinguish conditioned autonomic reactions.

It is argued nevertheless that a purely cognitive explanation of aversion therapy is as unsatisfactory as a purely non-cognitive explanation.

Theoretical problems

Experimental studies employing aversive stimuli can be described in terms of four main paradigms: punishment training, avoidance training, escape training and classical conditioning. These paradigms are defined operationally as follows:

Punishment: a reduction in the future probability of a specific response as a result of the immediate delivery of a stimulus for that response.
(Azrin and Holz, 1966)

Avoidance: a training procedure in which the learned movement circumvents or prevents the appearance of a noxious stimulus.
(Kimble, 1961 – p. 477)

Escape: an instrumental conditioning procedure in which the response terminates a noxious stimulus.
(Kimble, 1961 – p. 479)

Classical: behaviour change attributable to an operational paradigm consisting of a signal (CS) in temporal conjunction with a second stimulus (UCS) with the occurrence of the UCS not contingent upon behaviour of the organism being conditioned.
(Grings, 1965 – p. 71)

In the sections that follow, we shall consider the salient features of each of these paradigms in turn, mentioning methods of aversion therapy which have utilised them. We shall then attempt to suggest possible theoretical explanations for the success, or lack of it, of aversion therapy techniques which have been applied to the two main syndromes which have engaged the attention of clinicians: alcoholism and sexual disorders.

15

Theoretical analysis: punishment training

Consideration of the definition offered by Azrin and Holz, which was given above and which will be adopted for the purposes of our discussion, shows that punishment differs from both escape and avoidance training in that it does not necessarily generate new responses. In some cases, punishment may operate through the punished subject making responses incompatible with the punished response, e.g. a rat, having been punished for making a hurdle-jumping response, may crouch and 'freeze' in the experimental situation, such responses obviously being incompatible with jumping. However, the presence of such responses is not part of the operational definition, which concentrates on the reduction of the punished behaviour. The punishment paradigm differs from the classical paradigm in that, in the former, the aversive stimulus is always response-contingent, whereas, in the latter, the aversive unconditioned stimulus inexorably follows the conditioned stimulus, whether the subject makes a response or not. However, the punishment and classical paradigms are not mutually exclusive (e.g. Miller, 1967) and experimental and clinical procedures often have elements of both.

The definition of the punishment paradigm suggests that punishment is an apt model on which to base aversion therapy, the expressed purpose of which is the reduction in frequency of undesirable behaviour by use of aversive stimuli. Why, then, has it only been in the last few years (Kushner and Sandler, 1966) that aversion therapy techniques have been deliberately modelled on a punishment paradigm?

At least one reason for the relative neglect of punishment has been the myth, perpetuated among psychological circles for some years, that any suppression of responding obtained by the use of punishment can never be other than temporary. Solomon (1964), documenting this myth, points out that it seems to have originated in experiments such as those of Estes (1944) which found that punishment of a bar-pressing response in rats led to a suppression of the response, but that this suppression was only temporary. There are, however, numerous examples of permanent response suppression following punishment.

For instance, it is possible permanently to suppress eating in cats and dogs by a punishment procedure (Solomon, 1964). Such suppression effects can lead to fatal self-starvation. Azrin and Holz (1966) point out that by suitably manipulating the conditions of the punishment situation, especially the intensity of the punishing stimulus, almost any degree of response suppression, from the slightest and most evanescent to the completely irreversible, can be obtained.

Another factor contributing to the relative therapeutic neglect of the punishment paradigm has been the confusion existing over the actual effects of punishment on the punished behaviour. Far from universally producing a suppression of the punished response, the punishment of a given response may have no effect upon it, or may actually lead to an enhancement of that response. This topic is reviewed by Church (1963), who concludes:

In comparison with a procedure involving no aversive stimulation, the effects of punishment are varied. If punishment reinstates a condition of original training, or if it elicits a response similar to the act which is being punished, then the procedure may produce response facilitation. Otherwise, punishment will produce response suppression.

Church offers the following list of situations in which facilitation of the punished response may occur:

It may be
(a) that the punishment reinstated one of the conditions of training,
(b) that the aversive stimulus elicited fear which facilitated the response,
(c) that the aversive stimulus elicited skeletal acts compatible with the punished acts, or
(d) that the response associated with the termination of the aversive stimulus was compatible with the punished act.

For further discussion of the conditions in which punishment has a facilitatory rather than a suppressive effect, the reader is referred to Church's (1963) paper, and to the article by Azrin and Holz (1966). It seems that we now have sufficient knowledge to specify more or less the conditions where punishment will have a paradoxical effect. Thus, as long as we proceed with caution, there is no reason why the existence of such paradoxical effects should deter us from exploiting the possibilities of the punishment paradigm.

We have already suggested (p. 86) that most aversion therapy techniques employing electric shock as the UCS are best thought of operationally in terms of the punishment paradigm. This is also true of some chemical aversion procedures. Accordingly, we have suggested that for clinicians whose main interest is in the design of effective treatment procedures, consideration of the punishment paradigm would be most profitable. In line with this pragmatic approach, our discussion of punishment will be mainly at the level of empirical observation, rather than theoretical analysis.

During the course of this discussion it will become apparent that there are certain problems posed by the punishment interpretation of aversion therapy. These cannot easily be disposed of at a purely empirical level; a theoretical discussion of them will be given in later sections. For the moment, however, we shall remain largely at an empirical level of observation in our discussion, hoping that the evidence we cite will be of relevance to the actual design of a punishment-based aversion therapy procedure.

For an excellent recent review of experimental studies of punishment, the reader is referred to Azrin and Holz (1966). By way of summary of a most valuable contribution to the field of punishment, we shall quote their conclusions on how they would set about eliminating items of behaviour by punishment. Discussion of selected points will follow this quotation.

We have seen above that punishment can be quite effective in eliminating behaviour. Let us imagine that we are given an assignment to eliminate behaviour by punishment. Let us summarize briefly some of the circumstances which have been found to maximise its effectiveness: (1) The punishing stimulus should be arranged in such a manner that no unauthorized escape is possible. (2) The punishing stimulus should be as intense as possible. (3) The frequency of punishment should be as high as possible; ideally the punishing stimulus should be given for every response. (4) The punishing stimulus should be delivered immediately after the response. (5) The punishing stimulus should not be increased gradually but introduced at maximum intensity. (6) Extended periods of punishment should be avoided, especially where low intensities of punishment are concerned, since the recovery effect may thereby occur. Where mild intensities of punishment are used, it is best to use them for only a brief period of time. (7) Great care should be taken to see that the delivery of the punishing stimulus is not differentially associated with the delivery of re-inforcement. Otherwise the punishing stimulus may acquire conditioned reinforcing properties. (8) The delivery of the punishing stimulus should be made a signal or discriminative stimulus that a period of extinction is in progress. (9) The degree of motivation to emit the punished response should be reduced. (10) The frequency of positive reinforcement for the punished response should similarly be reduced. (11) An alternative response should be available which will not be punished but which will produce the same or greater reinforcement as the punished response. For example, punishment of criminal behaviour can be expected to be more effective if non-criminal behaviour which will result in the same advantages as the criminal behaviour is available. (12) If no alternative response is available, the subject should have access to a different situation in which he obtains the same reinforcement without being punished. (13) If it is not possible to deliver the punishing stimulus itself after a response, then an effective method of punishment is still available. A conditioned stimulus may be associated with the aversive stimulus and this conditioned stimulus may be delivered following a response to achieve conditioned punishment. (14) A reduction of positive reinforcement may be used as punishment when the use of physical punishment is not possible for practical, legal or moral reasons. Punishment by withdrawal of positive reinforcement may be accomplished in such situations by arranging a period of reduced reinforcement frequency (time-out) or by arranging a decrease of conditioned reinforcement (response cost). Both methods require that the subject have a high level of reinforcement to begin with; otherwise, no withdrawal of reinforcement is possible. If non-physical punishment is to be used, it appears desirable to provide the subject with a substantial history of reinforcement in order to provide the opportunity for withdrawing the reinforcement as punishment for the undesired responses.

Intensity of the punishing stimulus

In their discussion of this variable, Azrin and Holz conclude, 'all studies of the intensity of punishment have found that the greater the intensity of the punishing stimulus, the greater is the reduction of the punished responses'. For example, Hake and Azrin (1963) found that an increase of shock intensity from 50 to 60 volts (a 20% change) produced an instantaneous reduction of about 50% in the rate of punished responses.

The relationship of degree of suppression to intensity of punishment seems to hold both while the shock is contingent on the response, and after removal of the punishment contingency. Azrin (1960b) found that the likelihood of obtaining enduring suppression, following the removal of the punishment contingency, was a function of the punishment intensity; intense shocks were required to produce permanent suppression.

It seems to be the case that, if the punishment procedure is going to be effective, the reduction of responses seems to follow immediately upon the introduction of the punishment contingency. Further, once the behaviour has been completely suppressed, the response reduction seems virtually irreversible.

It is interesting to note that a recent study by Church et al. (1967) shows that the effects of increasing the *duration* of the punishing stimulus are similar to those of increasing its intensity; both procedures lead to increased suppression of a bar-pressing response in rats.

Frequency of the punishing stimulus

Azrin and Holz summarise their discussion of the comparison between continuous and intermittent punishment as follows:

Continuous punishment produces more suppression than does intermittent punishment for as long as the punishment contingency is maintained. However, after the punishment contingency has been discontinued, continuous punishment allows more rapid recovery of the responses, possibly because the absence of punishment can be more rapidly discriminated. At very high intensities of punishment, the relationship is probably more complicated. Continuous punishment would be expected to produce complete suppression, whereas intermittent punishment would produce only partial suppression. Since recovery is delayed or absent after complete suppression, it appears that at very high intensities continuous punishment would be more effective than intermittent punishment, in terms of permanence as well as the extent of suppression.

The preceding section suggested that it is necessary to employ a high intensity shock to obtain complete suppression of undesirable behaviour. From the passage of Azrin and Holz we have just quoted it seems advisable to use a continuous reinforcement schedule for maximum effectiveness.

Response-punishment interval

Early studies (e.g. Estes, 1944; Hunt and Brady, 1955) suggested that punishment delivered immediately after a response was no more effective than punishment delivered some time after the response. However, other psychologists, such as Azrin (1956), showed that this result depended on the relatively short experimental period (less than one hour) used in both the above experiments. If the experiment is continued beyond one hour, differences between the two procedures emerge; non-immediate punishment leads to substantial and often complete recovery of the response, whereas, with immediate punishment, the response is reduced indefinitely and often completely.

Azrin and Holz conclude: 'For enduring effectiveness, the punishing stimulus should be delivered immediately.' Church (1963), in his discussion of the importance of the contingency of the punishing stimulus on the punished response, reached an essentially similar conclusion.

Reduction of motivation to emit punished response

There is considerable evidence to suggest that reduction of the motivation to emit the punished response enhances the suppressive effect of punishment on that response.

Dinsmoor (1952) found that under severe food deprivation, punishment reduced the punished (food-rewarded) responses by a smaller proportion than under slight food deprivation. Azrin (1960b) and Azrin, Holz and Hake (1963) demonstrated that, although after a long history of variable interval food reinforcement the response rate does not change appreciably as a function of food deprivation, when punishment is introduced the punished response rate seems to be very sensitive to slight changes in food deprivation. Azrin, Holz and Hake found that they could render the punishment almost ineffective by increasing the degree of motivation to make the punished response.

It seems, however, that if the responses have been completely suppressed under low hunger motivation, an increase in motivation may not be effective in restoring the responses (Masserman, 1943; Storms, Boroczi and Broeu, 1962). The cases of fatal self-starvation already mentioned provide examples where the most intense hunger-drive was not capable of making the animals 'break training' and emit the previously punished response.

This finding is of extreme importance for aversion therapy, where many of the drives operating to maintain the undesirable behaviour may be at a relatively high level. It suggests that it should be worth while attempting to reduce drive level in the therapeutic setting to a degree where punishment can produce complete suppression of the undesirable behaviour. Hopefully, this suppression would be maintained when, once outside the therapy situation, the patient is again exposed to higher levels of drive. However, there is some evidence to suggest that the situation may not be as hopeful in practice; e.g. the patient successfully treated for transvestism by Blakemore (1963) using an electrical procedure showed a tendency to relapse to his deviant sexual behaviour during a period of heterosexual deprivation imposed by his wife's pregnancy.

The suggestion that, as part of one's efforts to eliminate an undesirable response, one should attempt to reduce the motivation for that response is, of course, sound clinical common sense, and could probably be applied with profit to most methods of eliminating a response. An example of the direct application of this principle to the practice of aversion therapy is provided by Blake (1965). This worker treated alcoholics by what was essentially a punishment procedure, punishing the response of drinking alcohol with faradic shock. There is some evidence to suggest that part of the motivation maintaining the drinking behaviour of alcoholics is an anxiety drive (Kessel and Walton, 1965).

In one group of alcoholic patients, Blake, in addition to applying the aversion therapy punishment procedure, trained the patients in relaxation in an attempt to reduce their general level of anxiety. At follow-up the group that had received the relaxation as well as the aversion therapy procedure was more improved than the group that had had aversion therapy without the relaxation procedure, though not to a statistically significant extent.

The combination of drive-reduction procedures with aversion therapy seems an important advance; it seems likely that aversion therapy will be most effective when used as part of a battery of therapeutic stratagems, each attacking different facets of the problem behaviour.

Reduction of positive reinforcement for the punished response

Many of the behaviour problems which are presented as candidates for aversion therapy are maintained by fairly powerful positive reinforcement on a more or less continuous schedule. Such reinforcements would include sexual gratification in the case of the sexual disorders, anxiety-reduction in the case of alcoholism, and reduction in the intensity of the craving in the case of the addictions to alcohol or drugs.

Removal of such positive reinforcement maintaining the undesirable behaviour would seem to be an important point of attack in the attempt to eliminate the behaviour. In the studies discussed by Azrin and Holz, this removal of positive reinforcement is relatively simple as most of them are concerned with punishment of instrumental behaviour maintained on a food reinforcement schedule. Removal of positive reward consists simply of disconnecting the food dispensing mechanism. The effect of this procedure is to enhance the suppressive effects of punishment.

In the types of behaviour to which aversion therapy is applied, the situation is not so simple. Much of this behaviour is of a consummatory nature, so that it is impossible to remove the primary reinforcer without destroying the behaviour which it is intended to punish, e.g. it would be difficult to punish the response of drinking alcohol without letting the patient drink alcohol. Thus, the drinking behaviour continues to be positively reinforced during the punishment procedure.

The only thing left to do in such a situation is to allow the maintaining reinforcer to follow the punished response but to try to change its sign from positive to negative. Indeed, this has been the main therapeutic approach of many aversion therapists, e.g. the early chemical aversion studies on the treatment of alcoholism appear to have been based on an attempt to substitute the negative reinforcement of nausea and vomiting for the positive reinforcement of anxiety-reduction and craving-relief.

There are obviously limits to the extent to which one can modify the qualities of a reinforcer; alcohol and drugs have definite physiological effects in reducing the specific drug deficit and sedating the addict; it seems unlikely that these reinforcing aspects can be altered by psychological means. However, reinforcement at the physiological level can follow the consummatory response only after an appreciable delay. By capitalising on the delay of reinforcement gradient, it should be possible, by psychological means, to make the immediate negative reinforcement of the response sufficiently powerful to offset the delayed positive physiological reinforcement and make the 'overall reinforcement' of the response negative.

In the case of alcoholism and drug addiction, this could perhaps be achieved by conditioning a nausea or anxiety response to the stimuli most intimately associated with the performance of the consummatory response. In the case of sexual responses, one could capitalise on the reciprocally inhibitory relationship which seems to exist between sexual arousal and anxiety (Wolpe, 1958; Gantt, 1949). Thus one could remove the arousal and reinforcing properties of the deviant sexual stimuli by conditioning anxiety to them (e.g. by electric shock). Similarly, conditioning anxiety to the stimuli associated with the performance of the deviant sexual act could disrupt sexual performance, thereby further reducing the reinforcement.

A more thorough discussion of the possibilities briefly outlined here is given below.

Provision of an alternative rewarded response

Several studies suggest that the effect of punishment in suppressing one response is markedly enhanced if another response, motivated by the same drive as and followed by similar reinforcement to the undesirable response, is available. The striking effects obtained in this way have been described by Solomon (1964) and Azrin and Holz (1966). Two examples cited by the latter authors will be given.

Azrin (unpublished data) studied pigeons punished by shock for a key-pecking response (maintained by a food reinforcement schedule). He showed that punishment had a far more dramatic effect in reducing responses on the punished key when another response key, on which responses could be made, be positively reinforced, and remain unpunished, was available, than when this key was not available.

The second study is by Herman and Azrin (1964), on humans. They showed that punishment of a manipulandum response (maintained by a cigarette reinforcement schedule) by a loud unpleasant sound produced only a slight degree of suppression. However, on provision of an additional manipulandum, responses on which produced only positive reward and no noise, the response rate on the punished manipulandum was reduced completely and almost immediately.

These results will surprise no one; clinicians have long recognised the importance of providing desirable, equally satisfying, alternative responses to the undesirable target responses of treatment. It is known, for example, that in the sexual disorders, prognosis for the elimination of aberrant sexual behaviour is better if normal heterosexual interests are present (MacCulloch and Feldman, 1967).

It seems unfortunately true that the great importance of providing rewarded responses, which can act as satisfactory alternatives to the undesirable responses, is matched by the great difficulty in providing such responses. For example, the problems for a homosexual in reorganising both his social and sexual life in a heterosexual rather than a homosexual direction are considerable. Similarly ponderous problems are posed in attempting to provide alcoholics and drug addicts with more satisfactory ways of coping with anxiety, frustration and depression than by the bottle or the needle.

Again, it would seem that aversion therapy should be only one aspect of a broad spectrum of treatment procedures. Provision of alternative rewarded responses seems extremely important to the success of aversion therapy, especially as such provision seems to allow elimination of the undesirable behaviour with the use of relatively mild punishment.

There are two further points which merit inclusion in our discussion and which are not mentioned in Azrin and Holz's summary given above. These can be posed in the form of two questions:

1 In a behaviour pattern consisting of several consecutive responses, at what part of the response chain should punishment be applied for maximum effectiveness?
2 Can subjects utilise safety signals which inform them that they can make previously punished responses without being punished?

The problems posed by the second question are complex, and discussion of them will be deferred until the first question has been considered.

At what part of the response chain should punishment be applied for maximum effectiveness?

Most of the undesirable behaviour patterns to which aversion therapy is applied consist of several responses chained together. The questions arise: Should we attempt to punish each component response of the behaviour, or should we punish only selected components of the behaviour? If we adopt the second strategy, which components of the behaviour should we choose to punish?

The classic experiment relevant to these questions is that of Solomon (quoted in Eysenck, 1964). In this study, the effects of punishing feeding behaviour in puppies by swatting them with a rolled-up newspaper were investigated. Two experimental conditions were used: in one group of puppies the animals were punished by swatting them as they approached the food; in the other group, they were punished as they were actually eating. Suppression of the eating response was obtained in both conditions, but was more lasting in puppies which had been punished while approaching the food.

This finding would suggest that punishment is most effective when applied early in the response sequence of the target behaviour. However, the situation is not quite so simple. It was found that when the animals eventually performed the 'taboo' act of eating, the group which had been punished while approaching the food showed no evidence of anxiety while eating, whereas the animals which had been punished while actually eating showed considerable evidence of anxiety while eating. Solomon draws a distinction between the 'ability to resist temptation' which is the length of time the animal will refrain from making the punished response, and 'guilt' which is the anxiety displayed when the animal eventually performs the previously punished response. In Solomon's experiment, the dogs punished while approaching the food showed greater ability to resist temptation but less guilt than the dogs punished while actually feeding.

We have suggested above that what Solomon calls guilt may be important in changing the overall reinforcement value of a behaviour. Thus, although punishment early in the response sequence seems most effective in delaying 'relapse' back to the performance of the previously punished behaviour, it may be that punishment late in the response sequence, producing more guilt, would be more effective in reducing the overall frequency of the undesirable behaviour over an extended period.

While not directly related to the topic under discussion, it is worth noting here what may seem entirely obvious, namely, that in order to eliminate a response by a punishment paradigm, the response has to be made. This point is illustrated in an experiment by Lichtenstein (1950). In this experiment, dogs were trained to eat food pellets, while they were restrained in a stock. One group of dogs was punished by electric shock as soon as they began eating. For a second group of dogs, the shock was administered as the food was presented (i.e. before they began to eat). The first group inhibited the act of eating after a mean of 1·7 shocks, and they did not eat again in the stock on three subsequent days of twenty trials per day. The second group failed to form a feeding inhibition; it seemed that, while they might have been afraid of the food, they were not afraid to eat it.

Although it may not be absolutely clear where in the response chain punishment should be applied for greatest effect, Lichtenstein's experiment seems to suggest quite strongly that aversive stimuli are most effective in eliminating behaviour if they are made contingent on the actual behaviour rather than simply on the situation in which that behaviour occurs.

Can subjects utilise safety signals indicating that they can make the previously punished response without receiving punishment?

A factor crucial to the use of punishment in aversion therapy is that the suppression of the punished response should generalise from the hospital situation in which treatment is performed to the situations in the patient's life in which the deviant behaviour normally occurs.

There are many experiments to show that if, in a punishment procedure, one provides rats with a safety signal to indicate when they can make the otherwise punished response without receiving punishment, they can make the discrimination. They perform the response in the presence of the safety signal and refrain from making the response in the absence of the safety signal (Azrin, 1956; Brethower and Reynolds, 1962; Dinsmoor, 1952; Hunt and Brady, 1955).

Patients receiving aversion therapy should be able to utilise the absence of shock electrodes as a safety signal and continue their deviant behaviour outside the hospital situation in which it has been punished. The surprising fact is that aversion therapy procedures incorporating the punishment paradigm seem to be at least moderately effective in producing suppression of the undesirable behaviour outside the hospital situation. Only one study seems to be based explicitly on a punishment paradigm (Kushner and Sandler, 1966); in this study, lasting changes in behaviour were obtained in three out of the four patients described. Many other studies also conform to a punishment paradigm; indeed, with the exception of the work of Feldman and MacCulloch, most of the studies employing faradic shock incorporate a punishment procedure. Further, some of the work employing chemical aversion therapy for alcoholism seems to fit a punishment paradigm. We are thus faced with the problem: extrapolation from experiments on animals suggests that punishment-based aversion therapy procedures are unlikely to produce lasting results outside the hospital situation; aversion therapy techniques incorporating punishment procedures seem to be moderately effective.

One possible reason for this is that the experiments with rats cited above incorporated a discrimination training procedure in which the rat was exposed to both the 'safe' and 'danger' conditions in the same training session. Aversion therapy procedures, typically, do not incorporate such a discrimination procedure; the patient only experiences the 'danger' condition in the training situation. It is known (Kimble, 1961, p. 346) that generalisation gradients are steeper following discrimination training than following procedures not employing discrimination. It could be that the aversion therapy procedures produce a flatter generalisation gradient of suppression (and, therefore, more suppression outside the hospital situation) because the training session in the hospital does not include a discrimination training procedure.

This seems unlikely because, although the aversion therapy procedure does not itself include discrimination training, the patient will have experienced repeated 'safe' performances of the undesirable response, in the absence of shock electrodes, before embarking on treatment. Further, it is likely that, despite the therapist's instructions, the patient will continue his undesirable behaviour between treatment sessions; again these 'safe' performances will be accompanied by the safety signal of absence of shock electrodes.

An obvious suggestion to explain the different outcomes in the animal and human situation is that we are dealing with different procedures. Throughout the section on punishment we have kept theoretical speculation to a minimum. We have included any procedure which falls within the *operational* definition of punishment given at the beginning of the section. This is an extremely broad definition, implying nothing about the mechanism involved in the reduction of response frequency. Many different mechanisms could be subsumed under the same definition if they all led to the same end result – reduction in response frequency.

That something of this kind is in fact happening is suggested by the varying effects of punishment on animal behaviour, depending on the nature of the response being punished. Thus, Solomon (1964) points out that consummatory responses are far more susceptible to the effects of punishment than are instrumental responses:

The interference with consummatory responses by punishment needs a great deal of investigation. Punishment seems to be especially effective in breaking up this class of responses, and one can ask *why*, with some profit. Perhaps the intimate temporal connection between drive, incentive and punishment results in drive or incentive becoming conditioned-stimulus (CS) patterns for aversive emotional reactions when consummatory acts are punished. Perhaps this interferes with vegetative activity: i.e. does it 'kill the appetite' in a hungry subject? But, one may ask why the same punisher might not appear to be as effective when made contingent on an *instrumental* act as contrasted with a consummatory act. Perhaps the nature of operants is such that they are separated in time and space and response topography from consummatory behaviour and positive incentive stimuli, so that appetitive reactions are not clearly present during punishment for operants.

As we pointed out earlier (p. 125) many of the behaviour problems to which aversion therapy is applied are consummatory responses. There we suggested that it was necessary to try to change the nature of the reinforcement of the punished response by the use of aversive stimuli. Solomon is suggesting that in the case of consummatory responses, punishment is effective by virtue of its effects in reducing the drive for the punished response.

Speculations of this kind seem somewhat removed from the type of instrumental behaviour, typified by the bar-pressing response of the rat, which has been the subject of most experimental investigations of punishment, including the article by Azrin and Holz (1966). It seems that what occurs in much aversion therapy is not adequately represented by the analogue of punishment of a bar-pressing response in the rat, especially as, to add another dimension of complexity, much aversion therapy employs punishment of the *imaginal* performance of the undesirable behaviour, rather than the undesirable behaviour itself. This is not to deny the usefulness of the punishment paradigm, operationally defined in terms of the contingency of the noxious stimulus on the to-be-punished response; aversion therapy employing this paradigm appears to have been moderately successful. What is required is an attempt to understand the mode of action of the noxious stimuli in the aversion therapy procedures themselves, with a view to improving their efficacy.

K

Some behaviourists are likely to object to our rejection of a solely empirical approach to the problem of aversion therapy. They would maintain that to point out that many aversion therapy procedures conform to the punishment paradigm is sufficient explanation of the efficacy of aversion therapy. It is therefore necessary to list some of our reasons for indulging in speculative theoretical analyses of the processes of aversion therapy in later sections:

1 The analysis ultimately offered seeks to explain the effectiveness of aversion therapy procedures employing diverse operational paradigms (punishment, avoidance, classical conditioning) by the same basic mechanism. It is thus more parsimonious than 'explanations' which consist of pointing out that aversion therapy procedures conform to a number of different operationally defined paradigms, each of which may or may not lead to response suppression.

2 Although the punishment model can accommodate a surprising amount of clinical information (especially that arising from electrical aversion), there are some findings which do not fit the model. Here we need mention only three such examples:

   (a) The clinical efficacy of the Feldman–MacCulloch method for treating homosexuality can only be accommodated by making numerous assumptions – on the face of it, their procedure is not response-contingent punishment. This is merely one instance of the difficulties which are encountered when treating any disorder in which the response cannot be carried out in the treatment setting. This objection can be overcome in the case of sexual disorders only by punishing sexual arousal to a secondary or symbolic stimulus. In the Feldman–MacCulloch method, the shock stimulus was not made contingent on a sexual response – but nevertheless produced results.

   (b) A second example is the efficacy of non-punishing contingencies in the chemical aversion treatment of alcoholism. The best model to account for these reports is one of classical conditioning.

   (c) A third example is our inability to account for some of the observed consequences of aversion therapy, such as the 'devaluation' of sexual stimuli reported by Marks and Gelder (1967).

3 The empirical evidence available from studies of the kind reported by Azrin and Holz cannot account for the generalisation of the suppressive effects of aversion therapy to situations outside the hospital, where there are many 'safety signals' to indicate to the patient that he can no longer be punished. The analysis which we offer below

suggests that this problem (of generalisation and retention of the effects of therapy in the presence of 'safety signals' outside the therapy situation) is not peculiar to punishment, but also occurs in the case of classical conditioning. The analysis, by bringing the problem in these two situations together, enables us to draw on more experimental evidence in our efforts to elucidate it.

4 We believe that an understanding of the underlying mechanisms involved in aversion therapy will lead to an improvement in technique, e.g.

(*a*) The idea that punishment involves the conditioning of 'anxiety' helps in an understanding of the situations in which punishment has a paradoxical effect (p. 120).

(*b*) Feldman and MacCulloch's attempts to elucidate the actual processes involved in their aversion therapy procedure have led to the realisation that their original technique should be modified (see next section).

To sum up, we feel that the punishment model tells us a great deal about the operation of aversion therapy; when we consider the processes involved, however, we are obliged to go beyond the operational model.

Summary

It is pointed out that experimental investigations employing noxious stimuli have looked at four main paradigms: punishment, avoidance, escape, classical conditioning. This chapter discusses punishment.

Many aversion therapy procedures conform to a punishment paradigm, and it is suggested that it is useful to view them in this light, especially with regard to designing treatment procedures. The failure of clinicians explicitly to adopt a punishment paradigm is discussed.

The variables determining the effectiveness of punishment in experimental situations are described. The fact that aversion therapy should be only one of a number of elements in a total therapeutic approach is illustrated by the findings that the effectiveness of punishment can be improved by the provision of an alternative rewarded response, and by steps taken to reduce the drive motivating the punished response.

Some limitations of the punishment approach, especially its difficulty in explaining the generalisation of punishment to the extra-treatment situation, are discussed. It is suggested that an attempt to offer a theoretical analysis of the processes involved in aversion therapy is worthwhile.

16
Theoretical analysis: avoidance conditioning models

Avoidance training, unlike punishment, is a procedure geared to the production of new responses. It can only eliminate responses by training new responses, incompatible with the old responses, to the stimuli which previously led to the behaviour it is desired to eliminate. Advocates of the use of an avoidance paradigm (e.g. Feldman and MacCulloch, 1965) stress that the advantages of this paradigm lies in the well-known resistance to extinction often observed in responses established by anticipatory avoidance learning.

The experiments which report such striking resistance to extinction have typically only measured the extinction of the overt motor avoidance response. In general, they have not looked at what happens to the anxiety response conditioned to the CS, which the two-factor learning theory of avoidance conditioning (Mowrer, 1960), and the work of Black (1965) suggest is an essential component in the acquisition of the motor avoidance response. Advocates of the use of the avoidance paradigm must thus base their position on the utility of the motor avoidance responses it produces, rather than on the utility of the classically conditioned anxiety component. Indeed, there is some evidence to suggest that the resistance to extinction shown by the motor avoidance responses may not be paralleled by that shown by the classically conditioned anxiety response. Thus, animals performing a well established motor avoidance response characteristically show little sign of anxiety. Further, Black (1965) has shown that, while the occurrence of a conditional heart rate change (the conditioned anxiety response) was essential to the occurrence of avoidance responses during the acquisition phase of training, no correlation appeared between the occurrence of changes in heart rate and the occurrence of avoidance responses in extinction.

It would seem that, to obtain a lasting suppression of undesirable behaviour by avoidance conditioning, we must use the avoidance procedure to train a motor response which will be incompatible with the performance of the undesirable behaviour. Where such undesirable target behaviour is dependent on objects in the external world, e.g.

homosexual partners, bottles of alcohol, cigarettes, hypodermic syringes, women's underwear, etc., the most effective incompatible response available is probably the shunning and physical avoidance of these objects. Thus, one is interested in producing a situation in which, when faced with the stimulus complex which formerly precipitated the undesirable behaviour, the patient, instead of making the old response (or simply making no response), prevents the occurrence of the undesirable response by withdrawing from the stimulus situation. For example, the treated alcoholic, on finding himself outside a bar or liquor store, should hurry quickly by instead of entering.

The problem of training shunning responses of such diversity that they will completely protect the patient from situations in which he might return to his undesirable habits is considerable.

The most prominent proponents of the use of the anticipatory avoidance paradigm in aversion therapy have been Feldman and MacCulloch (Feldman and MacCulloch, 1965; MacCulloch, Feldman and Pinschof, 1965; Feldman, 1966). These workers have applied their technique (which is described in detail on pp. 64 ff.) with considerable success to the treatment of homosexuality, and without success to the treatment of alcoholism (MacCulloch, Feldman, Orford and MacCulloch, 1966).

The avoidance response trained in the Feldman and MacCulloch procedure for the treatment of homosexuality is the depresssion of a button to remove a coloured slide of a naked male from a back-projection screen. On the face of it, there is not the slightest reason to think that this response is in any way incompatible with the homosexual behaviour which it is desired to eliminate. Further, as the homosexual is not provided with a button to carry around with him, it is not possible for the patient to make the actual trained response outside the hospital situation.

Feldman and MacCulloch's rationale for choosing this response was, presumably, based on the hope that generalisation would occur from the trained response (pressing a button to remove the slide of a naked male) to responses of avoiding, in the sense of shunning, homosexual acquaintances, haunts, etc., in the real life situation. This is generalisation of a fairly massive order, involving both response and stimulus generalisation. The only experimental examples we are aware of for generalisation of such an extent are where a powerful anxiety response has been established to a given stimulus, as in the experimental neuroses, and this then mediates a whole range of behaviour. Feldman and MacCulloch cannot adduce such examples as evidence in favour of their explanation of their treatment as they specifically reject the importance of the classically conditioned anxiety component of the avoidance response (see below). There seems to be no other evidence of generalisation on this scale, at least within the field of avoidance conditioning, and so we must reject their appeal to such generalisation as an explanation of the efficacy of their therapy.

It seems that there is a difficulty inherent in the use of the term 'anticipatory avoidance learning' to denote a certain paradigm of behaviour. Because one has established an 'avoidance response' (which can be any type of response one chooses) to a particular conditioned stimulus, there is a danger that one may assume that after training the subject will 'avoid', in the sense of shunning, the conditioned stimulus. There is no reason why this should necessarily occur, e.g. one could imagine a situation in which one trained an animal to make an 'anticipatory avoidance response' of approaching the conditioned stimulus.

The problem we have just mentioned may seem to be peculiar to the particular response trained by Feldman and MacCulloch in their aversion therapy situation. One might think that, given the right choice of avoidance response, avoidance training could be a powerful method of aversion therapy. However, there are several reasons to think this may not be the case.

One of these is that for the most effective conditioning in an avoidance conditioning paradigm, the avoidance response trained should be of an operant 'emitted' nature (Turner and Solomon, 1962), i.e. in humans, under a fair degree of voluntary control. Assuming that we train an avoidance response that will effectively prevent the occurrence of the undesirable behaviour, that this avoidance response is still under voluntary control, and that the undesirable behaviour is still attractive to the patient, we are presented with the problem – why should the patient continue to make the avoidance response after he has left hospital? This problem seems basic to the use of the avoidance paradigm.

In choosing suitable responses to train by the avoidance method we can either choose ones which will be incompatible with responses early in the response sequence of the undesirable behaviour, e.g. entering a bar in the case of the alcoholic, or late in the response sequence, e.g. for the alcoholic, lifting a glass of alcohol to his mouth. The problem with using responses incompatible with early parts of the behaviour sequence is that we have to train a vast number of such responses, e.g. going into bars, liquor stores, visiting friends who would offer drink, etc. The problem with using responses late in the sequence is that it is difficult to imagine the patient, employing voluntary control and close in time to the performance of his highly gratifying behaviour, not continuing his behaviour sequence through to its satisfying conclusion. For example, if, in an alcoholic, we had trained him to avoid shock by putting down a glass of alcohol he had already partially lifted to his mouth, it is hard to see why, if the avoidance response trained is susceptible to voluntary control, once he has left the hospital and entered a bar, he should not continue lifting the glass to his mouth and start drinking.

The fact remains, however, that the anticipatory avoidance procedure employed by Feldman and MacCulloch is impressively effective in eliminating homosexual behaviour. In the light of what we have just said, it is important to ask how this can be so.

The work of Black (1965) seems to suggest that the classical conditioning of 'anxiety' to the conditioned stimulus (CS) is an essential prerequisite for the emergence of the motor avoidance response in the anticipatory avoidance training procedure. In line with this observation, MacCulloch, Feldman, and Pinschof (1965) claim that only those patients who developed conditioned cardiac responses to the CS of the male slides developed consistent motor avoidance behaviour, and showed improvement from treatment. (There are, however, reasons to question the validity of this claim – see p. 68.) We have, then, as a possible concomitant of the development of the motor response, the classical conditioning of anxiety to the CS. This classical conditioning will be even more pronounced in the procedure employed by Feldman and MacCulloch, in which, in its main phase, shock is delivered on one-third of the trials irrespective of whether the patient makes a button-pressing response or not. Thus one-third of the treatment trials are actually classical conditioning trials.

We are suggesting that the effective process operating in Feldman and MacCulloch's procedure is not the development of a motor avoidance response, but the classical conditioning of anxiety to the homosexual stimuli. It is suggested that, by virtue of the reciprocally inhibitory relationship which seems to exist between anxiety and sexual arousal (Wolpe, 1958; Gantt, 1949), the classical conditioning of anxiety to the homosexual stimuli 'devalues' them of their sexual arousal properties. A more detailed discussion of the mechanism of this 'devaluation' will be given in a later section. This suggestion stands in contrast to that proposed by Feldman and MacCulloch to account for the results of their method of treatment; they emphasise the operant aspects of their procedure. Indeed, Feldman and MacCulloch specifically reject the use of 'Classical Pavlovian Conditioning' on the grounds that 'this technique results in unstable learning, and easy extinction' (Feldman and MacCulloch, 1965). While this may be true for classically conditioned motor responses, it is not inevitably true for all classically conditioned autonomic responses. Solomon and Brush (1956) make this point in their extensive review of the literature on avoidance conditioning:

We are led to conclude from the experimental studies concerning the relative effectiveness of classical aversive conditioning and avoidance training procedures that the latter produce better and more stable aversive motor behaviour, while the former produces more anxiety or emotion.

The problem of whether classically conditioned autonomic responses are retained for appreciable periods will be discussed at some length below. For the moment, let it be said that there are studies which demonstrate the retention of classically conditioned autonomic responses over very long periods of time. As an example of the distinction between the motor and autonomic aspects of classical conditioning we shall cite a study by Gantt (1964). This study demonstrated that, following a single reinforcement with faradic shock, one could condition a cardiac response in a dog, which was extremely resistant to extinction and which was retained over at least thirteen months. The motor conditioned reflex did not even appear with the single reinforcement given.

Feldman and MacCulloch have reported a failure to obtain any therapeutic improvement when applying to alcoholism essentially the same technique as they had found successful in the treatment of homosexuality (MacCulloch et al., 1966). On their hypothesis that they are training the patient to 'avoid' the stimuli that trigger the undesirable behaviour, their technique should be as applicable to this behaviour as it is to homosexuality. Feldman and MacCulloch suggest that the reason for this failure may have been the inconsistent pattern of development of the avoidance response, and the failure to develop a conditioned cardiac response to the CS, both of which were indicators of poor prognosis among their homosexual patients. An alternative hypothesis, assuming that a classical conditioning paradigm is the effective component of the Feldman and MacCulloch procedure, is that the incentive and reinforcement values of visual stimuli associated with alcohol are less susceptible to 'devaluation', by conditioning anxiety to them than are those of sexual stimuli. If sexual stimuli are rendered affectively neutral then they lose most of their motivating and reinforcing qualities; rendering visual stimuli associated with alcohol affectively neutral has much less effect on the reinforcing properties of alcohol, which retains its physiologically reinforcing properties such as anxiety reduction, or relief of a specific 'alcohol hunger'.

On this view, the patients in the MacCulloch *et al.* procedure for treatment of alcoholism are in an analogous position to those dogs in the Lichtenstein experiment (p. 129) which received shock in the presence of food before they had had a chance to start eating. The patients are shocked in the presence of visual stimuli associated with alcohol, without making any drinking movements; the dogs are shocked in the presence of visual and olfactory stimuli associated with food, without making any eating movements. These dogs in Lichtenstein's experiment did not develop an inhibition of feeding behaviour. While they might have been afraid of the food, they were not afraid to eat it. It seems possible that a similar phenomenon may account for Mac-Culloch *et al.*'s therapeutic failure in the case of alcoholism. Indeed, if part of the reinforcement of drinking in the alcoholic is anxiety reduction, one might expect conditioning anxiety to the visual stimuli associated with drinking alcohol to increase, rather than decrease, drinking behaviour (but see p. 169).

Feldman and MacCulloch (1968) recently obtained the preliminary results of a comparative trial of three procedures for the treatment of homosexuality. One of these is their original anticipatory avoidance procedure. The second is a classical conditioning procedure in which the patients are shocked on every trial in every session in the presence of a slide representing a homosexual stimulus. The female 'relief stimulus' is given after the shock, as in the anticipatory avoidance procedure. In this procedure no attempt is made to develop an avoidance response (pressing the button to remove the homosexual slide). The third treatment procedure is psychotherapy.

While the results are still at a preliminary stage, the tentative conclusion seems to emerge that both learning theory techniques are superior to psychotherapy but do not differ between themselves, i.e. the simple classical conditioning procedure is as effective as the anticipatory avoidance procedure. This result lends support to the argument presented here that the *essential* element in Feldman and MacCulloch's original procedure was its classical conditioning component. Further, it suggests that it is unnecessary to employ the complicated procedure required for the development of avoidance responding to obtain therapeutic effects.

The discussion of the work of Feldman and MacCulloch may seem unduly critical of a treatment technique which appears to produce an impressive improvement in homosexual patients. It is by no means intended to belittle what Feldman and MacCulloch have attempted and achieved. However, it should be pointed out that, ironically, the procedure does not seem to work in terms of the learning paradigm which dictated its design. It seems to be another example of the happy occurrence of reaching the desired goal by taking the wrong route.

It is greatly to the credit of Feldman and MacCulloch that, having produced an effective treatment technique, they are continuing their research in an attempt to disentangle the actual mechanisms operative in their treatment.

Feldman and MacCulloch stress the attempt they have made to base their therapy technique upon 'the knowledge derived from the many thousands of experiments on animal and human learning which appear in the literature'. It is instructive to see just how relevant much of the experimental literature is to the actual problems of detail in the design of a treatment technique. To take two examples – the first parameter of the treatment procedure that Feldman and MacCulloch (1965) discuss is the intertrial interval. On the basis of a paper by Feldman (1963) dealing with the extinction hypothesis of warm-up in motor behaviour, such as pursuit-rotor tracking, the authors conclude: 'The too frequent occurrence of unspaced training trials might be expected to lead to reactive inhibition, and hence to the possibly permanent decrement of the avoidance response. Trials should therefore, be distributed rather than massed.' The connection between warm-up-motor behaviour and the problem of intertrial interval in avoidance learning seems indirect, and one wonders why the authors have based their conclusion concerning intertrial intervals on such an apparently unrelated finding. The reason is that a search of the readily accessible literature on avoidance learning provides no data related to this problem; Solomon and Brush in their extensive (1956) review of parametric studies of avoidance training make no mention of the variable of intertrial interval. One is thus forced back, as Feldman and MacCulloch were, on to 'psychological common sense', which suggests that spacing of trials should be advantageous. Even having reached this conclusion, practical factors will probably force the therapist to employ relatively short intertrial intervals.

A second example of the discontinuity between their theoretical guidelines and actual treatment procedures is seen in Feldman and MacCulloch's ninth proposition, 'quantity of reinforcement'. This states that McClelland and McGowan (1953) showed that varying the quantity of reinforcement in a random fashion also increased resistance to extinction. In the present situation, randomly varying the level of shock, administered on non-reinforced trials, would therefore be expected to have this effect (*Feldman and MacCulloch, p. 168*).

Leaving aside the fact that they are attempting to apply a method of variable *reinforcement* to *non-reinforced* trials, the McClelland experiment describes the effect of variations in the manner of giving food pellets to rats running down an alley. Greater resistance to extinction was noted in the group of rats which received 'general' rather than 'specific' reinforcement. Both groups received the same amount of food, but the 'general reinforcement' group was rewarded in varying *sections* of the alley and after varying *types* of response. In our view, extrapolation from this experiment to a homosexual patient receiving unavoidable shocks of varying strength in the presence of male slides is not valid. There is no reason for supposing that McClelland's findings imply that the homosexual patients will be less likely to relapse because the shock intensities are varied on non-reinforced trials.

Like the earlier example of intertrial spacing, Feldman and Mac-Culloch's ninth proposition seems to derive from 'psychological common sense' considerations rather than from the laboratory.

The field of aversion therapy suffers from the lack of experimental studies, particularly on humans, which might help to answer directly the questions which therapists ask. It would seem that the solution to this problem is for users of aversion therapy themselves to try to disentangle what is going on, as Feldman and MacCulloch are doing.

Escape training

From the definition of escape training (p. 118), it can be seen that part of the stimulus situation in which the response occurs, necessarily involves the noxious stimulus which is terminated by the escape response. If the escape response is trained in a hospital situation with reinforcement by the termination of some unconditioned noxious stimulus, such as electric shock, there is no reason for the patient to emit the response outside the hospital unless he experiences electric shock. The usefulness of such a response is obviously limited.

The only way one could train useful escape responses, which would persist outside the hospital situation, would be to employ a conditioned noxious stimulus, such as 'anxiety', which the escape response terminates. As escape from conditioned noxious stimuli is in fact the usual model for *avoidance training*, it will not be discussed further here. It is also worth mentioning that patients treated by aversion therapy rarely show signs of escaping from the CS after treatment. Transvestites, for example, do not report a need to escape from female clothing.

Summary

The use of the avoidance conditioning paradigm in aversion therapy is discussed, with particular reference to the work of Feldman and MacCulloch. It is suggested that this paradigm is of limited use for the following reasons:

1 The considerable resistance to extinction of avoidance responses seems to be mainly at the level of motor responses, and it is difficult to provide the patient with a sufficiently wide variety of motor responses such that he will consistently 'shun' the situations in which he is likely to indulge in his undesirable behaviour.
2 For greatest resistance to extinction, the motor response trained should be of an operant, voluntary, nature. If we train such responses, why should the patient continue to make them once outside the hospital situation, if they are under his voluntary control?
3 It is suggested that the effective component of Feldman and Mac-Culloch's procedure is not the operant conditioning of the motor response, but the classical conditioning of anxiety to the homosexual stimuli. A new study by Feldman and MacCulloch seems to confirm this hypothesis and to suggest that it is unnecessary to employ the relatively cumbersome anticipatory avoidance procedure, when a simple classical conditioning procedure is equally effective.
4 Feldman and MacCulloch's avoidance training procedure was ineffective when applied to the problem of alcoholism.

It is suggested that the links between Feldman and MacCulloch's actual procedure and the experimental and theoretical literature are not as strong as one might desire. This reflects the lack of relevant experimental data in the literature.

The possible use of escape training in aversion therapy is briefly discussed and dismissed.

17

Theoretical analysis: classical conditioning models

The majority of the early attempts at aversion therapy seem to have been based on a classical conditioning paradigm: the intention of the therapist appeared to be to condition feelings of 'aversion' to the previously attractive stimuli. We have also suggested that a classical conditioning process is important to the success of Feldman and MacCulloch's 'avoidance method' of treating homosexuals. Punishment training often involves classical conditioning procedures. Indeed, Mowrer (1960) has suggested that the classical conditioning of fear to the internal stimuli produced by the punished response is the basis of punishment. This hypothesis, which we will utilise later, points to an intimate connection between the processes of classical conditioning and punishment. It thus seems likely that classical conditioning is an important component of much aversion therapy.

For the moment we will consider a problem which is central to our ideas about how classical conditioning may operate in aversion therapy. This is the problem of establishing conditioned responses which will be resistant to extinction and independent of the subject's voluntary control. Obviously, it is valueless to establish classically conditioned responses in the hospital treatment situation, if, on leaving hospital, the responses rapidly extinguish. Such conditioning will be equally useless if the patient, knowing that he is no longer in danger of receiving electric shocks, can nullify the effects of the conditioning.

To anticipate the results of our discussion of this problem, let it be said that no satisfactory solution is reached. The discussion will illustrate the problem, and then consider various suggestions which have attempted to resolve it. While each of these is of some value, none of them is completely convincing. This is unfortunate but, in our view of the present state of knowledge, inevitable.

As discussed in Chapter 14, there is evidence which demonstrates that, following a conditioning procedure involving the UCS of faradic shock, informing the subject that he will no longer receive shocks produces an extremely rapid extinction of the conditioned response. In contrast with these findings on the fragility of conditioned autonomic responses, and their high susceptibility to cognitive control, stand many results which suggest an extreme resistance to extinction and immunity to cognitive control. Thus, Sanderson et al. (1963) employing a one-trial conditioning procedure, with the extremely traumatic UCS of respiratory paralysis, produced autonomic CRs which, far from extinguishing over time, actually increased in strength with repeated presentations of the CS.

A learning theory approach to neurotic disorders (e.g. Eysenck and Rachman, 1965) suggests that neuroses provide excellent examples of conditioned autonomic responses, which may persist for many years. These responses are typically quite beyond the voluntary control of the patient. Patients commonly state: 'I know, rationally, that my fear is silly and groundless, but there's nothing I can do about it.'

Another example of persisting conditioned autonomic responses is provided by aversion therapy itself. Many of the patients who received chemical aversion therapy for alcoholism did develop persistent 'aversion' responses to the alcoholic CS. For example, Hammersley (1957) reports that, following treatment, almost all of his patients showed conditioned nausea to the CS of alcohol, while 25% actually acquired a conditioned vomiting response to this CS. These patients' conditioned responses did not extinguish as soon as they left the hospital and knew they were in no danger of being given emetic drugs. Indeed, one of Hammersley's patients decided deliberately to undo the effects of the conditioning procedure so that he could drink again, and only succeeded in doing so after persisting for four hours of drinking and vomiting.

The resolution of the problem posed by these conflicting findings is extremely important to aversion therapy. It is essential to elucidate the conditions which lead to relatively permanent conditioned autonomic responses – the underlying aim of aversion therapy.

One reason for the different results obtained in these two classes of experiment may be the nature of the conditioned stimulus employed. Razran (1939) showed that, in human salivary conditioning, both extinction and forgetting were much slower following conditioning in which the CS was a pattern of stimuli rather than when it was a single component of such patterns. This was true even when the original conditioned responses to each type of stimulus were equal. Those experiments which have shown rapid extinction of the conditioned response have typically employed simple stimuli, such as pure tones. In the case of the phobias and aversion therapy, the CS's seem to be of a more complex nature.

More light may be thrown on the apparently contradictory results of the two classes of experiment by a consideration of the existence of 'levels of learning' discussed by Razran (1955). This writer considers the problem we have mentioned and concludes that experiments investigating the 'classical conditioning' paradigm (operationally defined) in fact are dealing with learning which occurs at least at two levels. One level of learning, described as 'conditioning without perception' or 'mere conditioning' is typified by the learning reported in experiments on conditioning animals low in the phyletic scale (e.g. Protozoa, Coelenterata). In such cases the occurrence of perceptual processes, as the term is used in relation to the 'higher processes' in man, seems improbable. The second level, which Razran describes as perceptual, is evident in experiments on human 'classical conditioning' when the course of conditioning is suddenly changed as the subject 'catches on' to the stimulus relationships in the experiment. Razran holds that 'the chief determinant of the division is the presence or absence of perceived – or reacted – relations between stimuli and reactions involved in learning'. These two levels of learning are not mutually exclusive: 'whenever learning takes place, it involves the operation not of one kind *or* the other kind, but of either (*a*) the lower kind or (*b*) the higher *and* the lower kinds'. The scope for the occurrence of learning in which both levels are involved seems particularly great in human subjects, where the ability to perceive relations between stimuli is higher than in all other animals. Mere conditioning still seems to operate even where perceptual factors are apparently dominant. In cases where the subject is made aware of the stimulus relations and instructed to oppose the processes of 'mere conditioning', some non-perceptual conditioning often occurs.

It seems likely that the two levels of conditioning will respond differently to extinction. Information to the effect that the UCS will no longer be delivered after the CS, given explicitly by the experimenter or by the subject's self-instruction (e.g. on leaving the hospital) will have a more powerful effect at the 'perceptual-relational' level than at the 'non-perceptual' level. This is well illustrated in the experiment of Bridger and Mandel (1964), who compared conditioning of the GSR to actual shock and to threat of shock. They found that, while the conditioned GSR acquired was the same in amplitude in the two conditions, the GSR conditioned to real shock was more resistant to extinction, following removal of the shock electrodes and an assurance that no more shock could be given, than was that conditioned only by threat of shock. The greater perceptual-relational element in the threat of shock condition is apparent.

It would seem, then, that we might try to explain the contradictory evidence on the resistance of conditioned reactions to extinction in terms of the relative proportions of non-perceptually conditioned and perceptually conditioned components of the conditioned reaction. It is possible that conditioning occurring to a large extent at the perceptual level precludes the occurrence of much conditioning at the non-perceptual level.

If the above suggestions are correct, the conditioning procedure which should lead to conditioned responses most resistant to extinction would be one occurring predominantly at the non-perceptual level.

A good example of such a procedure, and one which might repay exploitation by aversion therapists, is the phenomenon known as 'Interoceptive conditioning'. This phenomenon is discussed in a paper by Razran (1961), in which he defines interoceptive conditioning as 'classical conditioning in which either the conditioned stimulus (CS) or the unconditioned stimulus (US) or both are delivered directly to the mucosa of some specific viscus'. Such conditioning stands in contrast to the more usual procedure of exteroceptive conditioning, where CS and UCS are both delivered to sense organs responding to external stimuli. As an example of one type of interoceptive conditioning (known as interoexteroceptive as only the CS is of visceral origin) we shall describe an experiment by Lotis (1949). A fistula was formed in the surgically exteriorised uterine horn of a female dog. This gave access to the internal surfaces of the uterus. The uterine interior was stimulated by a jet of air. After ten seconds of such stimulation, an electric shock was administered to the animal's right hind-paw. Conditioned paw withdrawal to the mere air stimulation first appeared after five trials and became stabilised after ten to eleven trials. The extent of the conditioned paw withdrawal appears to have been no less, and even greater, than the unconditioned response elicited by the shock. We have here a situation in which the internal stimulation of the uterus functions as a CS in just the same way as an exteroceptive stimulus, such as a light or tone.

Razran provides numerous examples of similar and more complex phenomena in both animals and man. Of particular interest is the fact that similar results seem to be obtained whether one employs an artificial interoceptive stimulus, such as the jet of air in the Lotis experiment, or natural interoceptive stimuli, e.g. those arising from 'natural' gastric contractions (Goncharova, 1955, p. 165).

Selected quotations from Razran's summary and conclusions will indicate the direct relevance of the phenomenon of interoceptive conditioning to the problems of obtaining classically conditioned responses which are resistant to extinction and independent of the subject's voluntary control:

1 Unlike the continuum of exteroceptive stimulation which is the body material of all our conscious experience, the continuum of interoceptive stimulation leads largely to unconscious reactions.

2 Interoceptive conditioning, whether involving conditioned or unconditioned interoceptive stimuli, is readily obtainable and is by its very nature largely unconscious in character.

3 While interoceptive conditioning is by its nature more limited than is exteroceptive conditioning with respect to total kinds and variety of stimulations, the interoceptive kinds of stimulations are, on the other hand, by their very nature much more recurrent, periodic and organism-bound, making interoceptive conditioning an almost built-in function that is constantly generated and regenerated in the very process of living and acting.

4 Interoceptive conditioning is somewhat slower in formation than is exteroceptive but, once conditioned, it is more fixed and irreversible (less readily extinguished).

5 When equal but opposing interoceptively produced and exteroceptively produced reactions are juxtaposed, the interoceptive reactions dominate the exteroceptive ones, with the final result that preceding exteroceptive stimuli become conditioned stimuli for succeeding interoceptive reactions whereas preceding interoceptive reactions become strengthened by exteroceptive reactions succeeding them.

6 The juxtaposition of conditioned interoceptive and exteroceptive stimuli of the same conditioned reaction, unlike similar juxtapositions of exteroceptive stimuli of different modalities, produces a certain amount of conflict and decrementation of conditioning.

Of the six propositions, the last three, the more specific ones, might still be in need of further empirical evidence to settle fully their status and parameters. However, there should be absolutely no doubt about the finality of the first three general propositions – the ubiquity, largely unconscious character, and ready all-round conditionability of interoceptive stimulations (*Razran, 1961*).

From this summary it is evident that aversion therapists would do well to investigate the possibilities of interoceptive conditioning. Of particular relevance to the problem of obtaining persistent conditioned responses are the unconscious character of interoceptive conditioned responses, their resistance to extinction, and their dominance over reactions produced by exteroceptive stimuli, such as 'You have now left the hospital treatment situation, and can no longer receive unpleasant stimuli'.

It is interesting to note that two of the examples of well-retained

L

conditioned autonomic responses given above, the Sanderson *et al.* study, and the aversions resulting from chemical aversion therapy, are extero-interoceptive responses. In both, the noxious UCS has its effect on the viscera of the body and so qualifies as an interoceptive stimulus.

However, not all those aversion therapy procedures which seem therapeutically successful appear to conform to an interoceptive conditioning paradigm. For example, Marks and Gelder's (1967) procedure seems to conform to an exteroceptive paradigm; the UCS of faradic shock (exteroceptive) follows the CS of either the real fetish or transvestite stimulus (e.g. panties) or the imaginal representation of the patient performing his deviant behaviour involving these stimuli. The CS of the real fetish stimulus is obviously exteroceptive. It is difficult to say what the nature of the imaginal stimulus is; it is not exteroceptive, in that the stimuli involving the deviant behaviour are of internal origin; however, it is not obviously interoceptive as it does not directly involve the stimulation of any internal viscera, and it is most definitely not unconscious in nature. Perhaps classical conditioning involving imaginal stimuli is peculiarly resistant to extinction. The surprising success of aversion therapy involving *wholly* imaginal stimuli would suggest that this might be the case.

Alternatively, these apparently exteroceptive conditioning situations may, in fact, involve elements of interoceptive conditioning. That is, the exteroceptive stimuli may produce interoceptive stimuli which themselves become conditioned to the UCR. For example, Marks and Gelder noted that their exteroceptive and imaginal stimuli produced penile erectile responses, as measured by the phalloplethysmograph. Such erectile responses involve changes in the stimulation of internal viscera, e.g. the distention of the penile blood vessels. These interoceptive stimuli and the exteroceptive unconditioned stimulus of faradic shock could form the basis of an interoexteroceptive conditioned response. This could underly an apparently exteroceptive conditioned response to the exteroceptive stimuli of panties, etc. Obviously, the exteroceptive stimuli must exert some influence, otherwise anxiety would be conditioned to sexual arousal *per se*, rather than specifically to the sexual arousal provoked by deviant stimuli.

One way of testing this hypothesis would be to compare the effects of applying the faradic UCS (*a*) very shortly after the presentation of the exteroceptive CS, before interoceptive responses could be initiated, with (*b*) the effects of applying it after the exteroceptive CS had been present for some time, when interoceptive stimuli would also be acting.

Mowrer's theoretical analysis of punishment (1960) is somewhat similar to what is being proposed here. Mowrer suggests that during the course of punishment training the internal stimuli associated with the performance of the punished response have anxiety conditioned to them by virtue of their repeated association with the noxious stimulus. After such training, inception of the punished response will produce internal stimuli which will, in turn, produce conditioned anxiety. This will inhibit the response which has been punished, leading to the response suppression usually observed following punishment training. Mowrer's ideas are transmitted well in an experiment which he quotes (p. 398, 1960). A dog had his right forepaw passively lifted by the experimenter. This produced internal stimuli associated with the response of leg lifting, without the dog actually initiating the leg lifting movement. Every time the experimenter lifted the leg, the dog was severely shocked. After a number of trials on which shock had followed the experimenter's lifting the animal's leg, the dog began actively to resist the experimenter's attempt to lift its leg. It is suggested that this is mediated by anxiety conditioned to the internal stimuli associated with lifting the leg. Mowrer suggests that a similar mechanism operates in the usual punishment procedure where the response is initiated by the animal, rather than by the experimenter.

We have already pointed out that many of the procedures employed by aversion therapists conform, in part, to both classical and punishment paradigms. Mowrer's suggested mechanism of punishment is of considerable interest as it may provide a bridge between our discussion of classical conditioning and punishment.

We shall now leave the discussion of interoceptive conditioning, and the distinction between conditioning at the perceptual and non-perceptual levels. For a fuller discussion of these topics the reader is referred to the articles by Razran (1955, 1961) and Grings (1965).

Before leaving the problem posed by the permanence or impermanence of classically conditioned autonomic responses, we shall describe a recent attempt by Eysenck (1968) to resolve the paradox.

Eysenck was primarily concerned with the phenomenon of the incubation of anxiety/fear responses. He distinguishes two types of incubation phenomena, and deals mainly with one of these. This type is exemplified by an experiment of Napalkov (Eysenck, 1967). This worker, studying dogs, found that various noxious stimuli produced increases in blood pressure of less than 50 mm., complete adaptation occurring after twenty-five presentations of the noxious stimulus. However, if a single reinforced trial (i.e. CS followed by noxious UCS) was given, repeated unreinforced presentations of the CS after this reinforced trial produced increases in blood pressure of 30–40 mm. at first, rising on subsequent presentations to 190–230 mm. Further, the hypertensive state produced lasted over a year in some cases. That is, repeated unreinforced presentations of the CS, far from producing extinction of the conditioned blood pressure response, actually led to a progressive increase in the size of the conditioned blood pressure response.

This conditioned response rapidly became considerably larger than the original unconditioned response to the unconditioned noxious stimulus.

Eysenck presents several examples of similar situations, including the study by Sanderson *et al.* on respiratory paralysis which we have already mentioned. In all these examples, repeated unreinforced presentations of the CS leads to an increase in the size of the CR, rather than to the fall in the size of the CR characteristic of such an extinction procedure.

To account for such anomalous results, Eysenck postulates that the unreinforced presentation of a CS for an anxiety/fear CR leads to the activation of two mechanisms, one of which operates in the direction of reducing the size of the response to subsequent presentations of the CS, the other operates in the direction of increasing the size of the CR to subsequent presentations of the CS. If the former mechanism is dominant, extinction occurs; if the latter mechanism is dominant, incubation occurs. The first mechanism, that leading to extinction is not discussed further by Eysenck as he feels that it is an already well explored mechanism. Eysenck suggests that the mechanism leading to incubation effects is as follows: presentation of a CS which has previously been paired with a noxious UCS produces a conditioned response of fear or anxiety. The feedback stimuli from these responses are themselves noxious and in turn produce responses of anxiety/fear. In this way, by means of a positive feedback loop, the overall anxiety/fear response to the CS is increased. The temporal contiguity of the CS and this augmented anxiety response leads to a strengthening of the CR, so that on the next presentation of the CS the CR is larger, the same processes are repeated, and the CR will continue to increase in magnitude with repeated presentations of the CS. This situation is obviously not what is usually observed, and its rarity is attributed to the fact that the extinction mechanism ordinarily dominates the incubation mechanism.

It is interesting to note that the main examples of persisting conditioned autonomic responses we have presented, namely, neuroses, experimental and clinical, the Sanderson *et al.* experiment, and the persisting effects of aversion therapy, are all included in Eysenck's discussion as possible examples of the occurrence of incubation. It is obvious that the effectiveness of aversion therapy would be considerably enhanced if we could arrange treatment conditions to produce conditioned autonomic responses which showed incubation rather than extinction. What these conditions are is not clear. Eysenck suggests that increasing intensity of the noxious UCS, and increasing neuroticism of the subject, would be two factors that would lead to incubation rather than extinction. Both of these would have the effect of increasing the intensity of the CR, so that the positive feedback system is more likely to dominate the extinction process.

Eysenck acknowledges that his hypothesis is still at the level of untested speculation. Its heuristic value seems considerable, however, and early testing would be important both for theoretical clarification of the problem we have been discussing, and for the design of more effective treatment procedures.

This chapter has concerned itself entirely with the problem of obtaining permanent conditioned autonomic responses. The variables which are usually considered in relation to the efficiency of classical conditioning, e.g. CS–UCS interval, etc., have not been considered. The reason for this is that the first problem seems critical to an understanding of aversion therapy and has been relatively little discussed, whereas problems of the second type have received considerable attention, and form the material of standard texts (e.g. Kimble, 1961).

As indicated at the beginning of the chapter, none of the suggestions we have considered gives a definitive answer to the problem in hand. All have some merit, and receive some support from what evidence is available. Unfortunately, little work has been done directly to test them in the context of the problem we have been discussing. Consequently, their value is somewhat limited.

The possibility of producing relatively permanent conditioned autonomic responses does seem established, however, and the analyses offered in the next two chapters will make use of this phenomenon.

Summary

It is suggested that the phenomena of classical conditioning are of importance to aversion therapy techniques, both those which are explicitly based on this paradigm, and those based on the other paradigms of avoidance conditioning and punishment.

It is suggested that a major problem in the use of classical conditioning in aversion therapy is to obtain conditioned responses which are resistant to extinction, and are beyond the patient's 'cognitive control'. Evidence is presented to show that while some classically conditioned responses are not resistant to these two processes, others most definitely are. The problem of obtaining such resistant responses is discussed in relation to Razran's two 'levels of conditioning', interoceptive conditioning, the complexity of the conditioned stimulus, and Eysenck's recent discussion of 'incubation effects' in classically conditioned anxiety responses.

18

An analysis of aversion therapy for sexual disorders

As our starting point for this discussion we shall consider a classic experiment performed by Crespi in 1942. This experiment studied the behaviour of rats running down an alleyway for food reward. It was designed to answer the question, 'What are the effects of variation of magnitude of incentive upon level of performance, namely (a) an upward shift of incentive-amount and (b) a downward shift of incentive amount?'

Only the downward shift will be discussed here. Three groups of rats were given an equal number of daily training trials in the alleyway under standardised conditions of deprivation. One group ran to an incentive of 16 units weight of food, the second to an incentive of 64 units weight of food, and the third group to an incentive of 256 units weight of food. The groups were run until the learning curves for speed of running down the alleyway were substantially flattened. On the following day the incentive shift was performed as follows:

16-unit group: held at the same value of incentive
64-unit group: shifted to 16-unit incentive
256-unit group: shifted to 16-unit incentive

The results of this procedure are shown in Figure 11.

The running speeds of the shifted groups fell to a level significantly below (for trials 4–6) that of the group which continued on the 16-unit incentive.

This experimental outcome can be considered in terms of the simple Hullian equation:

Excitation Potential = habit strength × drive

For the experimental situation under discussion, the level of drive to be inserted in the above equation would be largely determined by the number of hours of food deprivation the rat had experienced before being placed in the runway. As we have mentioned, the extent of food deprivation for all rats at the time that they were put into the alleyway

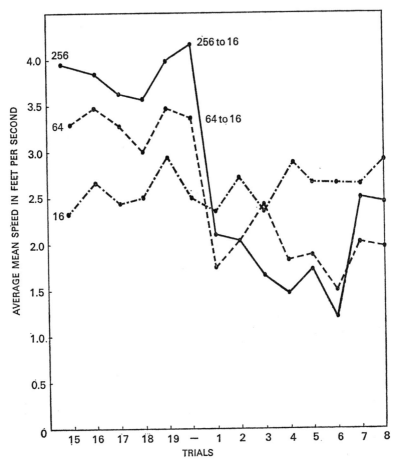

Figure 11 Curves from shifted groups. Effect of downward shifts of amount of incentive in comparison with non-shifted control groups. From Crespi, *American Journal of Psychology,* 1942.

was the same throughout the experiment. The change in behaviour resulting from the shift in incentive value cannot thus be explained in terms of changes in drive level, as measured by hours of food deprivation. The alternative is to assume that on the trials following the shift in incentive, the habit strengths of the two previously highly rewarded groups are lower than the habit strength of the group which continues at 16-unit incentive. This is clearly impossible. Before the shift, the speed of running is greater for the 64- and 256-unit incentive groups. If we assume inhibitory factors are equal in the three groups, this means that the excitatory potential is greater in the 64- and 256-unit groups than in the 16-unit incentive group. As drive is equal for all groups, habit strength, from the equation above, must be greater in the higher incentive groups before the incentive shift is performed.

The increment in habit strength resulting from the first trial in the shifted condition should be the same for all groups as they have received the same reinforcement. Thus, the 64- and 256-unit incentive groups should continue to perform at a level above, or at worst equal to, the 16-unit incentive group.

The simple Hullian equation is obviously inadequate to account for this situation. Clearly, the size of the reinforcement is having an effect on the performance of the rats, independently of its effects in reinforcing the hypothetical bond between stimulus and response (habit strength). Hull recognised this phenomenon and introduced the concept of 'incentive motivation, K, to account for it. The need for some such formulation which recognises the necessity for distinguishing strength of learning (conceived as the strength of the stimulus-response connection) and strength of performance (as measured by response latency, speed, vigour, etc.) is now generally accepted. Spence includes the factor of incentive motivation in his revision of Hull's equation:

$$E = H\,(D + K).$$

E is Hull's concept of excitatory potential, H is habit strength, D is drive, as indexed by hours of food deprivation, etc., and K is the incentive motivation factor. K is determined by the qualities of the reinforcement for the response. Spence conceives of it as adding to the motivational component of the excitatory potential; the more 'desirable' the reward, the greater the motivation to perform the rewarded action.

Spence's theory clarifies the difference between learning (measured by H) and performance (indexed by E). He summarises his position as follows:

This theory is, then, a reinforcement theory so far as excitatory potential is concerned; that is, the presence or absence of a reinforcer, and differences in its properties when present, do make a difference in the strength of the instrumental response. It is not, however, a reinforcement theory in the traditional sense of the term, for the habit or associative factor is not assumed to vary with variations in reinforcement (*quoted by Hilgard (1956) p. 419*).

The majority of the responses one is interested in, in aversion therapy are of a highly practised nature, i.e. the patient has performed them, and been reinforced for this performance, many times. It seems likely that in such a situation, where habit strength has probably reached an asymptotic value, the variables affecting the occurrence or non-occurrence of the response are not those determining learning but those determining performance. Put in everyday language, we are saying that the transvestite patient is always capable of putting on female clothing, in the sense of knowing what motions to go through; the factor which determines the occurrence of this action at any particular time is not habitual skill but inclination.

Having accepted that the quality of the reinforcement can affect the vigour of the response other than through its effect on the strength of the $S - R$ bond, it is necessary to ask how this effect is mediated. Obviously, there must be some process through which the effect of the quality of reinforcement is mediated before the reinforcement is actually received. That is to say, *previous* experience with the quality of the reinforcement determines the vigour of the response on any one trial before the reinforcement for that trial is received. How is this effect of previous experience mediated?

Spence utilised Hull's 'fractional anticipatory goal response mechanism, $r_G - s_G$' as the mediating process identified with incentive motivation, K. On this model, the stimuli associated with the performance of the goal response acquire incentive qualities by virtue of their association with the reward reinforcing the goal response. Components of the goal response then become conditioned to the stimuli, either internal or external, which precede the goal response. These stimuli trigger the fractional anticipatory goal response, r_G, which in turn produces stimuli s_G, which have incentive qualities and which constitute the incentive motivation. The following excerpt from Spence's Silliman lectures illustrates his view on this topic:

The essential notion of this formulation . . . is that learning in instrumental reward sequences involves classical conditioning of the goal or consummatory response to stimulus cues throughout the chain as well as an increase in the habit strengths of the instrumental acts themselves. There is, of course, nothing new about this notion of the conditional fractional anticipatory goal response. Indeed Hull introduced the concept in his early theoretical articles on maze learning (1930, 1931), although he never described its possible role in simple instrumental conditioning. The major difference between Hull's use of this theoretical mechanism and mine is that I have regarded it primarily as a motivator and have identified it with Hull's more recently formulated incentive motivational construct (Spence, 1951a, 1951b) (*Spence 1956, p. 126*).

Thinking similar to that of Spence is evident in Seward's (1950) concept of 'tertiary motivation' and Mowrer's (1960) concepts of 'hope' and 'fear'. The parallel with Spence's ideas are evident in the following quotation from Seward:

Our theory may be restated in the following nutshell: A reinforcer, in the case of positive cathexis, gains its potency through its ability, native or acquired, to arouse a consummatory response in the presence of the relevant need. In a learning situation this becomes conditioned to stimuli associated with the preceding instrumental act. When these stimuli recur they therefore arouse tertiary motivation, which in turn facilitates the act in progress (*Seward 1950, p. 372*).

While each of these authors' concepts differs to some extent, and there are difficulties associated with each of them, there seems to be a measure of agreement on some basic idea such as the following: the incentive or reinforcing qualities of the primary reinforcer become classically conditioned, to some extent, to the stimuli associated with the performance of the instrumental act on which the reinforcement is contingent; these conditioned incentive or reinforcing properties are of vital importance in determining the occurrence and strength of the response.

For a fuller discussion of the problems we have been discussing here, the reader is referred to Mowrer (1960, especially p. 261 onwards).

Let us turn now to the problem at hand, namely, what goes on in aversion therapy for sexual disorders. For ease of exposition, we shall concentrate on Spence's formulation of the ideas we have been discussing, as exemplified in his equation, $E = H(D + K)$.

The aim of aversion therapy is to reduce E for the deviant sexual behaviour. We have suggested above that variations in H will tend to be relatively unimportant in a highly practiced habit, and that we are interested in the factors which govern performance rather than learning. Our attempts at reducing E must thus involve manipulations of D and/or K. If D is conceptualised as sex-drive underlying all forms of sexual behaviour, then it would be undesirable to reduce this in treating sexual deviates, as this might interfere with the acquisition of more socially acceptable forms of sexual behaviour. Further, it is possible that drive of this nature, that is, a persistent need in the absence of sexual satisfaction, may be of relatively minor importance in determining sexual behaviour in the human male. Thus, Beach (1956) writes:

To a much greater extent than is true of hunger or thirst, the sexual tendencies depend for their arousal upon external stimuli. . . . When he encounters a receptive female, the male animal may or may not become sexually excited, but it is most unlikely that in the absence of erotic stimuli he exists in a constant state of undischarged sexual tensions. This would be equally true for the human male, were it not for the potent effects of symbolic stimuli which he tends to carry with him wherever he goes.

Similarly, Mowrer (1960) writes:

Appetitive excitement, or 'passion', in the region of a goal is a universal experience and is particularly striking in the realm of sex (where the primary drive is comparatively weak and the 'arousal' element prominent).

It seems then that our efforts in aversion therapy must be directed at K, the incentive motivation factor. K is mediated by conditioning of the incentive or reinforcing properties of the primary reinforcer to the stimuli associated with the responses leading up to the reinforcer. In the case of sexual behaviour, the importance of K seems unusually great; Ford and Beach (1952) have pointed out that, in man, the arousing properties of sexual stimuli are largely dependent on learning. McGuire, Carlisle and Young (1965) have proposed an interesting theory for the origin of sexual deviations. Although it is incomplete and not entirely satisfactory, the theory contains important elements. It is argued that patients with sexual disorders repeatedly masturbate to fantasies of their deviant sexual behaviour. As a consequence, the deviant stimuli and the associated behaviour acquire increments in their sexually arousing properties. The incentive and reinforcing properties of the primary reinforcement, in addition to becoming conditioned to the external deviant sexual stimuli, also become conditioned to the internal stimuli produced by the responses which constitute the ritual. It is hardly necessary to cite evidence that deviant sexual stimuli acquire sexually arousing qualities, e.g. Marks and Gelder (1967) showed that for fetishists and transvestites, the appropriate sexual stimuli evoked sexual arousal at both physiological and subjective levels. In the case of humans, the stimuli associated with imaginal rehearsal of the deviant act are capable of acquiring arousing properties as well.

The experiments on artificially induced fetishism by Rachman (1967) and Rachman and Hodgson (1968) support the idea that deviant sexual stimuli can acquire their reinforcing properties by a process of classical conditioning.

There seems a strong case for basing aversion therapy on an attempt to reduce K, or, ideally, to change its sign from positive to negative. We can reduce K by either or both of the following methods:

1 Changing the quality of the primary reinforcement, which would then lead to a change in the conditioned incentive motivation.
2 Changing the quality of the conditioned incentive motivation.

Obviously, for a persistent change in the quality of incentive motivation one must also change the reinforcing properties of the primary reinforcement. Otherwise, any change we may make in the qualities of K will be counteracted by the reconditioning of the original qualities of incentive motivation. This would occur by the repeated pairings of the stimuli associated with the reinforced behaviour with the unchanged (i.e. still positive) qualities of the primary reinforcer.

In the case of sexual arousal and reinforcement we are very fortunate in having a readily usable antagonist. It seems fairly well established that under many conditions there exists a mutually inhibitory relationship between sexual arousal and anxiety (Masters and Johnson, 1966; Wolpe, 1958; Gantt, 1949). We can thus eliminate the primary reinforcement attendant on masturbation or homosexual intercourse by conditioning anxiety to the situations in which these occur such that gratifying sexual performance is disrupted. Further, we can eliminate the arousal and reinforcing qualities of the incentive motivation attached to stimuli preceding primary reinforcement by a similar procedure. Where such stimuli are external ones, the procedure employed would fit the paradigm of classical conditioning of anxiety; where such stimuli are of an internal, response-produced, variety, the procedure employed would fit a punishment paradigm. As anxiety, in addition to being antagonistic to sexual arousal, is a negative reinforcer, we can choose either to change the quality of reinforcement and incentive of K from positive to neutral, or, by continuing the same procedures, to negative.

From our discussion we would predict that a procedure which employed electric shock to classically condition anxiety to the external stimuli associated with the deviant behaviour, and to punish the responses involved in the deviant behaviour, would be effective in eliminating the deviant sexual behaviour. Further, one would make the following predictions as to the outcome of such a procedure:

1 The excitatory potential of the deviant behaviour would be reduced, i.e. there would be a reduced frequency of occurrence of the behaviour after treatment.

2 The habit strength of the deviant behaviour would be unchanged, i.e.
   the patient would still be able to go through the motions of the
   deviant behaviour.
3 The deviant sexual stimuli, e.g. panties, boots, would no longer be
   sexually arousing; they would either be affectively neutral or have
   negative affective value.
4 The performance of the component responses of the deviant behaviour
   would no longer engender sexual arousal; they would be accompanied by no arousal at all or by arousal of a negatively reinforcing
   state.

The reader will recall that the method of treatment employed by
Marks and Gelder (1967) fits the requirements of the procedure outlined
above. Further, reference to the results obtained following this treatment shows that all four of these deductions were confirmed to some
extent by the treatment outcome.

It thus seems that the suggestions we have made may be useful in
allowing a better understanding of the processes involved in aversion
therapy for sexual disorders. As we see it, the crucial element involved
is the classical conditioning of anxiety to the stimuli, both internal and
external, associated with the deviant sexual behaviour. The problems
involved in obtaining conditioning which is resistant to extinction, and
the patient's 'cognitive control', have already been discussed. However,
once such conditioning has been obtained, the patient's 'cognitive
control' is no longer of much importance in restricting the efficacy of
therapy; even acting freely, he will not choose to indulge in the deviant
behaviour as he no longer gets any satisfaction from it.

We seem then, at least in the case of aversion therapy for sexual
disorders, to place crucial significance on the process of classical conditioning (punishment is included under this head, in line with Mowrer's
[1960] views on this phenomenon). It may be profitable at this stage to
reconsider the views of Feldman (1966), who explicitly rejects the importance of classical conditioning procedures in favour of operant conditioning procedures, especially avoidance training. (It should be remembered, however, that the distinction between these two forms of learning
does not seem as clear cut and rigid as was once thought to be the case.)
Feldman argues that 'Irrespective of the conditioning technique used,
the underlying aim (although this is frequently not specifically stated) is
to suppress the visual response of looking – in reality or fantasy – at an
attractive but inappropriate stimulus.' This view contrasts markedly

with the one proposed here. From our analysis, it is irrelevant whether the patient looks at the inappropriate stimulus or not; the crucial factor is whether or not the inappropriate stimulus arouses incentive motivation.

Feldman (1966) advances two main reasons why an operant model of aversion therapy is preferable to a classical conditioning one:

1 The changes resulting from classical conditioning are 'rather poorly resistant to extinction'.

2 In a study by Morgenstern, Pearce and Rees (1965), investigating the capacity of various psychological tests to predict the outcome of apomorphine aversion therapy for transvestites, the group with a favourable outcome showed significantly more conditioning in a test of verbal conditioning than did a group with an unfavourable outcome. Feldman argues that as verbal conditioning is an operant conditioning procedure, Morgenstern *et al.*'s results support his contention that aversion therapy is essentially an operant conditioning procedure.

The first of these points has been questioned earlier (p. 138). The significance of the second point is doubtful as serious reservations must attach to the relevance of Morgenstern *et al.*'s finding to the present problem. The reasons for this will appear on a detailed examination of their actual procedure. This is best conveyed verbatim:

The patient sat on one side of the table, the examiner on the opposite. The patient had a stack of one hundred test cards, and two trial cards. Their form was to contain one verb, and below this, the pronouns 'he', 'she', or 'we' in random order. The patient was instructed to make up a sentence from each card, using one pronoun and the verb, and to work rapidly. At the end of any sentence using the pronoun 'she' a reinforcement of 'good' was clearly used by the experimenter. The recording system was to use 1 for 'he', 2 for 'she' and 3 for 'we', no mark being made until the patient had finished speaking the sentence. Assessment of the results was by a comparison of the number of sentences containing the reinforced pronoun 'she' which occurred in the first thirty and the last thirty sentences.

The general level of verbal conditioning was low, as shown by an overall mean difference of only 1·3 between the number of 'she' sentences on the first thirty and the last thirty sentences. The subjects were split into groups, depending on the outcome of aversion therapy, into a 'cured', 'relapsed' and 'failed to attend' group. An analysis of variance was then performed as below. It is nowhere stated in the report of the study that the patients received the verbal conditioning procedure on more than one occasion, and so it must be assumed (although not stated in the text) that 'occasions' in the analysis of variance table means the two blocks of thirty sentences, and that the analysis was performed on the total number of 'she' sentences in each of these blocks.

Source	ss	df	VE	VR	p
Total	666·98	37			
Due to subjects	535·48	18	29·74	8·26	0·001
Due to occasions	19·19	1	19·19	5·33	0·05
Due to groups	57·97	2	28·98	8·05	0·01
Interactions					
Occasions × groups	3·89	2	1·94	0·97	ns.
Residual	50·45	14			

This table suggests that although there was a significant learning effect between the two blocks of sentences (significant 'occasions' effect) and between the groups divided according to treatment outcome (significant 'groups' effect) there was no difference between the groups in the rate at which they learned. That is, the overall level of 'she' sentence responding was higher in the group that responded well to treatment both in the first block of sentences and in the last block of sentences. The absence of a significant 'occasions × groups' interaction means that the extent of learning was not different across the groups. If this is the case, then Morgenstern et al.'s conclusion that their measure of learning in the verbal conditioning procedure was significantly related to treatment outcome is unjustified.

It seems at first sight odd that the level of producing 'she' sentences before any conditioning had occurred should differentiate the groups divided by treatment outcome. However, it was also found that these groups were differentiated by their scores on Slater's Masculinity–Femininity interest scale. These differences were in the direction of patients with successful outcome having the highest disproportion of feminine interest. It seems likely that this group of transvestites would thus be more likely to choose 'she' sentences in the verbal conditioning procedure than the groups with a lower disproportion of feminine interest.

In any event, the Morgenstern et al. study cannot be adduced as evidence in favour of aversion therapy being an operant procedure. Thus, neither of Feldman's main points seem to constitute a valid objection to the position advanced here, namely, that the crucial features in aversion therapy entail classical conditioning procedures.

Summary

A theoretical analysis of the processes involved in aversion therapy of sexual disorders is offered. The analysis stresses the importance of distinguishing learning and performance. It suggests that the occurrence of well-established behaviour patterns such as those which are presented for aversion therapy is determined largely by the factors of motivation and reinforcement, variations in habit strength being relatively unimportant.

Incentive motivation is identified as the important factor mediating the effects of variations in the quality of reinforcement on the occurrence of a habit. The processes of aversion therapy are examined in relation to Spence's equation: $E = H(D + K)$ where E is excitatory potential, H is habit strength, D is drive, and K is incentive motivation. It is suggested that aversion therapy is effective by virtue of its effects on K. Where aversion therapy is directed towards changing the K associated with external stimuli, the therapy procedure conforms to a classical conditioning paradigm; where it is directed towards changing the K associated with internal response-produced stimuli the therapy procedure fits a punishment paradigm.

It is suggested that there are two possible methods by which K can be altered:

1 By changing the nature of the primary reinforcement.

2 By directly attacking the incentive motivation conditioned to internal and external stimuli.

For enduring changes in behaviour, aversion therapy should employ both these methods.

In the case of sexual behaviour, incentive motivation seems to be the crucial factor in determining the occurrence of the behaviour, as drive, in the sense of a persistent need, seems relatively unimportant. It is suggested that sexual deviations originate by the classical conditioning of incentive motivation to inappropriate sexual stimuli, and to the response-produced stimuli associated with the sexually deviant behaviour. This incentive motivation can be eliminated by exploiting the reciprocally inhibitory relation which seems to exist between sexual arousal and anxiety. Aversion therapy for sexual deviations is thus effective by virtue of its conditioning anxiety (removing incentive motivation) to the deviant sexual stimuli (classical conditioning), and to the internal response-produced stimuli associated with the performance of the deviant behaviour (punishment).

Deductions are made from the theoretical analysis offered, and find some support in the results of Marks and Gelder's studies.

The position taken here stresses the importance of classical conditioning in aversion therapy. This contrasts with the views of Feldman and MacCulloch who stress the importance of operant factors. Evidence is presented in support of the classical hypothesis and against the operant hypothesis.

19

An analysis of aversion therapy for alcoholism

The analysis proposed in the case of aversion therapy for alcoholism is similar to that proposed for sexual deviations in the preceding chapter.

Again, our emphasis will be on factors modifying performance of a previously well-established habit, rather than on actual habit strength (H). We shall use Spence's equation: $E = H (D \times K)$ as the basis of our discussion.

The situation in the case of alcoholism differs in some respects from that obtaining in the sexual disorders. Firstly, the incentive motivation factor probably constitutes a smaller proportion of the total motivation driving the act of drinking alcohol than it does for sexually deviant behaviour. Either or both of the following components of the total motivation for the drinking response may be present in the absence of stimuli, either real or symbolic, associated with the drinking act: (1) anxiety, (2) a specific 'alcohol hunger' or craving in the physically dependent alcoholic, based on physiological deficit.

Neither of these can be considered as incentive motivations. Any total therapeutic approach to alcoholism should include techniques to reduce both of these drives. These techniques would not, however, be pure aversion therapy techniques. Techniques for the reduction of the anxiety drive could include relaxation training (e.g. Blake, 1965) and systematic desensitisation. The drive based on the physiological need for alcohol in the physically dependent alcoholic must be reduced or eliminated by subjecting the alcoholic to a withdrawal procedure, so that his physiology is no longer dependent for its adequate function on the presence of alcohol in the body. Having eliminated these two sources of motivation, we would regard the remaining components of the total motivation as incentive motivation, which might be susceptible to reduction by aversion therapy.

The existence of incentive motivation is more difficult to demonstrate in the case of alcoholism than in the case of sexual deviation. With sexually deviant stimuli, an excellent indicator of the physiological arousal (incentive motivation) which they provoke is available in the phalloplethysmograph. With alcoholic stimuli, no such indicator is available, and we have to rely for evidence of incentive motivation on anecdotal evidence such as the following from an alcoholic:

What annoys me is that I can last for as long as ten months, but then it all starts up again. First I have an urge to start for two or three days, set off by fortuitous happenings, a drink advertisement which catches my eye or a brewery wagon passing. Then I succumb (*Kessel and Walton, 1965*).

The importance of incentive motivation in triggering a bout of drinking, and as a potent factor in leading to relapse following treatment, seems obvious from quotations such as these. It is interesting to note that Mowrer (1960), after a discussion of incentive motivation-type phenomena, uses the case of alcoholism as an illustrative example:

Take the question of why human beings drink alcoholic beverages, i.e. why they engage in responses which lead to their becoming intoxicated (in whatever degree). The present analysis suggests that when an individual drinks he does so, not just because he is tense, anxious, depressed, but because when he *merely thinks* of drinking, his tensions drop somewhat – and come right back up again when he thinks of *not* drinking! It is, we hold, this *token* relief of tension that 'drives' the individual to drink – and to do all the other things he 'habitually' does. It seems most unlikely that a person would 'habitually' drink if each time he *thought* of it he got *more* tense. In fact, one well-known method of treating alcoholism consists of deliberately conditioning a specific drive (nausea) to the stimuli associated with alcohol consumption (*p. 270*).

In line with Mowrer's emphasis on the secondary reinforcing aspects of incentive motivation, the above passage concentrates on the drive reduction properties of stimuli associated with the performance of the consummatory response. It fits in very well, however, with the general position we are advancing, namely that the incentive qualities of stimuli, often symbolic, associated with the reinforced act, are of crucial importance in determining the occurrence or non-occurrence of that act.

Accepting then, that attempts to reduce K by aversion therapy procedures should be a valuable approach to the treatment of alcoholism, we recall that there are two points of attack, either or both of which we can use to reduce K:

1 Changing the quality of the primary reinforcement, which would then lead to a change in conditioned incentive motivation.
2 Changing the quality of the conditioned incentive motivation.

Now there seems to be a difference between sexually deviant behaviour and alcoholic behaviour in the extent to which we can implement the first of these approaches. Theoretically, in the case of sexual behaviour, we can condition intense anxiety to the situation in which the sexual behaviour is performed and thereby disrupt the performance of this behaviour. Hence, the primary reinforcement of the sexual behaviour is eliminated. In alcoholism, however, the alcohol can have two reinforcing effects at the physiological level:

1 Correction of a physiological need for alcohol in patients who have reached the stage of physical dependence.
2 Reduction of anxiety.

The first of these we cannot alter, unless we could condition a response which reliably evacuated alcohol from the stomach before it was absorbed, e.g. vomiting. The results of chemical aversion therapy for alcoholism suggest that while such therapy may lead to a conditioned nausea response to drinking alcohol, a conditioned vomiting reaction only occurs in a tiny minority of treated cases.

In connection with the second point, it should be pointed out that the effects of drugs on mood, while based on a physiological change, are not inevitable, automatic, consequences of ingestion of the drug but depend to a large extent on psychological factors such as the setting in which the drug is taken and the 'set' of the subject (Blum, 1965; Lindemann and Clarke, 1952).

However, with respect to both these physiological effects of alcohol, it should be remembered that reinforcement at the physiological level for the response of drinking alcohol can only occur after an appreciable delay, for absorption, circulation, etc., of the alcohol, following the response. The immediate reinforcement attendant on the presence of alcohol in the mouth must be of a secondary nature. By having the patient experience nausea and vomiting, or intense anxiety, as he drinks, we can change the immediate reinforcement of the drinking behaviour from positive to negative. In this way, even if the response is followed by a delayed positive reinforcement at the physiological level, the overall reinforcement of the drinking behaviour can be negative; few patients, if any, report enjoyment of the overall experience of chemical aversion therapy for alcoholism.

It thus seems feasible to regard aversion therapy in the light of our ideas on the importance of incentive motivation, and base aversion therapy procedures on an analysis similar to that for sexual disorders. These techniques should include a means for changing the quality of primary reinforcement for drinking alcohol from positive to negative, and of changing the incentive motivation conditioned to stimuli (including symbolic stimuli) associated with the drinking response from positive to negative.

When we examine the procedures and results of chemical aversion therapy for alcoholism, we see that the aims of this procedure seem highly similar to the approach we have outlined. Thus, there was the intention to change the quality of primary reinforcement for drinking behaviour from positive to negative by conditioning nausea and vomiting to the act of drinking. Further, there was often an intention to condition a vomiting and nausea response to the sight, taste, smell and thought of alcoholic beverages (Voegtlin and Lemere, 1942). The results reported in Chapter 3 show that in a proportion of patients treated, this aim was realised. This would have the effect of changing the incentive qualities of these stimuli, leading to a reduction in the frequency of drinking behaviour, which was observed in a proportion of patients.

Thus, in conditioned nausea and vomiting we have available an antagonist to oppose the incentive qualities conditioned to the stimuli associated with drinking alcohol, including those internal stimuli produced by the actual drinking behaviour. It seems intuitively apt that nausea and the pleasure anticipated from drinking should be antagonistic. However, as has been pointed out in Chapter 5, there are certain disadvantages inherent in the use of chemical methods of aversion therapy. This has led to the substitution of unconditioned responses other than nausea as the basis for the aversion procedure. Imaginal aversive events, such as imagined nausea, have been employed instead of chemically induced nausea and seem promising. To date, however, the main alternative to the use of chemical methods in the treatment of alcoholism seems to have been electric shock (Chapter 8).

As has been suggested earlier (pp. 86 ff.), procedures employing electric shock can be profitably thought of in terms of the punishment paradigm. We have also adopted Mowrer's view that punishment consists of the classical conditioning of anxiety to the internal response-produced stimuli characteristic of the punished behaviour. In terms of incentive motivation, punishment leads to a change from positive to negative in the incentive qualities conditioned to the response-produced stimuli associated with a previously positively reinforced response. In Mowrer's terms, this change would be from 'hope' to 'fear'.

In terms of our analysis, punishment and classical conditioning of an aversive CR to an external stimulus differ only in that the former involves internal response-produced stimuli, the latter external stimuli.

Our aversion therapy procedure must attempt to change the incentive qualities of both types of stimuli associated with the undesirable behaviour. The experiment by Lichtenstein and our proposed explanation of MacCulloch *et al.*'s failure in their treatment of alcoholism seem to suggest that changing the incentive qualities of external stimuli associated with eating or drinking behaviour is insufficient to suppress that behaviour. It seems particularly important to condition 'anxiety' to both external and *internal* stimuli associated with such behaviour. The reason for this may be that conditioned responses to internal stimuli are more persistent to extinction than those to external stimuli (p. 147).

We predict that electrical aversion therapy would change the quality of the incentive-motivation conditioned to both internal and external stimuli associated with drinking. This would occur by the conditioning of anxiety to these stimuli. Unfortunately, no data comparable to Marks and Gelder's measurements on changes in phalloplethysmograph responses during treatment of sexual disorders are available in the case of treatment of alcoholism. It is thus impossible directly to support the hypothesis proposed. However, the evidence that is available (mainly clinical anecdotal in nature) seems to support the hypothesis, e.g. MacGuire and Vallance (1964) report that one of their patients experienced a panic attack on going into a pub and ordering a whisky after treatment.

If, as Mowrer suggests, the incentive value of stimuli associated with drinking consists of their anxiety-reducing qualities, then it is obvious that we can oppose these qualities by conditioning anxiety to them. A problem does arise, however, when we remember that we have assumed that part of the motivation for the drinking response is anxiety. If we are conditioning anxiety to the stimuli associated with drinking, why do we not get a positive feedback vicious circle as below?

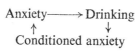

The success of Blake's (1965) electrical method of treating alcoholism by what is essentially a punishment procedure using faradic shock, shows that this situation does not occur. An answer to this problem can be found in Mowrer's revised theory of habit (1960). This theory eliminates the concept of 'habit strength' as a connection between stimulus and response. In the revised theory, drive will only motivate responses which produce internal stimuli which have conditioned to them drive-reduction properties for that drive. After a punishment procedure, the internal stimuli associated with the punished drinking response will have anxiety-increasing rather than anxiety-reducing properties conditioned to them. So this response will not be brought into action by increases in anxiety and the vicious circle will not revolve.

Support for our theory in the case of alcoholism is weaker than it is in the case of the sexual deviations, owing to the dearth of experimental data on what actually occurs during and after the course of treatment. It is hoped this situation will soon be rectified.

The theoretical analysis we have offered here is incomplete and inadequate in many ways. We have found it useful in conceptualising what occurs during aversion therapy, and in making testable predictions, and hope that it will serve this function for others.

Summary

The type of theoretical analysis developed in Chapter 16 is applied to the case of aversion therapy for alcoholism.

In the case of alcoholism, support for the hypotheses presented is less strong than in the sexual deviations, owing to the lack of evidence on the actual changes resulting from aversion therapy with alcoholics. Incentive motivation conditioned to visual stimuli seems less important in alcoholism than in the sexual deviations. Aversion therapy procedures for the treatment of alcoholism should thus include attempts to change the incentive motivation conditioned to a variety of modalities of external stimuli (e.g. taste, smell) and also that conditioned to internal stimuli associated with the response of drinking alcohol (punishment).

A further difference from the case of the sexual deviations is that, in alcoholism, drive, D, for the performance of the drinking response may be present at an appreciable level, in the form of anxiety, or physiological need for alcohol. Aversion therapy procedures for alcoholism should include techniques for the reduction of these drives.

In the case of alcoholism, there does not exist any technique for changing incentive motivation which is as well validated as the reciprocally inhibitory relation between sexual arousal and anxiety in the case of the sexual deviations. Intuitively, conditioned nausea would seem a suitable means for reducing the positive incentive motivation associated with drinking alcohol. The moderately successful results of chemical aversion therapy, and the encouraging results from the covert sensitisation treatment of alcoholism, support this suggestion. There are certain theoretical problems associated with the use of faradic shock to condition anxiety, as a means of reducing positive incentive motivation for drinking alcohol. However, the success of punishment procedures using electrical stimuli seems to confirm the usefulness of this technique.

It is suggested that the analysis offered is useful in aiding conceptualisation of the processes of aversion therapy, and in generating testable predictions.

M

20
Conclusion

The establishment and recognition of Behaviour Therapy is a recent event, and it is only within the past few years that clear lines of development have emerged. Of the numerous therapeutic possibilities which have been considered, only three have achieved satisfactory support to date: aversion therapy, desensitisation, operant (re)training.

Broadly speaking, aversion therapy and desensitisation can be used in the treatment of surplus disorders, and operant methods have been found to be particularly useful with deficit disorders (Eysenck and Rachman, 1965). The most *common* clinical uses of these three predominant methods are illustrated in Table 2.

Table 2 Common clinical uses of behavioural treatments

Treatment	*Areas where used*
Desensitisation	Neurotic disorders featuring anxiety (especially phobic states)
Aversion therapy	Sexual disorders (especially electrical aversion) Alcoholism (especially chemical aversion)
Operant training	Speech deficits, encopresis, deficient social relationships, mild conduct disorders

Both aversion therapy and desensitisation are techniques for reducing or eliminating unwanted, undesirable or unacceptable behaviour. Desensitisation is primarily designed to reduce anxiety and, for practical and theoretical reasons, is currently the treatment of first choice. If, however, the disorder is not characterised by anxiety then one can consider the use of a suppressive technique such as aversion therapy.

As we have attempted to demonstrate, the simplest practical guide is to use a punishment training paradigm. The aversive stimulus should be administered contingent on the occurrence of the deviant behaviour. Although this simple formulation has theoretical and practical limitations, it does provide a useful way of assessing, designing and conducting aversion therapy.

Where it is not possible directly to administer response-contingent aversion, the noxious stimulus can be made contingent on imaginal rehearsals and/or physiological arousal. In regard to the choice of an aversive stimulus, there are many reasons for selecting electrical stimulation, but in certain disorders chemical means may be preferred. An alternative possibility which is now being investigated involves the use of imaginal aversive stimulation. If successful, the substitution of covert (imaginal) sensitisation would be a highly desirable advance.

The punishment training paradigm has some theoretical limitations and a deeper analysis of aversion therapy is required. This analysis is facilitated by adopting Mowrer's view that punishment training necessarily implies the classical conditioning of autonomic responses. A classical conditioning model has wider explanatory value than that of punishment, and it also reveals large patches of ignorance. Apart from other investigations, it is essential to gather more and better information about the physiological changes which take place during aversion therapy. The role of cognitive factors also requires detailed study. It is suggested that a key question in the whole field of aversion therapy is why successfully treated patients refrain from carrying out their deviant activities outside the hospital.

In general, punishment training produces the following sequential changes: temporary suppression, partial suppression and, finally, total suppression. The commonest exceptions to this sequence are observed 'if punishment reinstates a condition of original training, or if it elicits a response which is similar to the act which is being punished' (Church, 1963). In these instances response *facilitation* may occur.

In relation to aversion therapy, the most important parameters involved in punishment training are: intensity of the aversive stimulus, frequency of administration, immediacy of delivery, manner of introduction, distributed practice, provision of alternative responses, response-contingent delivery of aversive stimulus. Other things being equal, the most successful type of aversion therapy (based on punishment training) would be conducted in this way.

Throughout treatment, a strong aversive stimulus should be delivered immediately the deviant response occurs. This procedure should be repeated frequently but under conditions of spaced practice and an alternative response to the eliciting stimulus conditions should be provided, if this is possible.

Aversion therapy should only be offered if other treatment methods are inapplicable or unsuccessful *and* if the patient gives his permission after a consideration of all the information which his therapist can honestly supply.

Finally, the substitution of effective, but less unpleasant, alternative methods of treatment should be carried out as soon as this becomes feasible.

References and author index

ANANT, S. (1967) 'A note on the treatment of alcoholics by a verbal aversion technique', *Canadian Psychologist*, 80, 19–22, *101*

ASHEM, B. and DONNER, L. (1968) 'Covert sensitization with alcoholics: A controlled replication', *Behav. Res. Ther.*, 6, 7–12, *31, 102–4*

AYLLON, T. (1963) 'Intensive treatment of psychotic behaviour by stimulus satiation and food-reinforcement', *Behav. Res. Ther.*, 1, 53–61, *6, 12*

AYLLON, T. and HAUGHTON, E. (1962), 'Control of the behaviour of schizophrenic patients by food', *J. Exp. Anal. Behav.*, 5, 343–52, *6*

AZRIN, N. H. (1956) 'Effects of two intermittent schedules of immediate and non-immediate punishment', *J. Psychol.* 42, 3–21, *123, 129*

AZRIN, N. H. (1958) 'Some effects of noise on human behaviour', *J. Exp. Anal. Behav.*, 1, 183–200, *8*

AZRIN, N. H. (1960) 'Effect of punishment intensity during variable-interval reinforcement', *J. Exp. Anal. Behav.*, 3, 123–42, *122, 124*

AZRIN, N. H. and HOLZ, W. C. (1966) 'Punishment', in W. K. Honig (ed.): *Operant Behaviour*. New York: Appleton-Century-Crofts, *8, 34, 37, 49, 52, 54, 55, 58, 86–7, 91, 118, 120–7, 131*

AZRIN, N. H., HOLZ, W. C. and HAKE, D. F. (1963) 'Fixed-ratio punishment', *J. Exp. Anal. Behav.*, 6, 141–8, *124*

AZRIN, N. H., HUTCHINSON, R. and SALLERY, R. (1964) 'Pain-aggression toward inanimate objects', *J. Exp. Anal. Behav.*, 7, 3, 227–33, *93*

BANCROFT, J. (1966) *Aversion Therapy*, D. P. M. Dissert, University of London, *34, 56–60, 62, 63, 70, 78, 79, 86, 90, 99*

BANCROFT, J. (1968) *Personal communication, 16, 96*

BANCROFT, J., GWYNNE JONES, H. and PULLAN, B. (1966) 'A simple transducer for measuring penile erection, with comments on its use in the treatment of sexual disorders', *Behav. Res. Ther.*, 4, 234–41, *28, 44, 79, 80*

BARRETT, B. (1964) 'Reduction in rate of multiple tics by free operant conditioning methods', in *Experiments in Behaviour Therapy* (ed. H. Eysenck), Pergamon Press, *8*

BEABRUN, M. H. (1967) 'Treatment of alcoholism in Trinidad and Tobago', 1956–65. *Brit. J. Psychiatry*, 113, 643–58, *20*

BEACH, F. A. (1956) 'Characteristics of masculine "sex drive"', in Jones, M. R. (ed.): *Nebraska Symposium on Motivation*. Lincoln: University of Nebraska Press, *157*

BEECH, R. H. (1960) 'The symptomatic treatment of writer's cramp', in *Behaviour Therapy and the Neuroses* (ed. Eysenck, H.), Pergamon Press, *90*

BEECH, R. H. (1963) 'Some theoretical and technical difficulties in the application of behaviour therapy', *Bulletin of the British Psychological Society*, 16, 25–33, *90*

BLACK, A. H. (1965) 'Cardiac conditioning in curarised dogs: the relationship between heart rate and skeletal behaviour', in W. F. Prokasy (ed.): *Classical Conditioning: A Symposium*. New York: Appleton-Century-Crofts, *134, 137*

BLAKE, B. G. (1965) 'The application of behaviour therapy to the treatment of alcoholism'. *Behav. Res. Ther.*, 3, 75–85, *3, 12, 72, 76, 124, 165, 169*

BLAKE, B. G. (1967), 'A follow-up of alcoholics treated by behaviour therapy'. *Behav. Res. Ther.*, 5, 89–94, *73–4, 76*

BLAKEMORE, C. B. (1964) 'The application of behaviour therapy to a sexual disorder', in *Experiments in Behaviour Therapy* (ed. H. J. Eysenck). Pergamon Press, *40, 41, 74, 80, 82, 83*

BLAKEMORE, C. B. (1967) *Personal communication, 82*

BLAKEMORE, C. B. *et al.* (1963) Follow-up note. *Behav. Res. Ther.*, 1, 191, *3, 40, 41, 124*

BLUM, R. *et al.* (1965) *Utopiates: the use and users of LSD-25*, Tavistock, *167*

BRANCA, A. (1957) 'Semantic generalisation at the level of conditioning', *Amer. J. Psychol.*, 70, 541–9, *112*

BREGER, L. and MCGAUGH, J. (1965) 'Critique and re-formulation of "learning theory" approaches to psychotherapy and neuroses', *Psychol. Bull.*, 63, 338–58, *4*

BREGER, L. and MCGAUGH, J. (1966) 'Learning Theory and Behavior Therapy: Reply to Rachman and Eysenck', *Psychol. Bull.*, 65, 170–5, *4*

BRETHOWER, D. M. and REYNOLDS, G. S. (1962) 'A facilitative effect of punishment on unpunished behaviour', *J. Exp. Anal. Behav.*, 5, 191–9, *129*

BRIDGER, W. and MANDEL, I. (1964) 'A comparison of, GSR fear responses produced by threat and electric shock', *J. Psychiat. Res.* 2, 31–40, *74, 109, 145*

BRIDGER, W. and MANDEL, I. (1965) 'Abolition of the PRE by instructions in GSR conditioning', *J. exp. Psychol.*, 69, 476–82, *113, 114*

BURCHARD, J. and TYLER, V. (1965) 'The modification of delinquent behaviour through operant conditioning', *Behav. Res. Ther.*, 2, 245–50, *9, 12*

CASTELL, D. (1967) Symposium at British Psychological Society Meeting at Belfast, *8*.

CAUTELA, J. (1966) 'Treatment of compulsive behavior by covert sensitization', *Psychol. Record*, 16, 33–42, *100, 101*

CAUTELA, J. (1967) 'Covert sensitization', *Psychol. Rep.* 20, 459–68, *101*

CHATTERJEE, B. and ERIKSEN, C. (1962) 'Cognitive factors in heart rate conditioning', *J. exp. Psychol.*, 64, 272–9, *112, 114*

CHURCH, R. (1963) 'The varied effects of punishment', *Psychol. Rev.*, 70, 369–402, *34, 59, 80, 91, 120–3, 173*

CHURCH, R. M., RAYMOND, G. A. and BEAUCHAMP, R. (1967) 'Response suppression as a function of intensity and duration of a punishment', *J. Comp. Physiol. Psychol.*, 39–44, *122*

CLANCY, J., VANDERHOFF, E., and CAMPBELL, D. (1966) 'Evaluation of an aversive technique as a treatment for alcoholism', *Quart. J. Stud. Alcohol*, 27, 739, *10*

COOK, S. W. and HARRIS, P. E. (1937) 'The verbal conditioning of the GSR', *J. Exp. Psychol.*, 21, 202–10, *109, 112*

CRESPI, L. P. (1942) 'Quantitative variation of incentive and performance in the white rat', *Amer. J. Psychol.*, 55, 467–517, *153–5*

DAVISON, G. (1968) 'The elimination of a sadistic fantasy by a client-controlled counterconditioning technique', *J. Abnormal Psychol.*, (in press) *98*

DINSMOOR, J. A. (1952) 'A discrimination based on punishment', *Quart. J. Exp. Psychol.*, 4, 27–45, *124, 129*

DINSMOOR, J. (1954) 'Punishment I', *Psychol. Rev.*, 61, 34–46, *86*

DINSMOOR, J. (1955) 'Punishment II', *Psychol. Rev.*, 62, 96–105, *86*

ESTES, W. K. (1944) 'An experimental study of punishment', *Psychological Monographs*, 47, Whole No. 263, *53, 119, 122*

EVANS, D. R. (1968) 'Masturbatory fantasy and sexual deviations', *Behav. Res. Ther.*, 6, 17–20, *46, 65, 69, 80*

EYSENCK, H. J. (1960) 'Summary and conclusions', in *Behaviour Therapy and the Neuroses* (ed. Eysenck, H. J.). Pergamon Press, *3, 72, 91*

EYSENCK, H. J. (1964) *Crime and Personality*, Routledge and Kegan Paul. Boston: Houghton Mifflin, *128*

EYSENCK, H. J. (1967) *The Biological Basis of Personality*, Springfield, Thomas, *35, 91*

EYSENCK, H. J. (1967) 'Single-trial conditioning, neurosis and the Napalkov phenomenon', *Behav. Res. Ther.*, 5, 63–5, *149–50*

EYSENCK, H. J. (1968) 'A theory of the incubation of anxiety/fear responses', *Behav. Res. Ther.*, 6, 309–22, *149–50*

EYSENCK, H. J. and RACHMAN, S. (1965) *The Causes and Cures of Neurosis*, Routledge and Kegan Paul, *xii, xiii, 1, 3, 34, 40, 70, 91, 92, 144, 172*

FARRAR, C., POWELL, B. and MARTIN, L. (1968) 'Punishment of alcohol consumption by apneic paralysis', *Behav. Res. Ther.*, 6, 13–16, *10*

FELDMAN, M. P. (1963) 'A reconsideration of the extinction hypothesis of warm-up in motor behaviour', *Psychol. Bull.*, 60, 452–9, *140*

FELDMAN, M. P. (1966) 'Aversion therapy for sexual deviations: A critical review', *Psychol. Bull*, 65, 65–79, *xii, 79, 87, 135, 160–1*

FELDMAN, M. P., and MACCULLOCH, M. J. (1965) 'The application of anticipatory avoidance learning to the treatment of homosexuality. I. Theory, technique and preliminary results', *Behav. Res. and Ther.*, 2, 165–83, *3, 7, 34, 63–6, 87, 134–41*

FELDMAN, M. P., and MACCULLOCH, M. J. (1967, 1968) *Personal communication*, *66, 80, 91, 139*

FELDMAN, M. P., *et al.* (1966) 'The application of anticipatory avoidance learning to the treatment of homosexuality. III', *Behav. Res. Ther.*, 4, 289–99, *63*

FERSTER, C. B. (1958) 'Reinforcement and punishment in the control of human behavior by social agencies', *Psychiat. Res. Rep.*, 10, 101–18, *9.*

FESTINGER, L. (1957) *A theory of cognitive dissonance.* Evanston, Illinois: Row, Peterson, *53*

FLANAGAN, B., GOLDIAMOND, I. and AZRIN, N. (1958) 'Operant stuttering', *J. exp. Anal. Behav.*, 1, 173–7, *8*

FORD, C. S. and BEACH, F. A. (1952) *Patterns of Sexual Behaviour*, Eyre and Spottiswoode, *158*

FRANKS, C. (1960) 'Alcohol, alcoholism and conditioning'. Reprinted in Eysenck, H. J. (ed.) *Behaviour Therapy and the Neuroses*, Pergamon Press, *19, 22, 32*

FRANKS, C. M. (1963) 'Behaviour Therapy, the principles of conditioning and the treatment of the alcoholic', *Quarterly Journal of Studies on Alcohol*, 24, 511–29, *1, 2, 3, 32*

FRANKS, C. M. (1966) 'Conditioning and Conditioned Aversion Therapies in the Treatment of the Alcoholic', *The International Journal of the Addictions*, 1, 61–98, *1, 3, 19*

FRANKS, C., FRIED, R. and ASHEM, B. (1966) 'An improved apparatus for the aversive conditioning of smokers', *Behav. Res. Ther.*, 4, 301–8, *12*

FREUND, K. (1960) *Die Homosexualitat beim Mann*, Birzel Verlag, Leipzig, *26, 63, 79*

FREUND, K. (1963) 'A laboratory method for diagnosing predominance of homo- or hetero-erotic interest in the male', *Behav. Res. Ther.*, 1, 85–93, *44, 79*

FREUND, K. (1965) 'Diagnosing heterosexual paedophilia by means of a test of sexual interest', *Behav. Res. Ther.*, 3, 229–34, *27*

GALE, D., STRUMFELS, G. and GALE, E. (1966) 'A comparison of reciprocal inhibition and experimental extinction in the psychotherapeutic process', *Behav. Res. Ther.*, 4, 149–57, *76*

GANTT, W. H. (1949) 'Psychosexuality in animals', *Psychosexual Development in Health and Disease*. New York: Grune and Stratton, *126, 137, 159*

GANTT, W. H. (1964) 'Autonomic conditioning', in Wolpe, J., Salter, A., Reyna, L. J. (eds.): *The Conditioning Therapies*. New York: Holt, Rinehart, and Winston, *108, 138*

GELDER, M. and MARKS, I. (1968) 'Aversion treatment in transvestism and transsexualism', in *Transsexualism and Sex Re-Assignment* (ed. Green, R.). Baltimore: Johns Hopkins Univ. Press, *54, 78*

GLYNN, J. and HARPER, P. (1961) 'Behaviour therapy in transvestism', *Lancet*, 1, 619, *25, 83*

GOLD, S. and NEUFELD, I. (1965) 'A learning theory approach to the treatment of homosexuality', *Behav. Res. Ther.* 2, 201–4, *97*

GONCHAROVA (1955) cited by Razran (1961), *146*

GRANT, D. (1964) 'Classical and operant conditioning', in *Categories of Human Learning* (ed. A. Melton). Academic Press, New York, *2*.

GRINGS, W. (1965) 'Verbal-perceptual factors in the conditioning of autonomic responses', in *Classical Conditioning* (ed. W. Prokasy). Appleton: New York, *109, 118, 149*

GRINGS, W. and LOCKHART, R. (1963) 'Effects of "anxiety-lessening" instructions and differential set development on the extinction of GSR', *J. exp. Psychol.*, 66, 292–9, *114*

HAKE, D. F. and AZRIN, N. H. (1963) 'An apparatus for delivering pain-shock to monkeys', *J. exp. Anal. Behav.*, 6, 297–8, *122*

HAMMERSLEY, D. W. (1957) 'Conditioned Reflex Therapy', in Wallerstein, R. S. (ed.) *Hospital treatment of Alcoholism*, Menninger Clinic Monographs, 11, *18, 19, 20, 21, 22, 83, 84, 115, 144*

HEARST, E. (1965) 'Stress-induced breakdown of an appetitive discrimination', *J. exp. Anal. Behav.*, 8, 135–46, *31*

HERMAN, R. C. and AZRIN, N. H. (1964) 'Punishment by noise in an alternative response situation', *J. exp. Anal. Behav.*, 7, 185–8, *127*

HESS, E. H., SELTZER, A. and SHLIEN, J. (1965) 'Pupil response of hetero- and homosexual males to pictures of men and women', *J. Abnormal Psychol.*, 70, 165–8, *79*

HILGARD, E. R. (1956) *Theories of Learning*, Second Edition. New York: Appleton-Century-Crofts, *155*

HODGES, W. and SPIELBERGER, C. (1966) 'The effects of threat of shock on heart rate', *Psychophysiology*, 2, 287–94, *109*, *110*

HOFFMAN, H. (1966) 'The analysis of discriminated avoidance', in *Operant Behavior* (ed. Honig, W.). New York: Appleton-Century-Crofts, *50*

HOLZINGER, R., MORTIMER, P. and VAN DUSEN, W. (1967) 'Aversion conditioning treatment of alcoholism', *Amer. J. Psychiat.*, 124, 150–1, *10*

HSU, J. (1965) 'Electroconditioning therapy of alcoholics: a preliminary report', *Quart. J. Stud. Alcohol*, 26, 449–59, *75*

HUNT, H. F. and BRADY, J. V. (1955) 'Some effects of punishment and inter-current anxiety on a simple operant', *J. comp. Physiol. Psychol.*, 48, 305–10, *123*, *129*

HUNTER, R. and MACALPINE, I. (1963) *Three Hundred Years of Psychiatry 1535–1860*, Oxford University Press, *5*, *8*

JONES, H. G. (1960) 'The behavioural treatment of nocturnal enuresis', in *Behaviour Therapy and the Neuroses* (ed. H. J. Eysenck). Pergamon Press, *36*

KANTOROVICH, N. (1935) 'An attempt at association reflex therapy in alcoholism', *Psychol. Abstracts*, 4, 493, *2*, *14*

KESSEL, N. and WALTON, H. (1965) *Alcoholism*, Penguin Books Ltd., *124*, *166*

KIMBLE, G. (1964) *Conditioning and Learning*, Methuen, *118*, *130*, *151*

KIMMEL, H. D. (1965) 'Instrumental inhibitory factors in classical conditioning', in *Classical Conditioning* (ed. Prokasy, W.). New York: Appleton Crofts, *68*

KNIGHT, R. (1941) 'Evaluation of the results of psychoanalytic therapy', *Amer. J. Psychiatry*, 98, 434–44, *73*

KOLVIN, I. (1967) 'Aversive imagery treatment in adolescents', *Behav. Res. Ther.*, 5, 245–8, *99*, *105*

KUSHNER, M. (1965) 'The reduction of a long-standing fetish by means of aversive conditioning', in *Case Studies in Behavior Modification* (ed. Ullman, L. and Krasner, L.). New York: Holt, Rinehart and Winston, *60*, *80*, *82*

KUSHNER, M. and SANDLER, J. (1966) 'Aversion Therapy and the concept of Punishment', *Behav. Res. and Ther.*, 4, 179–86, *61*, *119*, *129*

LANG, P. J. and HNATIOW, M. (1965) 'Learned stabilisation of cardiac rate', *Psychophysiology*, 1, 330–6, *115*

LAVIN, N. *et al.* (1961) 'Behaviour therapy in a case of transvestism', *J. Nerv. Ment. Dis.*, 133, 346–53, *25*, *92*

LEITENBERG, H. (1965) 'Is time-out an aversive event?', *Psychol. Bull.*, 64, 428–41, *9*

LEMERE, F. and VOEGTLIN, W. (1950) 'An evaluation of the aversion treatment of alcoholism', *Quart. J. Stud. Alcohol*, 11, 199–204, *15*, *17*

LIBERMAN, R. (1968) 'Aversive conditioning of drug addicts: A pilot study', *Behav. Res. Ther.*, 6, 229–32, *12*, *28*, *84*

LIBERMAN, R. (1968) 'A view of behavior modification projects in California', *Behav. Res. Ther.*, 6, 331–42, *1*

LICHTENSTEIN, F. E. (1950) 'Studies of anxiety: I. The production of a feeding inhibition in dogs', *J. comp. Physiol. Psychol.*, 43, 16–29, *76, 77, 129, 169*

LINDEMANN, E. and CLARKE, L. D. (1952) 'Modification in ego structure and personality reactions under the influence of the effects of drugs', *Am. J. Psychiat.*, 108, 561, *167*

LOTIS (1949) cited by RAZRAN (1961), *146*

LOVAAS, I. (1966) Lecture given at Maudsley Hospital, *9*

LOVIBOND, S. (1963) 'Intermittent reinforcement in behaviour therapy', *Behav. Res. Ther.*, 1, 127–32, *36*

LYNN, R. and EYSENCK, H. J. (1961) 'Tolerance for pain, extraversion and neuroticism', *Percept. Mot. Skills*, 12, 161–2, *35*

MACCULLOCH, M. J. and FELDMAN, M. P. (1967) 'Personality and the treatment of homosexuality', *Acta Psychiatrica Scand.*, 43, 300–17, *127*

MACCULLOCH, M. J., FELDMAN, M. P., ORFORD, J. and MACCULLOCH, M. L. (1966) 'Anticipatory Avoidance Learning in the Treatment of Alcoholism. A record of therapeutic failure', *Behav. Res. Ther.*, 4, 187–96, *22, 49, 74, 135, 138, 139, 169*

MACCULLOCH, M. J., FELDMAN, M. P., and PINSCHOF, J. M. (1965) 'The application of anticipatory avoidance learning to the treatment of homosexuality. II. Avoidance response latencies and pulse rate changes', *Behav. Res. and Therapy*, 3, 21–44, *65–9, 78, 135, 137*

MADILL, M. F., CAMPBELL, D., LAVERTY, S., SANDERSON, K. and VANDERWATER, S. (1966) 'Aversion treatment of alcoholics by succinylcholine-induced apneic paralysis', *Quart. J. Stud. Alcohol*, 27, 483–509, *9*

MARKS, I. and GELDER, M. (1967) 'Transvestism and fetishism: Clinical, and psychological changes during faradic aversion', *Brit. J. Psychiat.*, 119, 711–30, *3, 44–55, 79, 80, 81, 87, 132, 148*

MARKS, I., RACHMAN, S. and GELDER, M. (1966) 'Methods for assessment of aversion therapy in fetishism with masochism', *Behav. Res. Ther.*, 3, 253–8, *53, 83*

MARKS, I. and SARTORIUS, N. (1968) 'A contribution to the measurement of sexual meaning', *J. Nerv. Ment. Dis.*, 145, 441–51, *78, 81, 82*

MARTIN, B. (1963) 'Reward and punishment associated with the same goal response: a factor in the learning of motives', *Psychol. Bull.*, 60, 441–51

MASSERMAN, J. M. (1943) *Behavior and Neurosis.* Chicago: Univ. of Chicago Press, *76, 124*

MASTERS, W. and JOHNSON, V. (1966) *Human Sexual Response,* Churchill, *159*

MAX, L. (1935) 'Breaking up a homosexual fixation by the conditioned reaction technique', *Psychol. Bull.*, 32, 734, *2, 39, 82*

MCCLELLAND, D. C. and MCGOWN, D. R. (1953) 'The effect of variable food reinforcement on the strength of a secondary reward', *J. comp. Physiol. Psychol.*, 46, 80–6, *140*

MCGUIRE, R. and VALLANCE, M. (1964) 'Aversion therapy by electric shock: A simple technique', *Brit. Med. J.*, 1, 151–2, *3, 36, 42, 43, 82, 83, 169*

MCGUIRE, R. J., CARLISLE, J. M., and YOUNG, B. G. (1965) 'Sexual deviations as conditioned behaviour: A hypothesis', *Behaviour Res. and Ther.*, 2, 185–90, *46, 69, 99, 158*

METZNER, R. (1963) 'Re-evaluation of Wolpe and Dollard/Miller', *Behav. Res. Ther.*, 1, 213–16, *72*

MEYER, V. and CRISP, A. (1964) 'Aversion therapy in two cases of obesity', *Behav. Res. Ther.*, 2, 143–7, *77*

MILLER, E., DVORAK, B. and TURNER, D. (1964) 'A method of creating aversion to alcohol by reflex conditioning in a group setting', in *Conditioning Techniques in Clinical Practice and Research* (ed. C. M. Franks). New York: Springer, *3*

MILLER, N. E. (1967) 'Psychosomatic effects of specific types of training'. Paper at Conference of N.Y. Acad. Sciences, *119*

MILLER, N. and BANUAZIZEA (1968) 'Instrumental learning by curarized rats of a specific visceral response, intestinal or cardiac', *J. comp. Physiol. Psychol* (in press), *119*

MORGENSTERN, F., PEARCE, J. and DAVIES, B. (1963) 'The application of aversion therapy to transvestism. Paper read at Reading Conf. of Brit. Psychol. Soc., *26, 33, 92*

MORGENSTERN, F., PEARCE, J. and LINFORD REES, W. (1965) 'Predicting the outcome of behaviour therapy by psychological tests', *Behav. Res. Ther.*, 2, 191–200, *25, 26, 161–2*

MOWRER, O. H. (1938) 'Preparatory set (expectancy) – a determinant in motivation and learning', *Psychol. Rev.*, 45, 62–91, *109*,

MOWRER, O. H. (1960) *Learning theory and behaviour.* New York: Wiley, *134, 143, 149, 157, 158, 160, 166, 169*

NOTTERMAN, J., SCHOENFELD, W. and BERSH, P. (1952) 'Conditioned heart rate responses in human beings during experimental anxiety', *J. comp. Physiol. Psychol.*, 45, 1–8, *114*

PAVLOV, I. P. (1927) *Conditioned Reflexes* (trans. G. Anrep), Oxford University Press, *1, 67, 106*

POSER, E. (1960) 'Der Figurale After-effect als Personlichkeitsmerkmal', XVth Congress Exp. Psychol., Bonn, *35*

QUINN, J. and HENBEST, R. (1967) 'Partial failure of generalisation in alcoholism following aversion therapy', *Quart. J. Stud. Alcohol.*, 28, 70–75, *22, 49*

RACHMAN, S. (1961) 'Sexual disorders and behavior therapy', *Amer. J. Psychiatry*, 118, 235–40, *3, 39, 54*

RACHMAN, S. (1965) 'Pain-elicited aggression and behaviour therapy', *Psychol. Record*, 15, 465–7, *92*

RACHMAN, S. (1965) 'Aversion therapy: chemical or electrical?' *Behav. Res. Ther.*, 2, 289–300, *1, 3*

RACHMAN, S. (1965) 'Studies in desensitization. I. The separate effects of relaxation and desensitization', *Behav. Res. Ther.* 3, 245–51, *87*

RACHMAN, S. (1967) 'Sexual fetishism: an experimental analogue', *Psychol. Record*, 16, 293–6, *28, 158*

RACHMAN, S. (1967) 'Systematic desensitization', *Psychol. Bulletin*, 67, 93–103, *1, 6, 87, 96, 103*

RACHMAN, S. and EYSENCK, H. J. (1966) 'Reply to a "critique and re-formulation of behavior therapy"', *Psychol. Bull.*, 65, 165–9, *4*

RACHMAN, S. and HODGSON, R. (1968) 'Experimentally-induced "sexual

fetishism": replication and development', *Psychol. Record*, 18, 25–7, *28, 158*
RACHMAN, S., TURNER, R. K. and YOUNG, G. (1967) 'The effects of conditioning treatment of nocturnal enuresis'. Paper read at Brit. Psychol. Society, Ann. Conf., Belfast, *36*
RAYMOND, M. (1956) 'Case of fetishism treated by aversion therapy', *Brit. Med. J.*, 854–7, *3, 24, 83*
RAYMOND, M. (1964) 'The treatment of addiction by aversion conditioning with apomorphine', *Behav. Res. Ther.*, 1, 287–91, *26, 28, 32*
RAYMOND, M. and O'KEEFFE, K. (1965) 'A case of pin-up fetishism treated by aversion conditioning', *Brit. J. Psychiatry*, 111, 579–81, *25*
RAZRAN, G. (1939) 'Studies in configural conditioning. VI. Comparative extinction and forgetting of pattern and of single stimulus conditioning', *J. exp. Psychol.*, 24, 432–8, *144*
RAZRAN, G. (1955) 'Conditioning and Perception', *Psychol. Rev.*, 62, 83–95, *145, 149*
RAZRAN, G. (1961) 'The observable unconscious and the inferable conscious in current Soviet psychophysiology', *Psychol. Rev.*, 68, 81–147, *146–8, 149*
SANDERSON, R. E., CAMPBELL, D. and LAVERTY, S. G. (1963) 'Traumatically conditioned responses acquired during respiratory paralysis', *Nature*, 196, 1235–6, *9, 50, 144*
SANDERSON, R., CAMPBELL, D. and LAVERTY, S. (1964) 'An investigation of a new aversive conditioning technique for alcoholism', in *Conditioning Techniques in Clinical Practice and Research* (ed. C. M. Franks). New York: Springer, *95*
SCHMIDT, E., CASTELL, D. and BROWN, P. (1965) 'A retrospective study of 42 cases of behaviour therapy', *Behav. Res. Ther.* 3, 9–20, *11, 92*
SEWARD, J. P. (1950) 'Secondary reinforcement as tertiary motivation. A revision of Hull's revision', *Psychol. Rev.* 57, 362–74, *157*
SKINNER, B. F. (1953) *Science and Human Behavior*. New York: Macmillan, *86*
SOLOMON, R. L. (1964) 'Punishment', *American Psychologist*, 19, 239–53, *34, 119, 120, 126, 131*
SOLOMON, R. L. and BRUSH, E. S. (1956) 'Experimentally derived conceptions of anxiety and aversion', in Jones, M. R. (ed.), *Nebraska Symposium on Motivation*. Lincoln: Univer. Nebraska Press, *138, 140*
SOLOMON, R. L. and WYNNE, L. C. (1953) 'Traumatic avoidance learning: the outcomes of several extinction procedures with dogs', *J. Abnorm. soc. Psychol.*, 48, 291–302, *66*
SOLYOM, L. and MILLER, S. (1965) 'A differential conditioning procedure as the initial phase of the behaviour therapy of homosexuality', *Behav. Res. Ther.*, 3, 147–60, *60, 61–3, 78*
SPENCE, K. W. (1956) *Behaviour theory and conditioning*. New Haven: Yale University Press, *157*
SPENCE, K. (1965) 'Cognitive factors in the extinction of the conditioned eyelid response in humans', *Science*, 140, 1224–5, *109, 114–16*
SPENCE, K. and GOLDSTEIN, H. (1961) 'Eye-lid conditioning performance as a function of emotion-producing instructions', *J. exp. Psychol.*, 62, 291–4, *110*
STEVENSON, I. and WOLPE, J. (1960) 'Recovery from sexual deviations through overcoming non-sexual neurotic responses', *Am. J. Psychiat.*, 116, 737–42, *96*

STORMS, L. H., BOROCZI, G. and BROEN, W. E. (1962) 'Punishment inhibits an instrumental response in hooded rats', *Science*, 135, 1133–4, *124*

THIMANN, J. (1949a) 'Conditioned reflex treatment of alcoholism: I', *New England J. Med.*, 241, 368–70, *17*

THIMANN, J. (1949b) 'Conditioned reflex treatment of alcoholism: II', *New England J. Med.*, 241, 408–10, *17*

THORPE, J., SCHMIDT, E. and CASTELL, D. (1964) 'A comparison of positive and negative (aversive) conditioning in the treatment of homosexuality', *Behav. Res. Ther.*, 1, 4, 357–62, *10, 11, 76, 90*

TURNER, L. H. and SOLOMON, R. L. (1962) 'Human traumatic avoidance learning: Theory and experiments on the operant-respondent distinction and failures to learn', *Psychological Monographs*, 76 (Whole No. 559), *66, 90, 136*

TYLER, J. and BROWN, G. (1967) 'The use of swift, brief isolation as a control device for delinquents', *Behav. Res. Ther.*, 5, 1–9, *9*

ULRICH, R. and AZRIN, N. (1962) 'Reflexive fighting in response to aversive stimulation', *J. exp. Anal. Behav.*, 1962, 5, 511–20, *92*

ULRICH, R., HUTCHINSON, R. and AZRIN, N. (1965) 'Pain-elicited aggression', *Psychol. Rec.*, 15, 111–26, *91–3*

ULRICH, R., STACHNIK, T. J., BRIERTON, G. R. and MABRY, J. H. (1965) 'Fighting and avoidance reactions in response to aversive stimulation', *Behaviour, 33*

VALINS, S. and RAY, A. A. (1967) 'Effects of cognitive desensitization on avoidance behaviour', *J. Pers. Soc. Psychol.*, 7, 345–50, *59*

VOEGTLIN, W. L. and LEMERE, F. (1942) 'The treatment of alcohol addiction: A review of the literature', *Quart. J. Stud. Alcohol.*, 2, 717–803, *3, 14, 22, 29, 49, 168*

VOEGTLIN, W. L., LEMERE, F., BROZ, W. R. and O'HALLEREN, P. (1941) 'Conditioned reflex therapy of chronic alcoholism', *Quart. J. Stud. Alcohol.*, 2, 505–11, *2, 16*

WALLERSTEIN, R. S. (1957) 'Conclusions and Implication', in Wallerstein *et al.*, *Hospital Treatment of Alcoholism, 30*

WALLERSTEIN, R. S. and Associates (1957) *Hospital Treatment of Alcoholism*, Imago Press, *18, 19, 30*

WALLERSTEIN, R. S. and CHOTLOS, T. (1957) 'Purpose and method', in Wallerstein *et al.*, *Hospital Treatment of Alcoholism, 30*

WICKENS, D., ALLEN, C. and HILL, F. (1963) 'The effect of instructions and UCS strength on extinction of the conditioned GSR', *J. exp. Psychol.*, 66, 235–40, *114*

WEINER, H. (1962) 'Some effects of response cost upon human operant behavior', *J. exp. Anal. Behav.*, 5, 201–8, *12*

WEINER, H. (1965) 'Conditioning history and maladaptive human operant behavior', *Psychol. Rep.*, 17, 934–42, *12*

WEIST, W. (1967) 'Some recent criticisms of behaviourism and learning theory', *Psychol. Bull.*, 67, 214–25, *4*

WILDE, G. (1964) 'Behaviour Therapy for addicted cigarette smokers', *Behav. Res. Ther.*, 2, 107–9, *12*

WILDE, G. (1965) Letter, *Behav. Res. Ther.*, 2, 313, *12*

WILLIAMS, E. Y. (1947) 'Management of chronic alcoholism', *Psychiat. Quarterly*, 21, 190–8, *17, 20, 83*

WOLF, M., RISLEY, T. and MEES, H. (1964) 'Application of operant conditioning procedures to the behaviour problems of an autistic child', *Behav. Res. Ther.*, 1, 305–12, *6, 9*

WOLF, M., RISLEY, T. *et al.* (1967) 'Application of operant conditioning. A follow-up and extension', *Behav. Res. Ther.*, 5, 103–11

WOLPE, J. (1958) *Psychotherapy by Reciprocal Inhibition.* Stanford: Stanford Univ. Press, *5, 76, 96, 97, 126, 137, 159*

WOLPE, J. (1965) 'Conditioned inhibition of craving in drug addiction', *Behav. Res. Ther.*, 2, 285–7, *36*

WOLPE, J. and LAZARUS, A. (1966) *Behaviour Therapy Techniques*, Pergamon Press, *105*

YOUNG, F. (1965) 'Classical conditioning of autonomic functions', in *Classical Conditioning* (ed. Prokasy, W.). New York: Appleton Crofts, *33*

Index

Addiction 26, 36, 84, 99–100
Aggression 33–4, 90
Alcohol hunger 165
Alcoholics Anonymous 20
Alcoholism, treatment of 2–4, 14–23, 32–3, 43, 72–5, 101–5, 135, 138 ff, 169
Antabuse treatment 18
Anxiety 34, 43, 57, 68, 75–6, 78, 83, 90–3, 97, 126, 133–4, 137, 149 ff, 159, 165, 169
Apomorphine 1, 3, 15 ff, 24, 32–4, 161 ff
Attitudes, sexual 51–2, 81–5
Autonomic changes 53, 65, 74, 84–5, 107 ff, 138, 143 ff
Aversion – relief method 10–11, 62–3, 76
Aversion therapy,
  chemical, contraindications 17, 21
  electrical, apparatus 42
  contraindications 36
  side-effects 36
  ethical considerations 94–96
  generalisation of effects 47–52
  parameters 173
  selective effects 22, 47–52
  self-administered 36, 42
  subjective consequences 81–5

Behaviour therapy 1, 3, 172
Booster treatment 16, 36, 91

Cognitive factors 30–1, 65, 74–5, 105–17, 140–1, 143, 160
Cognitive set 109 ff
Combination treatments 11
Compulsive eating 76–7

Conditioning,
  avoidance 3–4, 34, 63–71, 74, 86–9, 90, 118, 133–42, 160 ff
  backward 19 ff, 30, 32–3, 102–3, 107
  classical 3–4, 14, 29–31, 40 ff, 69, 86–9, 103 ff, 118, 137–9, 143–52, 156, 158, 160 ff, 168 ff
  exteroceptive 146–9
  interoceptive 146–9
  verbal 161–2
Consummatory responses 131, 157
Covert sensitisation 12, 97–117
Crespi effect 153 ff

Desensitisation 1, 5, 96, 103, 165, 172
Devaluation, deviant stimuli 51 ff, 82 ff, 132, 137–8
Deviant stimuli, sexual 160
Drive 155 ff

Eating, compulsive 76–7
Emetine 17
Enuresis 36
Erectile responses 47 ff
Escape responding 66–70
Escape training 118, 141
Excitatory potential 153 ff, 159
Exhibitionism 61, 65, 69
Exteroceptive conditioning 146–9
Extinction 96, 112 ff, 142, 143, 148, 149–51, 160
Extraverts 35

Fantasy, latency 43, 46–9, 60–1, 80
Fetishism 24 ff, 39, 44 ff, 60–1, 99–100, 158
Frequency, aversive stimuli 123

Generalisation 65, 132
Generalisation, aversion therapy
  effects of 47–52, 132

Habit strength 155 ff, 160
Homosexuals 26, 56–60, 61–71, 74,
  91, 97–8, 135, 137
Hypnotherapy 18

Imagery, deviant 79–80
Incentive,
  amount 153 ff
  change 153 ff
  motivation 158 ff, 165 ff
Incubation 150
Intensity, aversive stimuli 122
Interoceptive conditioning 146–9
Introverts 35

Latency,
  image/fantasy 43, 46–9, 60–1, 80
  response 66–70

Masculinity–femininity scale 162
Masochism 83
Masturbation 69–70, 99, 104, 158
Milieu therapy 18
Morphine 1, 84
Motivation 123 ff, 165 ff

Napalkov effect 149 ff
Nausea, conditioned 1, 19, 32–3, 37,
  83, 100–4, 115, 167 ff
Noise, aversive 8
Non-specific therapeutic influences 30

Obsessions 101
Operant conditioning 1, 5, 40 ff, 172
Osgood, semantic differential 45 ff,
  78, 82–3

Paedophilia 44
Pain 35
Penile plethysmograph 27–38, 44 ff,
  57–60, 63, 79, 96
Physiological changes 78–9
Plethysmograph 62–3
Prognostic factors 66, 68, 71, 91
Pulse rate 66–9, 75
  paradoxical effects 120

parameters of 121 ff
Punishment,
  training 3–4, 59, 69, 77, 86–9,
    118–34, 149, 168 ff, 172 ff
  contrast 22, 39, 53
  recovery 39, 53
  generalisation of 49–52
  sequence of change 80

Reinforcers, negative 8–13
Relapse rates 36, 91, 166
Relaxation–training 72–5, 100–7, 165
Repugnance 12
Response, latency 66–70
Response suppression 120 ff, 134–5
  alternative 126 ff

Sadism 98–9
Safety signals 129 ff
Schizokinesis 108
Scoline 9, 95
Sexual attitudes 51–2
Sexual deviations, theory 69
Shock,
  immunity 40
  level 42
  threat 109 ff
Smokers 43
Stimulus,
  aversive 37, 95–6
  deviant sexual 160
  frequency 123
  intensity 122
  punishing 37
  timing of 123
Stress 51–2
Suppression, response 120 ff, 134–5
Symptom substitution 22

Testosterone 26–7, 63
Time-out 9
Transvestism 25 ff, 40 ff, 44 ff, 83–4,
  161 ff
Traumatic respiratory paralysis 9,
  95, 150
Two-factor learning theory 134, 149,
  173

Writer's cramp 90